Food DISHionary — Book 3

FOOD DISHionary

Book 3

1000 Recipe Ideas For Easy Meals

Juttee Armiss

As a dictionary is to language, this book is to food.

CONTENTS

1.

STARTERS

#	Dish	#	Dish
1	Mezze	26	Roasted Vibe Tomatoes With Sage, Feta, Black Olives And Olive Oil
2	Blue Vein Cheese Beignets	27	Bruschetta With Roasted Aubergine, Feta And Basil
3	Brie	28	Bruschetta Tomato And Feta
4	Parmesan Crisps	29	Prawn Bruschetta
5	Camembert Fondue	30	Prawn And Tomato Bruschetta
6	Goat's Cheese	31	Blue Cheese Bruschetta
7	Goat's Cheese With Tomatoes And Sesame Seeds	32	Bruschetta Hot
8	Baked Camembert	33	Pea And Mascarpone Bruschetta
9	Haloumi Cheese Wrapped In Bacon, Battered And Deep Fried	34	Calamari, Butter Bean And Chorizo Bruschetta
10	Grilled Haloumi Cheese	35	Crostini. Mozzarella And Tomatoes
11	Baked Filo Pastries	36	Blinis, Gravlax And Cream Cheese
12	Bagel Chips	37	Bruschetta With Caramelised Apple And Tomato
13	Filled Filo Pastries	38	Rarebit
14	Filo – Tunisia	39	Pear And Asparagus Bruschetta
15	Samosas	40	Tomato Crostini With Whipped Feta
16	Smoked Cheese Cigars	41	Crostini, Sun-Dried Tomatoes And Feta
17	Yorkshire Pudding Canapes	42	Smoked Salmon And Prawns
18	Yorkshire Pudding Canapes #2	43	Fresh Salmon Tartare Canapes
19	Bouchee Hollandaise	44	Bacon And Blue Cheese

Cheese

#1. Mezze

Feta, salami, tuna, olives, artichokes, bocconcini, prawns, sun-dried tomatoes, anchovies, pizza bread, sauce tomate (not ketchup) and olive oil. Use as a self-help tray for guests.

#2. Blue vein cheese beignets

Prepare a choux paste, mix in blue cheese and through a piping bag or using two tablespoons make small fritters and deep fry until golden brown. Serve with a blue cheese dip.

#3. Brie cheese

Deep fried. Cube the brie then put through flour, egg wash and breadcrumbs. Deep fry. Serve with a berry salsa.

#4. Parmesan crisps

Grate the Parmesan cheese and heap in small piles on a baking sheet. Oven bake till crisp. The cheese will spread out in the heat and look like potato crisps.

#5. Camembert fondue

Scoop out centre of the camembert and heat gently in a saucepan adding cream, garlic and wine. Pour it back into the centre of the camembert crust. Serve with vegetables/crudités and crackers.

#6. Goat's cheese

Dry fry in a frypan without oil then coat with a cracked pepper crust and serve on a salad.

#7. Goat's cheese with tomatoes and sesame seeds

Slice tomatoes and place on an oven tray. Slice goat's cheese, then dip in sesame seeds and place on tomatoes and grill for 2 minutes.

For sauce: Dice onions then add cranberries. Pour balsamic vinegar into a saucepan and reduce by 75 per cent then add the onions and cranberries and allow to heat through. Drizzle over cheese.

#8. Baked camembert

Remove top skin, add chopped thyme then bake. Serve with parsnip crisps and caramelised apples.

#9. Haloumi cheese wrapped in bacon, battered and deep fried

Haloumi cheese works well for this dish. Cut off a 10–15 mm slice of haloumi and wrap in fried streaky bacon. Prepare a frying batter then dip the cheese and bacon in flour then batter and deep fry.

#10. Grilled haloumi cheese

Cut the haloumi cheese and grill both sides. Remove from the pan and place on a plate where sesame seeds have been placed.

Pastry

#11. Baked filo pastries

Wilt spinach in very little water then drain well and dry off. Mix spinach with ricotta cheese and cubed feta. Add seasoning and grated nutmeg. Using four sheets of filo pastry, butter between each one. Cut into quarters and place the filling on each one in a line so that it will be rolled up cigar shaped, turning in the sides so that the filling will not escape during cooking. Brush with melted butter and bake at 200°C. Serve with natural yoghurt with harissa paste mixed through it as a dipping sauce.

#12. Bagel chips

Slice a bagel through to create thin strips at an angle and lay them on a baking sheet then bake at 160°C till they dry out. They can be used as an accompaniment for dips or to add toppings to for canapés.

#13. Filled filo pastries

Using four sheets of filo, brush between each sheet with melted butter. Cut the sheets in half so there will be two pastries from the four sheets. Prepare a filling with chopped wilted spinach, tomato slices, cream cheese, nutmeg, parsley, lemon juice and zest, sesame seeds. Fold the right corner of the filo to the left side then fold back to the right ensuring the filling remains in the pastry and forming a triangle. Butter the pastry and oven bake.

#14. Filo (Tunisia)

Use a 20 cm round piece of filo. To a mixing bowl add drained canned tuna, capers, chilli flakes, parsley and fresh prawns plus one raw egg unbeaten and mix together. Place some of the mixture in the middle of the filo then brush the edge with egg wash, fold in half, seal and deep fry. Serve with chilli sauce.

#15. Samosas

Slice leek, mushrooms, onions and sweat off in butter then cool. Cut out the filo pastry into 20 cm circles and place some of the filling in the centre. Cut a brie round into segments and put two with the filling. Brush with egg wash and seal the pastry with the seam being uppermost then bake.

#16. Smoked chicken cigars

Store-bought puff pastry sheets, char-grilled red capsicums, smoked chicken, pesto and cheddar cheese. Dice the capsicums and smoked chicken and place in a mixing bowl. Spoon over pesto, grated cheddar cheese and mix in with seasoning. Cut the puff pastry sheet into quarters then place some filling down the centre of each quarter and roll sealing the edge with beaten egg wash. Twist both ends so that the filling cannot escape while cooking. Bake at 220°C and serve with a tomato salsa and grapes.

#17. Yorkshire pudding canapés

Whisk up a Yorkshire pudding batter adding crumbled blue cheese. To the muffin tin moulds add oil and heat the muffin tin moulds in the oven till the oil is very hot. Then ladle in the batter and bake at 220°C. When cooked, fill the centre with smoked salmon, add a little more blue cheese and mayonnaise.

#18. Yorkshire pudding canapés No. 2

Whisk up a Yorkshire pudding batter. In the bottom of the muffin tin moulds, place hot, fried, black pudding with a piece of streaky bacon on top. Pour the batter over and put into a hot oven at 220°C.

#19. Bouchée hollandaise

Using store-bought puff pastry, cut out two circles using a crimped pastry cutter. Out of one of the circles, cut a smaller circle using a similar-style cutter at 40 mm. Egg wash the first circle, place the second circle on top and again egg wash then bake till golden brown. Leave to go cold then fill the centre with cold poached salmon with hollandaise sauce over the top.

#20. Bouchée smoked salmon

Produce the bouchée case as in #19 then when cold, fill with feta, sliced capsicum and smoked salmon slices and dress with a balsamic dressing.

#21. Onion tart

Blind bake a puff pastry case in a spring-form tin then when cold, coat with crème fraîche. Cook sliced onions in red wine, thyme, balsamic vinegar, brown sugar then reduce and cool. Spoon the onion mixture over the pastry then add crumbled feta onto the tart and keep in the refrigerator.

#22. Naan bread omelette

Prepare an omelette with a tuna and chilli filling. Do not fold the omelette but just place in centre of the naan bread then roll the naan bread with the omelette till completely enclosed then cut into slices for serving.

#23. Chicken and mushroom vol-au-vents

Poach the diced chicken breasts in stock then make a velouté from the stock adding fresh cream at the end. Add the small pieces of chicken to the velouté then fry the sliced mushrooms and add to the velouté. Chop coriander leaves and add to the sauce. Using store-bought puff pastry, cut out two 60 mm rounds with a pastry cutter. With the second 60 mm piece, cut out a centre round of 40 mm and keep separate. Egg wash then place the puff pastry ring onto the 60 mm whole pastry ring, i.e. 60 mm round with 60 mm ring on top, and 40 mm centre cut-out in a 220°C oven, fill with the chicken mix and place the lid on top.

#24. Chorizo and blue cheese canapé

With a pastry cutter, cut out from sliced white bread a 40 mm diameter crouton then deep fry till brown. In a frypan, fry sliced chorizo in butter and oil till golden brown then place on the crouton. Meanwhile soften the blue cheese in a food processor and add cream. Pipe some blue cheese on top of the chorizo and add a basil leaf.

Bruschetta

Bruschetta is an Italian antipasto dish consisting of grilled ciabatta bread, rubbed with fresh garlic and topped with olive oil and salt. The following are toppings that can be used for bruschetta but they are not limited to this list. As an alternative, the toppings can be served separately along with the ciabatta toasted slices so that guests can select their own toppings.

#25. Roasted vine tomato bruschetta with black olives

Olive paste, olives, roasted vine tomatoes, olive oil, thyme, basil, lemon juice.

#26. Roasted vine tomatoes with sage, feta, black olives and olive oil

Roast the vine-connected tomatoes in olive oil, sage and garlic. Process some of the tomatoes and keep some for garnish. Rub the ciabatta slice with garlic then spread over the tomato paste and add black olives with feta.

#27. Bruschetta with roasted aubergine, basil and feta

Mash the roasted aubergines with garlic, lemon juice, torn basil leaves, seasoning and olives. Spread over the ciabatta slices and garnish with cherry tomatoes and basil.

#28. Bruschetta tomato and feta

Ciabatta bread, butter, garlic, sliced tomatoes, feta cheese, fresh basil, black olives and olive oil.

#29. Prawn bruschetta

Slice ciabatta bread into 15 mm slices and toast or fry in butter on both sides. Make an anchovy spread using soft butter, anchovy fillets and a little anchovy oil. Spread over the fried ciabatta. Fry the prawns in butter and lemon juice and place on the anchovy butter. Grill when ready to serve or serve cold with aioli.

#30. Prawn and tomato bruschetta

Slice the ciabatta into a 15 mm slice and fry in garlic butter till golden brown on both sides. Roughly dice the tomato and marinate in balsamic vinegar, mint and garlic. Toss the prawns in butter and fry quickly then cool. Mix the prawns, tomatoes and a little of the vinegar together then lay out on the ciabatta.

#31. Blue cheese bruschetta

Soften the blue cheese with butter adding Worcestershire sauce and orange zest. Spread on the fried ciabatta slice and top with caramelised apple chutney.

#32. Bruschetta — hot

Tomatoes, basil, balsamic vinegar and brown sugar on a croute that has been fried in butter and garlic. Slice the tomatoes and place in a bowl then add balsamic vinegar and seasoning. Place the tomato slices on the croute along with basil and sliced feta and grill quickly.

#33. Pea and mascarpone bruschetta

Ciabatta sliced and toasted, spread with butter and garlic then with mascarpone and topped with minted pea mash. Mint or parsley to garnish.

#34. Calamari, butter bean and chorizo bruschetta

Using fresh calamari rings, fry very quickly in hot oil then cool. In the same pan put diced chorizo and fry it till coloured all over. Grill the ciabatta bread slice, rub with raw garlic then line with the calamari, butter beans and chorizo.

#35. Crostini, mozzarella and tomatoes

Baguette grilled with butter and rubbed with garlic, then coat with sliced mozzarella, cherry tomatoes and basil.

#36. Blinis, gravlax and cream cheese

To make the blinis, sift buckwheat flour and ordinary flour together. Add in baking powder and an egg and start whisking while adding buttermilk. Whisk to a smooth thick paste then add melted butter. Use two tablespoons of the batter in a frypan with hot oil to make the blinis. Top the blinis with cream cheese then sliced salmon.

#37. Bruschetta

Top with caramelised apple, tomato, thyme and fried feta.

#38. Rarebit

English mustard, Tabasco, Worcestershire sauce, cheese, flour. In a saucepan, melt butter then add flour along with mustard, Tabasco, Worcestershire sauce and cheese. Once the paste has cooked through, spread on ciabatta and grill. Could also use on top of steak, fish or toast.

#39. Pear and asparagus bruschetta

Hot and en croute. Toss pear and asparagus in a pan with garlic and oil. Toast ciabatta bread and rub with butter and garlic. Line with mozzarella, olive oil and balsamic vinegar. Top with pear slices and asparagus.

#40. Tomato crostini with whipped feta

Put feta and cream cheese in bowl and whisk. Add olive oil and lemon juice. In a dry frypan, fry pine nuts until brown all over. Make a dressing and add sliced tomatoes. Spread the cream cheese mix on the crostini, add tomatoes and pine nuts.

#41. Crostini, sun-dried tomatoes and feta

Slice baguette on an angle. Toast and toss in hot butter and oil then leave to cool. Top with feta and baked vine-ripened tomatoes or sun-dried tomatoes, parsley and mint.

#42. Smoked salmon and prawns

Cut a slice of white bread into three then fry in garlic butter on both sides. Cool then spread with lime aioli, a slice of smoked salmon and cooked garlic prawns.

#43. Fresh salmon tartare canapé

Chop the very fresh salmon so that it resembles coarse mince and place in a mixing bowl. Add finely diced shallots, olive oil, lemon zest, capers, sliced gherkins and seasoning. Mix well and spread on grilled baguette slices that have been toasted and spread with garlic butter. Top with capers and lemon zest.

#44. Bacon and blue cheese

Slice the ciabatta, fry in garlic butter then spread with blue cheese that had been softened with balsamic vinegar. Cut streaky bacon into batons, fry and cool then spread over the blue cheese and place under the grill.

#45. Cajun mushroom bruschetta

Fry sliced button mushrooms in butter, garlic and Cajun spice. When cooked, add in chopped parsley and spread over the sliced ciabatta toast.

#46. Creamy mushrooms

Sliced button mushrooms cooked in butter then added to a béchamel sauce along with mascarpone. Add seasoning and Worcestershire sauce and spread over the ciabatta.

#47. Mussel bruschetta

Steam the mussels in very little water and white wine. Once they have opened, remove the mussel from the shell then remove the beard. In a frypan, sweat off finely diced onions with smoked paprika in butter. Add in the mussels and toss. Toast the ciabatta slices then rub with garlic butter and sun-dried tomato pesto. Top with the mussels, coriander then serve.

#48. Roasted capsicum and basil bruschetta

On the toasted ciabatta slice, top with sliced roasted capsicum that has been drenched in a balsamic vinegar, virgin olive oil and garlic dressing. Garnish with basil leaves.

#49. Mushrooms with blue cheese and walnuts bruschetta

Use portobello mushrooms and fry in butter. Cook skin side last and add pieces of blue cheese on top along with roughly chopped walnuts. Serve on toasted ciabatta.

2.

BEEF

#50. Beef with blue cheese dumplings

Prepare a beef casserole with chuck steak. Put the beef through seasoned flour and brown in oil and garlic. Add thyme, Guinness, mustard, tomato paste, fresh chopped tomatoes, orange zest and juice, chopped onion, marmalade, mixed herbs and stock. Oven bake and cook slowly. The flour should thicken the casserole for the sauce. When the beef is nearly cooked divide the dumpling dough into equal sizes, roll between the hands to form a ball and put on the beef, brush with milk and return to the oven to brown. **Blue cheese dumplings**: 200 g self-raising flour, 100 g butter, 50 g blue cheese, seasoning and milk. Rub the butter and blue cheese lightly into the flour then add milk to make a dough. Handle carefully so that it does not become a tight dough. **Or herb dumplings**: 1½ cups self-raising flour, 60 g chopped butter, thyme leaves, chopped parsley, ½ – 1/3 cup of milk plus seasoning.

#51. Beef casserole potato top

Prepare the beef casserole as in dish #50. When the beef is cooked, ladle into a casserole dish and top the casserole with potato gems and return to the oven to cook the gems. Grated cheese could also be sprinkled on top. As an alternative, store-bought gnocchi can be cooked then cooled quickly and placed on top of the beef when ready. Like the potato gems, place back in the oven to reheat.

#52. Crusted beef ragout

Using a good braising steak or cubed steak, fry onions and garlic in a saucepan till brown then add beef and brown all over. Add tomatoes, caraway seeds, beef stock and oven bake on 160°C for 1 hour. When cooked transfer the beef to ramekins for individual portions then make a crust from cup flour, ¼ cup Parmesan, baking powder, chopped rosemary, butter, salt and milk. Place the crust on the ramekin and oven bake. When ready to serve, top with black olives, capers and rosemary or thyme and anchovy fillets.

#53. Fillet steak tarte Tatin

Very quickly brown the fillet steak on each side and cool. Prepare an onion marmalade with brown sugar and dried herbs. In a large pie tin, pack the fillet steak tightly together then add crushed garlic, onion marmalade and butter. Cover with puff pastry, tucking the overhanging pastry down the inside of the pan, egg wash and bake. When cooked, place the serving platter over the top of the cooked pastry and complete a 180-degree turn. The pastry now becomes the base. Keep your face away from the pan while turning, as you might get boiling liquid spilling from the pan.

#54. Barbecue beef fillet

Trim the beef and remove any fat or silver skin. In a mixing bowl, pour olive oil, chopped garlic, thyme, seasoning, cracked black pepper, smoked paprika and a few drops of smoke oil if available. Place the beef in a casserole and pour the marinade over the beef and keep in the fridge overnight. Remove from the fridge an hour before cooking. Place the beef in a barbecue fired by charcoal and cook till rare in the centre but nicely browned on the outside. Rest for 15 minutes before carving.

#55. Cola pot roast

Buy a boned and rolled blade of beef. Brown the beef in a frypan with sliced garlic in oil. Roughly chop root vegetables such as carrots, parsnips and sweet potato; pumpkin can also be used. Once the beef has been browned, place in casserole dish with lid. Brown the vegetables in the same frypan and place with the beef. Deglaze the pan with stock and pour it over the beef along with the cola and Worcestershire sauce. Cook the beef slowly in the oven and when cooked remove from the casserole and set aside to rest. Thicken the sauce with an instant gravy mix or make a roux from butter and flour. Check the sauce for taste and seasoning and return the joint back to the sauce briefly for 5 minutes then carve and serve.

#56. Corned beef in cola

Place the corned beef in a large saucepan in cold water and bring to the boil then tip out the water. This will remove some of the brine and salt in the meat. Wash the meat in cold water, pat dry then place back in the saucepan. Pour in cola but the meat does not have to be covered. Add whole cloves, cinnamon quill, onion cut into quarters, roughly chopped pieces of carrot and bring to a very slow simmer. Keep a lid on the saucepan while the meat is cooking. Check that the meat is cooked and leave to rest before carving. Serve with a mustard sauce.

#57. Braised beef in coffee, cinnamon and orange juice

In an oven dish, sweat off diced onion and sliced garlic till translucent then stir in coffee, orange zest, cinnamon, oil and brown sugar. Brown the beef in oil in a frypan till it is sealed all over then add to the coffee mixture in the oven dish. Put a lid on the oven dish and bake in the oven slowly at 150°C till the beef is cooked. Allow the beef to rest, reduce the cooking liquor then thicken with a roux. Check seasoning of the sauce before serving.

#58. Bacon and cheese meatloaf

Mix the beef mincemeat with chosen herbs, spices then add an egg and breadcrumbs. Once the meat has been mixed well, place half the meat into an oiled meatloaf tin. At halfway, top with cold fried bacon batons and grated cheese as a layer then top with more mincemeat. Bake in the oven till the meatloaf is cooked through.

#59. Beef short ribs

Cook the ribs in simmering apple juice, chilli, diced onions, garlic, celery and reduce then leave to cool. Make the barbecue sauce from ketchup, brown sugar, Worcestershire sauce, smoked paprika, white wine vinegar, bourbon and seasoning. Brush over the ribs and baste while cooking on the barbecue.

#60. Beef ribs

Brown the ribs in a frypan in oil and garlic, then transfer to a roasting dish and put aside. In a food processor blitz onion, chilli, root ginger and garlic to a paste then fry in oil in the same frypan. While the paste is heating, pour in beer, miso blended with water, grated lime zest and sugar. Pour the paste over the ribs and bake slowly in the oven. Meanwhile cook brown rice to serve with the ribs. Fry the cooked rice with chopped onions, carrots, peas, ginger and garlic. While the rice is frying make two holes in it with the base of a serving spoon and break in fresh eggs and mix in with the rice along with soy and fish sauce.

#61. Paprika beef and cream

Cut bacon into strips then fry in oil and butter and remove. In the same pan, fry beef schnitzel in oil and garlic till brown on both sides. When cooked, remove from the pan and cover with tinfoil. To the pan, add diced onions and fry adding paprika. Leave to cook out then pour in pomodoro sauce and sour cream. Simmer gently and allow to reduce. Return the beef back to the sauce for 5 minutes then serve.

#62. Steak bites

Cut sirloin or rump steak into 20–25 mm size pieces. Fry quickly in oil and butter till brown but rare. Remove when cooked then add more butter to the pan and cook diced onions and mushrooms. Return the beef back into the pan with the mushrooms. Add garlic butter and swirl the pan. Add a teaspoon each of mustard and sour cream. Stir and serve.

#63. Stuffed Wiener schnitzel

Use two small pieces of beef schnitzel or one large piece and fold in two to complete the dish. Prepare a bread stuffing of white bread, diced bacon and onions, mixed herbs, orange juice and zest. Once the stuffing is made, place in the middle of the schnitzel then top with the second piece. Egg wash the edges so that a good seal is made. Dip the schnitzel through flour, egg wash and breadcrumbs and fry in an oil/ butter medium on both sides.

#64. Garlic bread casserole

Using a baguette, slice into diagonal slices then butter both sides with garlic butter. Prepare a Bolognese sauce using beef mince. Butter a casserole dish and spread the base with a layer of meat sauce. Top with the sliced garlic bread and grated mozzarella over the top of that. At this point, spinach and sliced tomatoes could be added, then spoon in another layer of meat sauce. Top with a layer of bread then more meat sauce, followed by a thin layer of cheese sauce, grated mozzarella and sliced tomatoes. Bake in the oven till cooked through and golden brown then serve.

#65. Steak marinade

Oil, jalapeño, coriander, vinegar, garlic, lime juice, orange juice and seasoning. Pour the ingredients into a Ziploc bag and shake. Add the steak and leave in the fridge for 4 hours plus. Then cook the steak and freeze the marinade.

#66. Hungarian goulash

Dredge the meat through the flour and fry in a frypan in oil and garlic till brown then place in a casserole. In the same frypan, brown the diced carrots, onions, capsicums and hold the sliced mushrooms to the end. To the frypan, add tomato paste, Worcestershire sauce, paprika and 200 ml of beef stock and stir well to lift all the pan drippings. Pour the contents of the frypan into the casserole and bake in the oven for 90 minutes at 160°C. Check that the beef is tender then add sliced mushrooms that have been fried in butter. Check if any sugar is required to remove any acidity. After 30 minutes, check for taste, seasoning and serve.

#67. Beef and barley casserole

Cut the beef into 30 mm cubes, dredge in flour and brown in a frypan in oil, garlic and dried mixed herbs. Put the meat into a casserole dish then in the same pan fry diced carrots, onions, pumpkin and celery till brown and place with the meat. Pour tomato purée into the pan along with a can of crushed tomatoes to deglaze the pan then add all to the meat. Top the casserole up with beef stock then add barley and place in the oven. Stir occasionally early so that the barley mixes into the liquid and does not form a lump. Cook for 2 hours on 160°C then check for the tenderness of the beef. Check seasoning and thickness of the sauce and serve.

#68. Thai corned beef

Place the beef in a large saucepan of cold water without adding any salt, bring to the boil and as soon as it reaches the boil, drain out the water, wash off the beef and saucepan then place the beef back into the saucepan with hot water. Add tomato paste, coriander seeds, fish sauce, red curry paste store-bought, whole peppercorns, diced onions, carrots and whole baby potatoes. Bring to a gentle simmer and hold there for 90 minutes. Check that the beef is cooked then make a sauce from the cooking liquor and add coconut milk to the sauce to finish it off. Let the beef rest for 15 minutes before carving.

#69. Beef brisket in balsamic and blackberry sauce

Brown the brisket in oil in a frypan so that it is browned on both sides then place in a casserole dish with a lid. Pour in beef stock, garlic, balsamic vinegar and blackberry jam. Cook on low heat at 160°C and check for tenderness of the beef. Check taste and seasoning then remove the beef and allow to rest. Pour the cooking liquor into a saucepan, reduce and sweeten with sugar or blackberry jam if necessary. Thicken the sauce with cornflour mixed with water then serve.

#70. Bourbon bacon meatballs

Prepare meatballs with the addition of 100 ml of bourbon and bacon which has been chopped to a coarse mix in a food processor. Mix the beef mince and sausage meat mixture, breadcrumbs, beaten egg, dried mixed herbs then roll into balls. Brown in a frypan in oil and garlic then place in a casserole. Make caramelised onions and add to the meatballs then pour in a gravy. Bake in the oven till the meatballs are cooked.

#71. Meatballs in a nest

Prepare the meatballs as in dish #70. When ready to serve, cook spaghetti in boiling salted water to a point of being al dente. Drain quickly into a colander then using a pasta spoon, scoop out some spaghetti and place on a baking tray that has been oiled. Using a table fork, place in the middle of the spaghetti and turn the fork to create a cavity in the spaghetti. Place a meatball in the centre, top with Parmesan cheese and bake. Place on the serving dish and coat with some of the sauce.

#72. Meatballs in filo

Prepare the meatballs as in dish #70 then roll into balls. Push a thumb into the meatball to make a hole then fill with a piece of cheese then smooth over to form a whole meatball. Fry the meatballs in oil in a frypan till cooked through then leave to cool. Take three sheets of filo pastry and brush with melted butter but keep separate. Cut the sheets into four sectors then place the first piece into a muffin tin mould. Top with the second piece but keep it off centre from the first piece of filo then place the third piece of filo in the muffin tin hole. Put the meatball in the centre of the filo then sheet by sheet wrap the meatball. Brush with melted butter and bake.

#73. Meatballs in tomato and coconut sauce

Prepare the meatballs as in dish #70 then fry in oil in a frypan and finish in the oven. In a saucepan, fry sliced onions, Italian herbs, sage and garlic till opaque then pour in pomodoro sauce. Add in tomato paste and bring to a simmer. Pour in coconut cream to taste then pour it over the meatballs and oven bake.

#74. Sirloin steak with Captain Morgan

Cook the steak in a hot pan in butter, oil and crushed garlic 2 minutes on each side to brown the steak then remove and keep warm. Pour in the rum, Worcestershire sauce, beef stock and reduce. Thicken with cornflour and water, check seasoning then add a knob of butter and cream and simmer. Return the steak back to the sauce briefly then serve.

#75. Fillet of beef in puff pastry

Same principle as beef Wellington with a few changes. Trim and seal/brown the fillet of beef in oil in a frypan then leave to go cold. Lay out a sheet of puff pastry and spread with caramelised onions. Top with thin slices of ham and sliced camembert on top of the ham. Lay the cold beef fillet on top then envelop the pastry around the beef so that the sealed joint is underneath and the ends are folded under. Brush with egg wash and bake in the oven at 190°C till the pastry is golden brown. The beef should be rare. Serve with Béarnaise sauce.

#76. Roast fillet of beef with salsa verde

Using the head of fillet, stud the beef all over with slithers of garlic. Brown the beef in a hot frypan in oil with rosemary and sage. Transfer to a roasting pan and roast at a high heat for approximately 8–10 minutes for a rare roast beef. Leave to rest then top with salsa verde — capers, anchovies, garlic, Dijon mustard, vinegar, mint, parsley and olive oil.

#77. Beef and potato fricassee

Use a good beef steak for this dish and cut into 1 cm size fingers. Dip through seasoned flour and paprika then fry in a frypan with oil and garlic. Add to a casserole dish. In the same frypan, fry diced onions, carrots and celery, button mushrooms then add to the casserole. Deglaze the pan with beef stock and Worcestershire sauce, pour it over the beef then bake in the oven until the beef is tender. If the sauce requires thickening, make a roux and use the cooking liquid to mix into the roux. Cook out then check for seasoning. Pour in sour cream and serve.

#78. Osso bucco

This uses the shank of beef and the meat will include the bone which is dredged in flour then fried in a frypan in oil and garlic then placed in a casserole. Diced onions, thyme and dry mixed herbs are also fried along with diced celery and carrots. Pour in beef stock to deglaze the pan then some tomato paste. Pour it into the casserole then add a can of crushed tomatoes, a spoonful of brown sugar, seasoning and bake slowly in the oven. Because it is a tough cut of meat it does require slow cooking. When the meat comes away from the bone easily, check the seasoning. In a food processor blitz garlic, parsley and lemon zest and serve with the osso bucco.

#79. Italian stuffed schnitzel

Lay the schnitzel on a chopping board and spread half with a tomato and onion sauce. Top the sauce with spinach and basil leaves then add slices of mozzarella cheese. Fold the schnitzel in half and hold in place with toothpicks then fry in a frypan in oil/butter and finish cooking in the oven for 10 minutes till cooked through.

#80. Stuffed layered schnitzel

Sauté the schnitzel in oil and butter just to brown the surface then lay the cold schnitzel on a chopping board and look to cut three identical-size pieces which will form the schnitzel stack. Prepare a stuffing of cooked bacon lardons, diced cooked onions, dried mixed herbs, diced tomato flesh, torn white sliced bread, orange juice and finely diced zest, crushed garlic, chopped parsley and a beaten egg. Mix the stuffing well then spoon some of the stuffing onto the base layer of schnitzel. Top with a second slice of schnitzel then spoon more stuffing onto the second layer. Finally, top with the third piece of schnitzel and press down gently to push it all together. Place in a greased roasting pan and bake in the oven and serve with a brown onion sauce.

#81. Roast beef with grapefruit stuffing

If the beef is already boned and rolled, undo the strings and open out. Put sliced garlic, salt and pepper on the beef. Make a stuffing with torn white crustless bread, fried diced onions, garlic, dried mixed herbs, grapefruit juice and finely sliced grapefruit zest, an egg and seasoning. Mix all ingredients to combine well then place on the inside of the beef in an even layer. Re-roll the beef and tie with string or use skewers. Then roast the beef in the oven sitting on a bed of onions and roughly chopped root vegetables.

#82. Braised oxtails

Dredge the oxtail and braising steak in flour and fry in a frypan in oil and garlic till brown then place in a roasting pan or pressure cooker. Fry the bacon, onions, capsicum, celery, tomato paste and carrot in the same pan and brown. Add the chilli flakes then pour in the red wine and canned tomatoes. Bring to the boil then add to the oxtails. With all ingredients mixed in with the oxtails, cover the pan with tinfoil and bake on low for 8 hours then check for tenderness. The meat should just fall off the bone. Thicken the sauce by pouring off the sauce into a brown roux in a saucepan and let the flour cook out. The oxtail can be served with a fried mixture of breadcrumbs, chopped celery, garlic and chopped walnuts.

#83. Fried ginger beef fingers with sliced cabbage

Cut the beef into fingers then marinate overnight in soy, garlic, diced root ginger, oil and brown sugar. When ready to cook, remove the beef from the marinade and dry on kitchen paper.

Fry in a wok in batches if necessary, in garlic and some of the marinade when the pan is very hot, but don't allow the meat to stew. When the meat is complete, fry sliced onions, capsicums and snow peas adding to the beef. Finally fry the cabbage very quickly keeping it crunchy and al dente. Spoon over some of the sauce and serve. Cooked noodles can also be fried in the same wok and mixed in as an alternative to go with the beef and cabbage.

#84. Beef with sun-dried tomatoes and Parmesan

Place a whole piece of braising beef on a tray and sprinkle with pepper and salt on all sides. In a mixing bowl add sliced sun-dried tomatoes, Parmesan cheese, Dijon and a dash of oil. Spoon the sun-dried tomato mix all over the beef then place in a roasting dish with 500 ml of beef stock and cook on low for 5 hours. Check that meat is cooked and remove from the roasting pan, cover with tinfoil and leave to rest for at least 30 minutes. Pour in a pre-made brown sauce and red wine to deglaze the pan then carve the beef and serve with the sauce.

#85. Beef casserole with peanut sauce

Using braising steak, cut into cubes 25 mm, fry with diced onions, capsicum and garlic in a frypan till brown then place in a roasting pan. Add canned tomatoes, beef stock, chilli flakes and oven bake on 160°C for 2 hours. When the beef is getting tender, add crunchy peanut butter to the beef and pan-fried peanuts. When ready to serve, top with more chopped pan-fried peanuts and chopped coriander.

#86. Chimichurri beef roulade

Buy at your local butcher or supermarket a piece of beef thin enough to be rolled and slightly thicker than a beef schnitzel. In a food processor, blitz parsley, almonds, pine nuts, red onion, chilli, lemon juice and zest, red wine vinegar and olive oil but keep the mixture to a wet paste that requires spreading with a spoon. Lay the beef on a sheet of baking paper which is on a chopping board, season and wipe with a cut garlic clove. Lay slices of pastrami all over the beef then top with the paste. Lift one end of the baking paper then roll the meat into a tight roll and tie with butcher's twine. Brown the beef in a frypan all over then place in a roasting pan and roast. When the beef is cooked, top with a brown sauce which has garlic, maple syrup, olive oil and thyme added to it.

#87. Beef and asparagus kebabs

The kebabs require a good steak to be used such as sirloin or rump. Cut into 25 mm cubes and put in teriyaki marinade overnight. Cut the fresh asparagus into 30 mm lengths. Soak wooden skewers in water then start threading the cubes with two pieces of asparagus between each piece of steak. Either grill or barbecue the kebabs and serve with Béarnaise sauce.

#88. Pesto and herb stuffed roast beef fillet

Prepare a stuffing of white bread, dried mixed herbs, chopped onions, lemon juice and grated zest, garlic, pesto and seasoning. Bind with a beaten egg. Using the head of a fillet of beef, with a sharp knife slice it in half lengthways and open out. Line the bottom side with the stuffing approximately 15 mm thick. Fold the top back and tie with butcher's twine. Place the fillet on a wire cake stand in the roasting tray. Roast the beef quickly in a hot oven (210°C) so that it remains rare in the centre. Leave to rest for 15 minutes when it is cooked to desired degree.

#89. Beef and brandy

Dice a good cut of beef for this dish, either fillet, rump or sirloin. Brown the beef cubes in butter and while it is browning add bacon strips then pour in 60 ml of brandy and flame being careful not to burn yourself or equipment. Remove the meat then brown the onions and mushrooms. When cooked, return the meat and pour in red wine, tomato paste, gravy and simmer gently till the beef is cooked. Check the taste for seasoning then spoon in crème fraîche.

#90. Beef brisket braised in cider

With a 1.5 kg of boned and rolled piece of braising beef, brown in a frypan on all sides then place in a lidded casserole dish. In the frypan, add oil, sliced onions and garlic. Reduce heat and add rosemary, thyme, apple cider vinegar, cider and beef stock. Braise slowly in the oven till the beef is cooked. Around half an hour before the beef is going to be removed, add the sliced apples. Remove the beef from the cooking liquor then reduce the liquid. Either thicken the sauce with cornflour and water or make a roux and use the liquid to thicken the sauce.

#91. Beef with Guinness and prunes

Dice the beef into large dice and brown in a saucepan in oil and garlic then set to one side. To the saucepan add diced onions and when transparent add butter to the saucepan then add the same amount of flour to make a roux. Add the Guinness (slowly), tomato paste and a can of tomatoes and as the sauce thickens, add beef stock to make a smooth sauce. Return the meat to the saucepan and add the prunes which have been soaking in some of the Guinness. Simmer gently for 2 hours and check that the beef is cooked and tender. Serve with mashed potatoes.

#92. Spiced beef casserole

Cubed beef, stock, lime leaves, garlic, coriander, cumin, diced root ginger, soy sauce, chillies chopped. Process all ingredients except the meat, stock and lime leaves in a food processor. Fry the resultant paste in oil in a frypan then add meat. Place in a casserole dish along with stock and lime leaves and bake slowly in the oven. Check seasoning and when the meat is cooked, serve on rice.

#93. Moussaka

Sliced eggplant, courgettes and potatoes. Line a buttered casserole with potatoes, then eggplant and then courgette. Ladle in meat sauce and same layers again. Near top of casserole spoon over cheese sauce which has cubes of feta, top with grated cheddar and bake in oven at 170°C for approximately 40 minutes.

#94. Chilli, chocolate, beef and beans

Beef cubed, cumin, paprika, chilli, parsley, capsicum, chocolate and cannellini beans. Fry the beef in a frypan in oil and crushed garlic till brown on all sides then place in a roasting pan. To the same frypan add more oil, chilli flakes, cumin, paprika, sliced capsicum and beef stock. Place a lid on the beef or use tinfoil and roast slowly till the beef is tender. Once cooked, add drained cannellini beans and chocolate pieces. Test for seasoning and taste.

#95. Grilled fillet steak with lemon and herb sauce

Use a piece of fillet steak 50–60 mm thick. With a very sharp-pointed knife cut small slits 2 cm long by 5 mm deep in the steak. In a bowl, mix 2 Tbsp olive oil, 2 Tbsp oregano, 2 Tbsp parsley and ½ tsp grated lemon zest along with lemon juice and chopped garlic. Mix well then massage the mix into the steak 30 minutes before grilling. Spoon some of the mix over while it is cooking then leave the steak to rest before serving.

#96. Bloody Mary braised beef

Using a piece of whole sirloin or rump, brown in oil in a frypan with garlic and dried mixed herbs. When brown all over, place in an oven casserole. In the same frypan, brown sliced red onions and sliced celery. Deglaze the pan with the Bloody Mary mix — passata, Worcestershire sauce, Tabasco and vodka along with seasoning. Slow cook in the oven till the meat can be pulled apart using two table forks. Remove the meat and reduce the sauce. Check for seasoning then add three large knobs of butter and serve separately from the beef.

#97. Thai beef peanut sauce

A piece of sirloin, sesame oil, grated root ginger, chilli paste, brown sugar, lemongrass, soy and fish sauces, crushed garlic, spring onions, peanut butter mixed with a little warm water, dry pan-fried peanuts. Beat the lemongrass with the back of a knife then mix all ingredients together except the meat and peanuts and heat gently in a saucepan. Cook the steak in a frypan then pour the sauce over it and reduce heat. Add the whole peanuts last, check seasoning and serve with rice.

3.

LAMB

#98. Roast boned and rolled leg of lamb with brandy sauce

Prepare a meat stuffing of sausage meat, fried onions, crushed garlic, sage, thyme, lemon juice, lemon zest, beaten egg and breadcrumbs. Remove the ties from the boned and rolled leg then place the stuffing down the centre of the meat. Roll and tie the meat and roast in the oven with the meat placed on a bed of vegetables, rosemary, onion, garlic to prevent the bottom of the meat from frying. When the lamb is cooked, remove from the oven and allow to rest under a foil wrap. Place the roasting pan on an element and brown the vegetables then add a cup of brandy. Allow to reduce then add chicken stock and butter. Thicken with cornflour, season then serve with the lamb.

#99. Roast leg of lamb with anchovies and mint

Using a leg of lamb with bone in, take a sharp-pointed knife and stab the lamb 20 times all over. Push your finger into the knife cuts to widen the cut then insert a leaf of mint with half an anchovy fillet wrapped in it. Crush garlic then rub it over the lamb and forcing it into the knife cuts. Roast on 170°C till cooked, then leave to rest before carving.

#100. Lamb belly

Belly lamb tends to be quite fatty so some fat will need to be cut off before cooking. Leave the bones in but brown the lamb in a frypan on the stove and transfer to a casserole. Fry chopped onions, carrots, celery in the same pan adding thyme, rosemary and sage at the same time. Top the casserole with chicken stock and oven bake. When cooked remove the lamb and leave to cool. Peel and thinly slice some potatoes and line the bottom of a casserole dish. Pull the bones out of the lamb belly and cut the meat into 50 x 50 mm pieces. Add a layer to the casserole on the potatoes and layer to the top, with potatoes being the top layer. Use the stock to pour over the potatoes and lamb and oven bake.

#101. Lamb casserole

This dish uses a cheaper cut of meat from the belly. It tends to be a fatty part of the lamb but the fat can be cut out. Cut the lamb belly into 40 mm squares. Make a caramel of sugar and water in a large heavy-based saucepan. When the caramel begins turning brown, add the lamb and ensure each piece is coated. Add butter and flour then a stock cube, diced carrots, raw beetroot, garlic, thyme, onion diced, celery, Tabasco, a little brown sugar and chicken stock. Cook slowly and at the end add cut green bananas.

Herb dropped dumplings: 1 cup self-raising flour, 1 tsp baking powder, 60 gms butter, ½ cup buttermilk, spring onion, chopped parsley and coriander.

#102. Filo lamb and lentil pies

Filling of lamb mince, garlic, ras el hanout, lentils, pine nuts, chopped parsley, chopped tomatoes. Lay four sheets of filo on a chopping board, buttering in between each sheet. Cut the sheets in half and spoon some of the cooked lamb mixture into the centre of the filo then fold by lifting up each corner to the centre and tying with butcher's twine. The design is to look like a money bag. Brush with butter and bake in the oven till brown. Serve with **sauce tzatziki**: 1 cup yoghurt, crushed garlic, ½ cup cucumber flesh seedless and skinless, 1 Tbsp chopped mint.

#103. Lamb shoulder roast bone in

Place the roast in a ceramic pan or a dish that will not have a reaction to balsamic vinegar. Pour over the roast 3 cups stock and 1 cup of balsamic vinegar. Add in whole cloves of garlic and rosemary, cover with foil and roast slowly at 150°C. Check after 3 hours and then cook for as long as required to finish off. Make a pan gravy while the roast is resting. Heat chicken stock and add brown sugar, malt vinegar, chopped mint and pour it over the meat just before removing from the oven.

#104. Lamb casserole

In a frypan, brown the diced lamb (in batches) in oil, garlic, ginger and diced capsicum then add to a lidded casserole dish. Pour into the frypan mushroom soup, canned tomatoes then add the mint, thyme leaves and Worcestershire sauce. Cook on a low heat (160°C) till the lamb is tender. Check seasoning and serve with mint jelly. Root vegetables can also be added to the dish. This method could also be used to cook lamb shanks.

#105. Roast leg lamb chorizo

Lightly score the surface of the leg like you would roast pork. Rub the leg with a mixture of smoked paprika, crushed garlic, oil, ground pepper with a pinch of cayenne. Using a very sharp knife, insert into the flesh and make a 15 mm hole. Cut a slice of chorizo that will fit the hole, wrap with mint leaves and push into the hole. Make approximately 20–30 holes in the leg then roast slowly in the oven.

#106. Lamb meatballs

Place the minced lamb in a mixing bowl and to it add diced onions fried in butter along with garlic, chopped rosemary and dried mixed herbs. In a separate bowl soak fresh breadcrumbs in milk. Squeeze the milk out of the breadcrumbs and add to the lamb along with the onion mixture. Add seasoning and mix all the ingredients well. Add in a beaten egg to bind the mix then shape into meatballs. They can be fried or roasted in the oven or, once browned, placed in a sauce and braised. Serve with a mint yoghurt dressing.

#107. Lamb and chickpea meatballs

Use the same method as in #106 and include a can of drained chickpeas or soak dried chickpeas overnight then drain, cook and leave to cool. Add to the mincemeat and roll out to form meatballs. **Sauce**: Diced onions, canned chopped tomatoes, grated garlic, dried mixed herbs, sugar and seasoning. Fry the onions then add the tomatoes, garlic, mixed herbs and olive oil. Add sugar to taste to remove any acidic taste and adjust seasoning. A brown sauce could also be used.

#108. Lamb rump with Brazil nut sauce

Remove the skin and score the fat. Fry fat side down to render the fat then turn over so both sides are brown. Add butter and spoon it over the rump then add garlic and rosemary. Place in the oven for around 8–10 minutes then leave to rest. Serve with a salad and **Brazil nut sauce**: Into a food processor place Brazil nuts, apple cider vinegar, soy sauce and sesame oil. Blitz adding small amounts of water to bring it to a liquid.

#109. Lamb rump

Remove any sinew from the rump then place in a mixing bowl. Spoon in a mix of natural Greek yoghurt mixed with curry powder, garlic and diced shallot. Leave in the fridge for an hour, wipe off then fry quickly in oil in a frypan. When browned, remove and leave to rest for 10 minutes under foil. Slice the lamb and serve with a rosemary and mint sauce.

#110. Lamb backstrap dukkha

Remove any silver skin that may be on the backstrap then place in a mixing bowl along with seasoning, olive oil and garlic. Either prepare dukkha in-house (#492) or use store-bought dukkha. Place the oil-dipped lamb backstrap into the dukkha and pat the crumb mix onto the lamb. Fry in hot oil and allow to brown or bake in the oven on a greased baking tray. Keep the lamb rare and leave to rest before carving.

#111. Lamb tagine

Lamb steaks, oil, diced onions, garlic, cumin, cinnamon, coriander, ground ginger, cayenne pepper; chicken stock, lemon zest and pitted prunes. Sauté the onions, garlic, spices then add the lamb and cover with the spice mix. Add stock and lemon zest and cook on a low heat with lid on at 160°C. Add prunes and continue cooking. Check for seasoning and taste. Serve with couscous.

#112. Sweet potato top shepherd's pie

Shepherd's pie is so called because those minding the sheep, known as shepherds, would have roast lamb and the next day the leftovers would be used to make a pie. The cooked lamb is minced and mixed with whatever is available — tomatoes, carrots, parsnips, celery and gravy. The standard shepherd's pie is topped with mashed potato but in this instance, we are using mashed sweet potatoes. Peel and slice the sweet potato into even-size pieces, boil until cooked then mash with butter, seasoning, cream and milk if required to make a smooth mashed potato. Spread over the top of the meat in the casserole dish, rake with a table fork and bake in the oven.

#113. Braised lamb shoulder chops

Brown the chops in a frypan in oil, garlic and thyme then remove to a casserole pan. Brown the carrots, celery and lemon slices till brown then add to the chops and pour in red wine and chicken stock. Into a bowl put a can of crushed tomatoes, cumin, bay leaf, coriander, garlic and soy. Mix well and add to the vegetables and chops. Simmer slowly in the oven till cooked so check after

80 minutes for tenderness. Once the meat is cooked, remove the chops and thicken the sauce with a roux (flour and butter equal quantities) and add the cooking liquid stirring all the time till it thickens. Return the chops back to the sauce and top with chopped coriander.

#114. Lamb backstrap with deep-fried vegetables

In a mixing bowl place chopped rosemary, thyme, olive oil, crushed garlic, mint leaves, seasoning and Cajun spice. Put the lamb into mixing bowl and marinate for an hour. Prepare carrots, parsnip and sweet potato by peeling and cutting into similar-sized pieces then slice aubergine and courgettes. Parboil the root vegetables then plunge into iced water to stop them cooking. Place the lamb into a hot oven in a roasting pan (200°C) for 10 minutes with garlic along with the aubergine and courgettes until nicely browned then remove from the dish and set aside. Deep fry the root vegetables until brown then drain on kitchen paper. Arrange the vegetables on rocket on a serving dish, slice the rested lamb and place on the vegetables then dress with wasabi and sour cream dressing.

#115. Lamb with prunes and almonds

In a frypan, brown and seal the diced lamb in oil and garlic then place in an ovenproof casserole dish that has a lid. In the same pan on reduced heat add cinnamon, ground cardamom, turmeric and a pinch of chilli flakes. Add more oil and add sliced red onions and cook till they are transparent. Add a tin of crushed tomatoes, soaked dried prunes and deglaze the pan then add to the casserole. Peel and dice sweet potatoes, add to the casserole, add seasoning then bake in the oven. When the lamb is cooked, add a can of chickpeas and runny honey if it requires a little sweetening. Stir in thick natural yoghurt and top with flaked toasted almonds.

#116. Moroccan harissa lamb shank

Lamb shanks, Moroccan spice, harissa paste, onion, garlic, paprika, ground coriander, cumin, turmeric, cinnamon, canned whole peeled tomatoes, chickpeas, honey, carrots diced and grated, couscous, fresh coriander. Brown the lamb shanks in a frypan in oil, Moroccan spice and garlic then place in a casserole dish. To the frypan, add coriander, cinnamon, cumin, diced onions, carrots and brown. Pour in the tomatoes, drained chickpeas, harissa paste, paprika and honey. Top up with chicken stock and braise slowly in the oven till the meat pulls away from the bone. Remove the lamb shanks, thicken the sauce with a roux, season and serve with chopped coriander sprinkled over the top. Accompany with turmeric couscous mixed with raisins and grated carrot.

#117. Moussaka

Roast potatoes and slices of aubergine in a roasting pan in the oven with garlic. Remove them from the pan as they are cooked then set aside. Prepare a meat sauce similar to a Bolognese sauce with diced onions, garlic, tomato purée and paste, chickpeas and beef stock then set aside. Prepare a béchamel keeping it thick and creamy and at the end add grated cheese, crumbled feta and an egg yolk. Slice the potatoes and lay in a buttered casserole then top with meat sauce. Next layer is sliced aubergine and cheese sauce. Continue layering till the casserole is full; the top layer should be the white cheese sauce. Sprinkle with grated cheese and bake in the oven at 170°C till cooked through and glazed on top.

#118. Braised lamb in satay sauce

Cut the lamb into cubes and fry in a frypan in oil, garlic and sliced chilli to brown but not cooked through. Place in a casserole and in the same pan fry diced onion, chopped capsicum, diced smoked red capsicum, celery and carrot batons then add a can of tomatoes and add all to the browned lamb. Add satay sauce to the casserole. In a dry frypan, heat unsalted peanuts till they just start browning then cool and blitz in a food processor. Add to the casserole and check seasoning. Slow cook in the oven for 70 minutes and check the tenderness of the lamb. When cooked, thicken the sauce with cornflour and water if necessary, check seasoning and serve over rice.

#119. Lamb Kashmir rice

In a frypan add oil then brown sugar, a can of drained kidney beans, turmeric, cumin, cardamom, diced onions, cinnamon, celery, coriander and chilli flakes and heat on a low heat. In another frypan, brown cubed lamb in diced ginger and garlic then add a can of crushed tomatoes. Heat slowly and mix well then add uncooked rice. Add the spice pan contents to the lamb along with pistachios and whole almonds. Top with chicken stock, bring to a simmer than bake in the oven with a lid on the pan. Check seasoning, stir well and serve.

#120. Lamb harissa

Cut the lamb into 25 mm cubes then place in a mixing bowl with cumin, coriander and flour. Brown the lamb in oil, batch frying so that the pan is not overloaded. Add sliced onions and diced root ginger to brown then pour in white wine. Allow to reduce then add tomato purée, harissa paste, a can of crushed tomatoes, grated zest of a lemon, lemon juice and runny honey. Place a lid on the casserole and bake in the oven at 150°C for 90 minutes. When cooked add a can of cannellini beans and stir in sour cream. Serve with sliced ciabatta garlic bread.

#121. Lamb strudel

Using minced lamb, fry in oil, butter, diced onion, garlic, thyme and oregano till all the lamb is browned. Reduce heat, add a knob of butter and the same volume of flour and stir then slowly add chicken stock till it thickens. Let it reduce so that there is only a small amount of liquid. Leave to go cold then sprinkle in feta cheese, defrosted and well-drained spinach, seasoning and nutmeg. Mix well. Butter four sheets of filo pastry and place on top of each other on a sheet of baking paper. Spoon the lamb mixture over three quarters of the pastry and keeping in from the edges. Top the lamb with chopped pistachio nuts. Fold in the sides then roll the strudel into a log shape and place on a baking tray. Brush with butter and bake for 50 minutes at 190°C till golden brown. Serve with a lamb gravy.

#122. Roast lamb with a basil pesto crust

Remove any excess fat from the lamb and stud with garlic and rosemary pieces. In a mixing bowl put fresh breadcrumbs, crushed garlic, black pepper, chopped parsley, basil pesto, olive oil and a beaten egg. Mix well to a moist paste and apply to the lamb joint. Top the joint with a sheet of tinfoil and bake in the oven slowly at 160°C. When cooked, remove the foil and bake for 20 minutes uncovered allowing the crust to bake and brown. Leave to rest then carve.

#123. Lamb patties

Lamb patties — mince, grated onion, bulgur wheat. Filling — diced onions, pine nuts, bulgur wheat, cinnamon, allspice, chopped parsley and mint, chopped pistachios, seasoning. Into a mixing bowl put mince, onion, juice of a lemon and grated lemon zest and bulgur wheat that has soaked in cold water for 20 minutes then drained. Mix well by hand and if too wet add freshly grated breadcrumbs or if too dry add an egg and seasoning. Divide the mince into equal-size balls, roll and then press out onto a chopping board into an oblong about 15 mm thick. Add all the ingredients together for the filling and spread over each of the mince oblongs. Roll the mince into cigar shapes and place on a baking tray and bake in the oven at 180°C till cooked. Serve with yoghurt and mint sauce.

#124. Lamb turnover

Dredge diced lamb through flour and brown in a frypan with oil, crushed garlic, thyme and chopped rosemary then place in a lidded casserole dish. Deglaze the pan with red wine, tomato paste then add anchovies. Cook in the oven till the lamb is tender, the sauce has thickened then leave to go cold. With a sheet of store-bought puff pastry, cut out a circle 140 mm in diameter and place on baking paper on a baking tray. Spoon some of the lamb onto the pastry but don't overfill otherwise it will blow out the pastry while baking. Brush the edges with egg wash, fold in half then brush the top with egg wash and bake at 200°C till golden brown.

#125. Lamb curry

Fry diced lamb in oil, grated ginger, crushed garlic, turmeric, garam masala, chilli, chopped lemongrass stalk, cinnamon, fenugreek then add a can of crushed tomatoes and tomato paste. Top with chicken stock and simmer gently till the lamb is tender. Check seasoning then add fresh spinach leaves and plain yoghurt. Stir and serve on rice with naan bread.

#126. Lamb chop crust

In a mixing bowl, place panko breadcrumbs, cumin, mint leaves, ground coriander, pepper, garlic mixed with vegetable oil in a mortar and pestle. Add salt and cracked black pepper. The ingredients should be wet enough to form a paste. Spoon the mixture onto the chops and mound it. Bake the chops in the oven until cooked through and serve with mint jelly.

#127. Envelope of lamb

Cut the lamb into large pieces around 200 g each. Brown in a frypan on both sides then set aside. In the same pan brown finger-sized pieces of carrot and celery along with diced onions, mixed herbs, mint and oregano. On a bench top, lay out sheets of foil with baking paper on top. Lay a piece of lamb in the centre and top with the vegetables include sprigs of mint and seasoning. In the frypan add butter, a spoonful of Dijon and chicken stock and reduce quickly removing the pan drippings on the base of the pan. Spoon the sauce over the lamb and fold the baking paper and foil to the top so that leakage from the packet cannot occur. Bake in a slow oven for 2 hours or until the lamb is cooked. Take great care when opening the packages to inspect the contents. The steam can cause serious burns.

#128. Greek lamb and cheese filo

Wash the mince in a bowl of water so that it breaks apart into small pieces. Drain well then place on a baking tray and brown in the oven with oil, grated lemon zest, crushed garlic, seasoning. When brown spoon into a saucepan with cooked diced onions and add a small amount of passata sauce just to bind the mix together then leave to cool. Butter four sheets of filo pastry and stack on top of each other. Spoon the cold lamb onto the centre of the filo in a row then spread out keeping the edges clear. Top with frozen spinach that has been thawed and well drained then sprinkle with grated cheddar and a few flaked olives. Roll the filo and seal with butter. Place on a baking tray seam side down, slice a few cuts in the top to allow the steam to escape and bake at 200°C till golden brown.

#129. Lamb casserole with prunes and cinnamon

Cut lamb into 25 mm cubes then brown in a frypan in oil and garlic. Remove and place in a casserole and hold. In the same frypan brown diced onions, whole baby carrots, whole baby potatoes and baby sweet potatoes. Reduce the heat and add sliced garlic and root ginger, cumin, turmeric, cinnamon and chilli flakes. Pour in chicken stock and add prunes, bring to a simmer then add to the casserole. Bake in the oven on a low heat at 160°C for 2 hours. Check that the lamb is cooked and tender, season and serve.

#130. Lamb cutlets with sun-dried tomato butter

Prepare the butter by chopping the sun-dried tomatoes into small pieces then add some of the oil, chopped parsley, mint and black cracked pepper. Mix well with soft butter then roll in cling wrap to form a cylinder 30 mm in diameter. Hold in the fridge or the freezer. Season the lamb cutlets which could have the end of the bone end 'Frenched' and either grill or fry till both sides are browned but the centre is just cooked. Rest for 10 minutes then slice the sun-dried tomato butter and place on top of the cutlets. The butter should be melting as it is being served.

#131. Lamb and polenta casserole

Prepare the polenta as per the instructions on the packet whether it be instant or slow-cooking polenta. You can use any meat casserole or cooked mince (beef, chicken, pork, vegetarian) for this dish. When the polenta is cooked, smooth out onto an oiled flat tray approximately 10 mm thick and leave to cool. Lightly butter a casserole dish and spoon in cooked meat. Top with grated cheese then cut a slice of polenta to fit the casserole and place on top of the cheese. Complete a second layer, cover with tinfoil and bake in the oven till heated through, approximately 20 minutes. Remove tinfoil, brush with butter and sprinkle with grated cheese and grill till the cheese browns.

#132. Pastitso (Greek-style lasagne)

Lamb mince, oil, garlic, onions, bay leaf. Brown the mince in oil with onions and garlic then add red wine, bay leaves and reduce. Prepare a béchamel sauce and cook penne pasta and drain off before it's al dente. Into a casserole dish add the cold penne pasta, lamb mince and mix in the béchamel. Top with cheese and bake.

4.

CHICKEN

#	Dish	#	Dish
133	Chicken And Cashews	191	Fricassee Of Chicken With Potatoes
134	Roasted Satay Chicken	192	Chicken In Smoked Red Pepper Sauce
135	Roasted Butter Chicken	193	Crumbed Chicken Tenders
136	Butter Chicken And Vegetable Pie	194	Chicken With Cashews #2
137	Lemon Butter Chicken	195	Sesame Chicken
138	Chicken In Tomato And Basil Cream	196	Chicken In White Wine And Balsamic Vinegar
139	Jerk Sauce (Jamaican)	197	Braised Chicken With Lemon And Olives
140	Chicken Pieces With Yoghurt And Harissa Sauce	198	Chicken And Capsicum
141	Coconut Chicken Casserole	199	Chicken Meatballs Cordon Bleu
142	Fried Chicken	200	Deep Fried Chicken And Coconut
143	Quick Brined Chicken	201	Chicken Breast With Sun-Dried Tomato Cream Sauce
144	Baked Chicken And Pesto	202	Chicken And Pineapple Bake
145	Chicken In Pineapple	203	Chicken Breasts With Sun-Dried Tomatoes, Spinach And Cheese
146	Ritz Chicken	204	Chicken Parmigiana
147	Skewered Chicken	205	Chicken With Basil Pesto And Bacon
148	Chicken Limoncello	206	Chicken Breast Stuffed With Pesto And Cream Cheese
149	Chicken, Bacon And Smoked Red Pepper	207	Lemon And Herb Crust Chicken
150	Pistachio Chicken	208	Asian Style Chicken

#133. Chicken and cashews

Use chicken breast and cut into 30 mm cubes. Put the chicken in a bowl with crushed garlic, diced root ginger, soy sauce, sesame oil and sherry. Marinate for an hour. Drain off the chicken pieces and in a very hot frypan or wok, fry the chicken in oil and a few drops of sesame oil added till brown then hold in another pan till all is cooked. Don't overload the pan otherwise the chicken will stew. Once the chicken is cooked, in the same pan, fry sliced capsicums, sliced carrots and sliced onions. Put the cooked chicken in with the vegetables and pour the marinade over it then add roughly chopped dry-fried cashew nuts.

#134. Roasted satay chicken

Rub the chicken with turmeric, crushed garlic, diced root ginger and cumin then leave overnight in the fridge. Prepare a paste of lemon grass, garlic and root ginger in a mortar and pestle. Add coconut milk, lime juice and chilli flakes and mix well. Dry roast 250 g peanuts in a frypan then roughly blend in a food processor. Mix in kecap manis (Malaysian) and mix well. Spread the paste over the chicken keeping it thick then place in a roasting tray. Start on a low heat at 130°C for an hour then raise to 160°C till cooked.

#135. Roasted butter chicken

In a mixing bowl pour natural yoghurt, tomato paste, chilli, cumin and a store-bought butter chicken paste. Put the chicken into the marinade and leave for at least 2 hours. On the chicken breast, pull the skin back and put some of the marinade between the skin and the meat. Then put the chicken into a casserole dish and roast slowly, basting with the sauce every half hour. Leave to rest when cooked.

#136. Butter chicken and vegetable pie

Fry diced chicken in a frypan in oil, grated ginger, garlic, cumin and coriander then place in a saucepan and set aside. Into the same frypan, fry the onions, sliced zucchini, mushrooms and stock. Pour into the saucepan and cook the chicken and vegetables. Leave to go cold. Line a pie tin with short pastry and bake blind. Add yoghurt to the chicken then spoon into the cooked pastry case. Top with puff pastry, egg wash and bake in the oven at 200°C till the pastry is brown.

#137. Lemon butter chicken

Chicken breasts, chicken stock, baby spinach, paprika, cloves of garlic, butter, lemon juice, cream, thyme, Parmesan. Melt butter in a frypan then add chicken, garlic, paprika, thyme on a gentle heat then brown the chicken. Add lemon juice and stock then bake in the oven. When the chicken is cooked add the spinach, cream and top with Parmesan and put back in the oven for 10 more minutes then serve.

#138. Chicken in tomato and basil cream

In a frypan, fry the chicken breasts in oil, butter, crushed garlic and thyme. When the chicken breasts are brown pour in store-bought tomato pasta sauce style mix with chicken stock and oven bake for 20 minutes. When cooked remove from the oven, add torn basil leaves and stir into the sauce along with cream. Check seasoning and serve.

#139. Jerk sauce (Jamaican)

Rum and vinegar, nutmeg, all spice, thyme, bay leaves, scotch bonnet chilli, red onion, garlic, salt, caster sugar, oil — blitz in a food processor. Jerk sauce is a very hot spicy sauce — beware.

#140. Chicken pieces

Dice chicken pieces then put through flour, batter and deep fry till brown. When the batter is brown, remove and cool. Cook the chicken again on a barbecue and serve with a yoghurt and harissa sauce.

#141. Coconut chicken casserole

Sweat off sliced onions, sliced capsicum, smoked red capsicums, garlic and chilli then seal off chicken in the pan. Add chicken stock and coconut milk and bake in the oven. At the same time put shredded coconut on a baking tray and lightly colour. Season and thicken and finish off with coconut cream over the top followed by baked shredded coconut.

#142. Fried chicken

Chicken pieces, self-raising flour, eggs, onion, buttermilk, bacon, salt and water. Whisk salt, flour, buttermilk, eggs, garlic and pepper in a bowl and add chicken pieces. Remove the chicken and dip them through a flour and egg seasoning mix twice so that they are well covered. Fry in oil to brown then oven bake.

#143. Quick brined chicken

Brine is cold water and sea salt, caster sugar, garlic, bay leaves, lemon, peppercorns, thyme and rosemary. Stir well so that all ingredients have dissolved then brine the chicken.

#144. Baked chicken and pesto

Bake the chicken in a casserole or baking dish with sliced onions and garlic. Brush with butter and oil while baking. When nearly cooked brush with sun-dried tomato pesto and continue baking.

#145. Chicken in pineapple

Diced chicken, pineapple juice, garlic, ginger, brown sugar, soy sauce and chilli flakes. Brown the diced chicken in a frypan along with garlic and diced root ginger. When brown, place in a lidded casserole dish. In the same frypan, fry diced onions, diced capsicums then pour in pineapple juice, soy sauce and add chilli flakes. Heat and allow to reduce slightly. Adjust the sweet taste with brown sugar, malt vinegar and seasoning. Pour it over the chicken and bake in the oven for 30 minutes. Serve with rice.

#146. Ritz chicken

Break up a sleeve of Ritz crackers into crumbs. Cut the breasts into cubes then add beaten egg whites to the bowl and dip into the Ritz crumbs. Place on a baking tray and oven bake. When cooked pour a chilli lime dressing over the top and serve with aioli mayonnaise.

#147. Skewered chicken

Slice the chicken into thin slices. Whisk together rice wine, cornflour, egg white and place the chicken in the marinade and in the fridge for 30 minutes. Soak wooden skewers in water for at least 30 minutes or use metal skewers and thread the chicken onto the skewers and grill in the oven or on the barbecue. **Sauce:** Oil, grated ginger, minced garlic, Coca-Cola, hoisin sauce, soy, sesame oil, brown sugar, cornflour and spring onions. Fry the onions, garlic in oil and sesame oil then add the Coke, hoisin sauce, soy and brown sugar. Bring to a simmer and thicken with a cornflour and water slurry. Brush over the chicken while it is cooking and serve as an accompanying sauce.

#148. Chicken limoncello

Put the chicken breasts through seasoned flour and fry in butter till brown on both sides. Add chicken stock to the pan along with lemon juice, grated lemon zest and limoncello. When ready to serve, check seasoning, brown lemon slices on a hot plate and use as a garnish on the serving plate.

#149. Chicken, bacon and smoked red pepper

Prepare the chicken breast by beating with a rolling pin to flatten out. Crumb in flour, egg wash and breadcrumbs then fry. When cooked, top with cooked bacon pieces, slices of smoked red pepper, grated cheese then grill.

#150. Pistachio chicken

Cut the breasts and butterfly them. In a bowl, mix runny honey with a beaten egg and crushed garlic. Mix chopped pistachios with panko crumbs and chopped parsley. Flour, egg wash and crumb the chicken then fry quickly in the frypan in hot butter and finish off in the oven.

#151. Chicken Caprese

Flatten out the chicken with a rolling pin then fry in oil and butter till cooked. Remove from the pan and rest for a few minutes. Place the chicken on the serving plate then top with a round of mozzarella cheese, a slice of tomato then chopped basil. Drizzle with a balsamic vinegar reduction.

#152. Rolled stuffed chicken

Slice a chicken breast lengthways then open out so that it is shaped like a butterfly. Prepare a bread-based stuffing with herbs, breadcrumbs, cheese, parsley, eggs, sun-dried tomatoes then roll and tie the chicken and treat it like a thin roast meat.

#153. Rolled stuffed chicken breast with cheese

Slice the chicken breast in half lengthways and open out like a butterfly. In the centre place cheddar cheese sticks 10 x 10 mm and cream cheese. Season then roll up and tie. Roast in the oven.

#154. Chicken, sausage and mushroom casserole

Any cuts of chicken can be used whether they are bone in or out. Brown the chicken and sausages in a frypan with garlic to seal then place in a casserole dish. To the frypan, add diced onions, sliced smoked red peppers then place in the casserole. Cook the mushrooms in butter in the same pan then add chicken stock to deglaze pouring all into the casserole dish. Add tomato paste or canned tomatoes to the chicken along with diced potatoes 15 mm cubed. Bake the casserole in the oven with the lid on till the chicken and potatoes are cooked. Check seasoning then thicken the sauce if necessary and serve. This could also be cooked in a slow cooker.

#155. Fried chicken with blue cheese dressing

Slice chicken breasts into strips widthways. Mix flour with paprika and seasoning, and buttermilk with crushed garlic. Press the chicken pieces into the flour on both sides, dip into buttermilk then back into the flour and fry in oil till golden brown.

Dressing: Mayonnaise, blue cheese crumbled, crushed garlic, Worcestershire sauce and a few drops of Tabasco. Mix well.

#156. Chicken and sweet potato pie

This dish can use whatever chicken is available. It could be freshly cooked or leftover roast. Cut the chicken into large dice-style pieces. Peel and cut the sweet potato into uniform sizes and cook in boiling salted water till soft. Drain and set aside. Make a béchamel sauce to combine the chicken and sweet potatoes. Sweat off diced onions, garlic and ginger then toss in the sweet potato followed by the chicken. Spoon into a buttered casserole then spoon the béchamel over the mix. Top with caramelised onions, grated cheese then oven bake.

#157. Chicken and leek casserole

Brown the chicken breasts in a frypan then add sliced onions and leeks. Remove to a casserole then add more butter to the pan and fry sliced mushrooms adding to the chicken. Add a few sliced sun-dried tomatoes then braise in the oven. When cooked, remove the chicken and leave aside. Reduce the sauce then add cream and a little mustard to taste.

#158. Chilli chicken

Using tinned peaches, drain the can and pour the liquid into a small saucepan. Add chilli flakes, brown sugar, diced root ginger, butter and reduce till it becomes syrupy. Add Thai sweet chilli sauce then use this mixture to baste the chicken on a baking tray. Continue to baste the chicken while it is cooking in the oven. Serve with a bacon and avocado salsa.

#159. Cajun chicken strips

Slice the chicken breasts into large fingers. Dip them into buttermilk, garlic and egg mix then into flour that has paprika and Cajun spice added, then back into the buttermilk mix and fry in the frypan in oil. Serve with a tomato-based pasta sauce that has Cajun spice added to it.

#160. Rolled chicken breast

Lay the chicken breast on its side and with a sharp knife cut the chicken breast into two equal halves. Beat them both out lightly to a uniform thickness. Spread with sun-dried tomato pesto, a slice of smoked cheese and a piece of sliced cooked bacon. Roll up the chicken and hold with a toothpick. Dredge in flour, egg wash and breadcrumbs to which Parmesan and paprika have been added. Fry in a frypan in oil and butter till brown then finish off in the oven. Leave to rest.

#161. Lime marmalade chicken

Cut the chicken into pieces and brown in a frypan in oil and butter then place in a casserole. In the same frypan, add sliced onions, crushed garlic, diced ginger, and turmeric. Pour it on the chicken then add fresh lime juice and sliced zest, thick-cut marmalade and oven bake till the chicken is cooked. If necessary, thicken the sauce, add seasoning and serve on rice.

#162. Smoked paprika chicken

Chicken pieces, smoked paprika, diced onions, tomato paste, crushed tomatoes, caraway seeds, garlic, turned potatoes. Rub the chicken pieces through flour that has smoked paprika sifted into it then brown the chicken in a frypan in oil and crushed garlic. Remove when brown but not cooked through and in the same frypan, fry diced onions then add caraway seeds, canned tomatoes, tomato paste, smoked paprika and chicken stock. Bring to a simmer. Peel small potatoes and cut into shapes of small barrels then put into the saucepan with the chicken. The sauce should thicken due to the flour on the chicken but if not thick enough, remove the chicken when it has cooked and simmer the sauce to reduce. Season, return the chicken to the sauce, add crème fraîche and serve.

#163. Chicken breast with walnut and date stuffing

Prepare the stuffing by using fresh breadcrumbs, sliced dates, chopped walnuts, fried diced shallots, chopped coriander and an egg. Mix well and season the mix. Slice the chicken breast in half lengthways to form a butterfly cut. Place the stuffing on one side of the chicken breast, fold the other side back and hold in place with toothpicks. Fry the chicken breast in a frypan in oil and butter till brown on both sides. When the chicken is cooked, place on serving plate and drizzle the chicken with brown butter.

#164. Chicken in paprika and cream

With a rolling pin, beat the chicken breast so that they are all uniform in thickness. Fry in butter, oil, garlic and paprika till brown on both sides then set to one side. In the same pan brown sliced onions then pour in a half cup of chicken stock and allow to reduce. Add brown sugar then return the chicken to the pan and pour in cream, season and simmer gently. Fry sliced mushrooms in butter and add to the chicken.

#165. Chicken in cream and basil sauce

Dip the chicken through flour, egg wash and breadcrumbs and fry in a butter/oil mix with crushed garlic. Cook till brown on both sides then remove from the pan. Add a small amount of chicken stock to deglaze the pan then pour in cream. Heat gently adding basil, diced tomatoes, a half teaspoon of mustard and seasoning. Return the chicken to the pan and baste with the sauce then serve.

#166. Roast chicken with a cream cheese stuffing

Cut a bulb of garlic in half and bake in the oven till soft. Leave to cool then squeeze the cloves out and mix with cream cheese, chopped rosemary and chopped parsley. Cut the crusts off three slices of bread and tear into small pieces then mix with the cream cheese and a beaten egg. Spoon the stuffing into the chicken cavity and between the breast meat and skin. Place a piece of bread over the end of the cavity and hold with toothpicks then bake slowly in the oven till cooked.

#167. Chicken bruschetta and ravioli

Use chicken breasts or thighs and fry in oil till golden brown. Finish off in the oven if necessary. Slice and deseed fresh tomatoes then cut into 15 mm size slices and place in a mixing bowl. Add torn basil leaves, balsamic vinegar, oil and crushed garlic. In a saucepan of boiling water, cook ravioli till al dente. Place the chicken in a serving tray then add ravioli and the tomato mixture over the top and mix well. Serve with shaved Parmesan cheese.

#168. Miso-glazed whole roasted chicken

Prepare the roasting dish for the chicken by cutting root vegetables and placing on the bottom of the roasting dish. Add sliced bulbs of garlic, chunks of lemon and pieces of ginger. Prepare a miso glaze by mixing miso paste, sesame oil, dry sherry, a little warm water and sugar. Paint it on the chicken, splash with oil then bake the chicken. Continue basting while it is cooking.

#169. Braised Asian chicken

In a small bowl of water add soy sauce, brown sugar, hoisin sauce, sesame oil, Tabasco sauce, crushed garlic, root ginger and combine well. Add chicken breast to the sauce and allow to sit for 2 hours. Place the chicken in a casserole dish then pour in the sauce, cover with a lid or foil and bake in the oven. When the chicken is cooked add fried sliced mushrooms to the dish, check seasoning and serve.

#170. Bacon and sage chicken

Melt butter and paint the chicken all over. Wrap the chicken in streaky bacon which has leaves of sage stuffed underneath the bacon. Fill the chicken cavity with lemon halves. Roast slowly in the oven till golden brown and cooked through.

#171. Chicken lemon tenders

Beat out the chicken breast under a sheet of cling wrap to give a uniform thickness. Slice the breast in a diagonal cut then dip through a mix of flour/cornflour, into a mix of beaten egg, soy sauce and lemon juice, back into the flour mix and fry in oil till golden brown. When all the chicken is cooked, drain the frypan and add lemon juice to deglaze along with water, caster sugar then reduce. Add sliced lemon zest, thicken with cornflour and season. Put the chicken back into the sauce, stir then serve.

#172. Baked chicken Parmesan

Slice the chicken breast in half lengthways and beat out with a rolling pin. Dip through flour, egg wash then flour mixed with Parmesan. Place on an oiled baking tray and bake in the oven till cooked then spoon over pomodoro sauce and top with grated cheese. Bake in the oven to melt the cheese.

#173. Soy chicken wing casserole

Simmer the chicken wings quickly in salted water with spring onions, sliced ginger and garlic for 2 minutes only. Drain the chicken then fry in oil with garlic and ginger. When brown add soy sauce, brown sugar, rice wine and chicken stock. Simmer gently for 20 minutes to cook the chicken and reduce the sauce. Check the chicken for tenderness and seasoning and serve over noodles.

#174. Garlic chicken breasts

Remove the skin and place the chicken in a roasting tin. Season with salt and pepper then rub with soft garlic butter and bake in the oven. Continue to spoon the butter over the chicken while it is cooking. When cooked, top with grated cheese, chopped rosemary then grill.

#175. Orange chicken

Dice the chicken into 25 mm cubes then place in beaten egg then flour and fry till brown. For the sauce, put orange juice and zest in a saucepan with malt vinegar, brown sugar, garlic, diced root ginger and a sliced bird's eye chilli. The taste effect should be sweet and sour and that can be adjusted by using more malt vinegar or sugar. Check seasoning then place the cooked chicken into the sauce and serve with rice.

#176. Chicken moneybags

Lay a sheet of savoury short pastry (store-bought) on the bench and cut into four segments. Into a mixing bowl, place cooked diced chicken, melted butter, cream cheese, seasoning, diced onion, chopped spring onions and mix well. Place some of the filling into the centre of one of the pastry segments then fold up each corner to the top of the meat. Add more folds up if necessary to seal the pastry then tie in place with a piece of string. Brush with egg wash then bake at 200°C till golden brown.

#177. Ranch chicken

In a mixing bowl put olive oil, crushed garlic, sliced capsicum, lemon juice and zest, a pinch of cayenne and ranch dressing. Put the chicken thighs into bowl and mix well then brown in a frypan and brown on both sides. Place into a casserole and pour the mix over the chicken and the other ingredients and bake. Remove the chicken and rest. Check the sauce for thickness and taste. Add a little pouring cream, bring to the boil and return the chicken to the sauce then serve.

#178. Thai chicken with peanut sauce

Dice chicken and place in a mixing bowl. In another bowl put fish sauce, chilli flakes, 100 g brown sugar, oil, 300 g peanut butter, 1 tsp sesame oil and mix well. Brown the chicken in a frypan in oil then spoon some of the sauce over the chicken and bake in the oven. Continue to spoon more sauce over the chicken while it is in the oven. Serve on rice with the sauce spread over the chicken.

#179. Chicken with tomatoes and basil

Fry the chicken breast in oil and butter and when cooked, set aside and keep warm. In the same pan toss cherry tomatoes with chopped basil and a little chicken stock. Return the chicken to the pan, top the chicken with slices of mozzarella, put a lid on the pan, reduce the heat and leave to cook through.

#180. Roast black pepper chicken

Place the chicken pieces in a mixing bowl and pour over soy sauce, white vinegar, olive oil, diced ginger, pinch chilli flakes, runny honey and ground black pepper. Mix well and leave to marinate for an hour. Remove the chicken from the marinade, dry and fry in oil and butter till cooked through then pour in the marinade and simmer gently. Check the sauce for taste and adjust if necessary.

#181. Cream chicken casserole

Chicken breasts diced, cream cheese, cream of chicken soup, Italian dressing seasoning. Fry the chicken breasts in oil/butter till browned on both sides then set aside and keep warm. Pour the chicken soup into the pan then add the cream cheese and simmer gently. Pour into a casserole dish and oven bake till cooked through. Drizzle with the Italian dressing.

#182. Chicken breast with peppercorn, lime and caper sauce

In a frypan, cook the chicken breasts till just cooked through then set aside and keep warm. Deglaze the pan with lime juice then add capers and cracked pepper. Pour cream into the frypan and simmer gently then return the chicken breasts back to the frypan, check seasoning, add chopped parsley and serve.

#183. Braised chicken pieces in thyme and coconut cream

Use one particular cut of chicken, for example thighs or breasts. Fry in a frypan with fresh thyme, sliced onions and crushed garlic till brown then place in a casserole dish. Deglaze the pan with chicken stock and add to the chicken. Add seasoning and oven bake for 30 minutes slowly until chicken is cooked. Remove the chicken then add coconut cream to the sauce and reduce. Thicken the sauce with a roux or cornflour then return the chicken back to the sauce. Coat the top with dry-fried desiccated coconut and serve.

#184. Italian chicken

Line the base of a casserole dish with a pomodoro or tomato pasta sauce to 6 mm and add in defrosted spinach. Season the chicken breasts and place in the sauce. Spoon the breasts with basil pesto and spread it over then sprinkle with dried Italian herbs. Top with grated cheese and bake in the oven for 40 minutes. Check that it is cooked, top with fresh basil and serve.

#185. Chicken stir-fry

Cut slices from the chicken breast approximately 20 mm wide. Cut capsicum, onion, beans, celery and the base of bok choy thinly so that it will cook fast. Roughly chop the bok choy leaves. In a wok or frypan heat a vegetable oil then add chopped garlic, ginger and chilli. Quickly add vegetables and stir while cooking.

Don't overload the pan and cook in batches if necessary. Add the chicken pieces and cook through. Return the vegetables then pour over soy sauce, fish sauce and sprinkle through sesame seeds. Add cooked noodles and turn through the vegetables then serve immediately. Top with chopped coriander and sesame seeds.

#186. Baked chicken pieces

Chicken pieces of choice then for the egg wash put eggs, buttermilk, baking powder and baking soda into a bowl and mix well. Onto a tray put flour, smoked paprika, garlic, onion powder and sugar. Dip the chicken through the egg wash then into the flour mix. Repeat again then place the chicken into a hot baking dish that has hot oil in it. Oven bake for 20 minutes, turn over then bake for another 20 minutes or until the chicken is cooked.

#187. Chicken and broccoli casserole

Use either chicken thigh and legs or diced chicken. Brown the chicken in a frypan with oil, butter, garlic then place into a casserole dish. In the same pan, fry sliced onions and capsicums then add chicken stock to deglaze the pan and add to the casserole dish. Cut the florets off the broccoli and set aside. With the leftover root of the broccoli cut into dice and add to the chicken and oven bake. When it has cooked for 20 minutes, add the broccoli florets to the casserole and return to the oven for another 20 minutes or until the chicken is cooked. When cooked place the chicken in a serving dish, thicken the sauce with a roux then add crème fraîche at the end. Check seasoning, pour it over the chicken and serve.

#188. Chicken in paprika and spinach sauce

Fry the chicken breasts in a frypan in oil, garlic and butter turning over so that both sides brown. Add in sliced onions and when they begin to caramelise add a teaspoon of smoky paprika then baby spinach leaves. Allow the leaves to wilt then pour in cream. Bring to a gentle simmer, season then serve.

#189. Creamy jambalaya chicken

Fry the diced chicken breast in oil with Cajun spice then remove from the pan. Add sliced sausages to the same pan then sliced red onion and chopped capsicum. Lastly, add prawns and when they are nearly cooked pour in a tomato pasta-style sauce. Add cooked penne pasta to the frypan and mix all together. Stir in cream, check the seasoning and serve.

#190. New Orleans chicken

Into a mixing bowl pour teriyaki sauce and add brown sugar. Stir well, pour into a Ziploc bag, place the chicken pieces into the bag and marinate overnight. Dry the chicken off and brown in a frypan; sprinkle with sugar while it is browning. Then slice and cook smoked sausage in the same pan along with sliced capsicums, garlic, tomatoes. Pour the marinade into a saucepan and heat then add runny honey and a pinch of chilli flakes. Thicken the sauce with cornflour, season and pour it over the chicken. Continue to simmer till the chicken and sausage is cooked then serve with rice.

#191. Fricassee of chicken with potatoes

Cut the chicken into cubes and dredge with seasoned flour then fry in a frypan till sealed on all sides and doing by batches if necessary, then place in a casserole dish. In the same frypan, brown the carrot strips, diced onions and potatoes, crushed garlic, mixed herbs and add button mushrooms. Add all to the casserole, top with chicken stock and oven bake for 45 minutes. The sauce should be thick now through the flour, but should it not be thick enough, make a roux and add the cooking liquid to thicken it. Season, add chopped parsley, lemon juice and cream. Return the chicken back to the sauce.

#192. Chicken in smoked red pepper sauce

In a frypan, brown the chicken pieces in oil and garlic then add to a casserole dish. In the same pan, brown diced onion, roughly chopped red capsicum and tomato paste then add to the casserole. Slice smoked red pepper, which is sold in jars, and add to the chicken then bake in the oven for 45 minutes. Check for taste and seasoning and pour in sour cream. Top with chopped coriander.

#193. Crumbed chicken tenders

Dredge the chicken tenders in flour, egg wash and breadcrumbs then fry in butter, oil and garlic. When all are cooked, remove from pan. Pour 50 ml of bourbon into the pan and reduce by half then add cream and chopped chives. Check the seasoning and taste then pour it over the chicken.

#194. Chicken and cashews No. 2

In a mixing bowl, put soy, vinegar, ketchup, brown sugar, garlic and diced root ginger. Marinate the diced chicken in the liquid for three hours. Remove and dry the chicken then dredge through the flour. Fry the chicken in a wok then batch cook diced onions, capsicum, beans and broccoli adding a little of the marinade while frying. Place all the chicken and vegetables in a holding tray, thicken the sauce in the wok using cornflour, return the chicken and vegetables back to the wok. Add cherry tomatoes and top with dry pan-fried cashew nuts.

#195. Sesame chicken

Flour then brown the cubed chicken pieces in sesame oil and oil then place in a roasting pan. In a mixing bowl put soy sauce, a few drops of sesame oil, grated ginger, chopped garlic, brown sugar and sesame seeds and stir. Add a small amount of stock to the roasting pan if required. Cook the chicken on low for 20 minutes then check the chicken. Heat and thicken the sauce with a cornflour and water slurry. Put the chicken in a saucepan, pour the sauce over the chicken and top with white sesame seeds. Heat on an element for 4 minutes, check seasoning and serve over rice.

#196. Chicken in white wine and balsamic vinegar

With chicken legs and thighs, fry in butter, oil and garlic in a frypan then add in diced bacon and cook till they are nicely browned. Add in white wine and allow the wine to reduce then pour in balsamic vinegar and again reduce. Add pepper but check for salt as the bacon will be salty. Once the sauce becomes a little thicker and the chicken is cooked, place the chicken on a serving plate and coat with the sauce.

#197. Braised chicken with lemons and olives

In a saucepan sweat off diced root ginger in oil on a low heat. To the saucepan add chopped onions and garlic, cloves, cinnamon, ground black pepper, mustard seeds and chilli flakes. Set the mix aside and brown the chicken pieces in the same frypan then place into a casserole. Return the onion mix back to the frypan and add tomato paste and chicken stock along with juice from a lemon. Put the lid on and braise slowly for 60 minutes then check on the chicken for taste and tenderness. Add sliced lemons, green olives stuffed with pimentos and chopped coriander.

#198. Chicken with capsicum

Fry chicken legs and thighs in oil and garlic then add sliced red onions, chilli flakes, chopped coriander and spring onions and tomato wedges. Place all in a casserole dish. In a food processor, blitz capsicums to a liquid adding a small amount of chicken stock. Pour it over the chicken, add mint leaves and slices of lime and with a lid on, bake in the oven for 40 minutes. Check taste, seasoning and serve.

#199. Chicken meatballs cordon bleu

Place chicken mince in a mixing bowl and add crushed garlic, breadcrumbs, seasoning, smoked paprika, chopped parsley and a beaten egg. Mix well and add more breadcrumbs if the mixture is too wet. Mould into meatballs then using the thumb, push a large indent into the meatball. Fold a slice of ham and a slice of cheese and place into the indent. Reform the meatball so that the filling is well covered then place on a lined baking dish. Pour over a readymade brown sauce and bake in the oven till cooked.

#200. Deep-fried chicken and coconut

Either use the chicken tenderloin or cut a chicken breast into strips. Prepare a deep-frying batter and add desiccated coconut to the batter. Flour then batter the chicken strips and deep fry till golden brown. Drain on kitchen paper and serve.

#201. Chicken breast with sun-dried tomato cream sauce

Place the chicken breast on a chopping board, overlay with cling wrap and beat slightly with a rolling pin. Fry the chicken in oil, butter and garlic till just cooked then set aside and keep warm. In the same pan, sweat off more garlic with sliced onions and sun-dried tomatoes and a little oil from the sun-dried tomatoes. Bring to a simmer then pour in cream. Return the chicken back to the pan, check the seasoning and serve.

#202. Chicken and pineapple bake

Place the chicken breasts in a buttered baking tray and season on both sides. Top with diced pineapple, spoon over a small amount of barbecue sauce and knobs of butter then bake in the oven. When the chicken is cooked, pour over some runny honey, put it back into the oven for 5 minutes then serve.

#203. Chicken breasts with sun-dried tomatoes, spinach and cheese

Using a sharp knife, cut the chicken breast through lengthways so that it opens out like a butterfly but remains hinged. On one side lay a slice of cheddar cheese topped with spinach leaves and sliced sun-dried tomatoes. Fold back the other piece of chicken and secure with toothpicks. Fry the chicken breast in butter and oil on both sides and if necessary, finish off in the oven. Remove to rest on a covered plate and in the same frypan brown sliced onions, sliced sun-dried tomatoes, crushed garlic and sliced smoked red capsicum. Pour in cream and reduce the heat so that it just simmers. Season and return the chicken to the sauce, warm the chicken breasts and serve.

#204. Chicken Parmigiana

In a frypan, fry diced onions, garlic in oil then add sage and a can of crushed tomatoes. Allow to simmer gently. Meanwhile place the chicken breasts on a chopping board and beat with a rolling pin to flatten them out to uniform thickness. Put the chicken through flour, egg wash and breadcrumbs then fry in oil and butter. Brown both sides of the chicken then top with grated cheese and sliced mozzarella. Place the chicken on top of the sauce and grill in the oven till the cheese is glazed then serve.

#205. Chicken with basil pesto and bacon

Butterfly the chicken breast with a very sharp knife by cutting the breast lengthways and opening out. Coat one side with a layer of basil pesto and slices of mozzarella cheese. Close the chicken breast up. On a chopping board, lay out streaky bacon overlapping each other side by side. Place the chicken breast at one end of the bacon and roll the breast in bacon so that it is completely encompassed then fry in oil and oven bake till cooked.

#206. Chicken breast stuffed with pesto and cream cheese

With a skinned and boned chicken breast, use a sharp knife and slice the chicken breast in half, opening it out like a butterfly. Spread one side of the chicken breast with sun-dried tomato pesto then on top, spoon over cream cheese. Fold the breast back together and secure with toothpicks. Fry in oil in an oven friendly frypan then finish off in the oven.

#207. Lemon and herb crust chicken

Slice a chicken breast in half with a sharp knife but don't cut right through so that when laid on a chopping board it has the shape of a butterfly. Prepare a bread stuffing containing dried mixed herbs, orange and lemon juice, grated lemon zest, white crustless bread, chopped parsley, seasoning and a beaten egg. Mix the stuffing well and spread over one side of the chicken breast then fold the other half back. Line the top with thin slices of lemon then fold prosciutto or bacon around the whole breast. Brown in a frypan in oil then finish cooking in the oven.

#208. Asian-style chicken

Brown the chicken breasts in a frypan in oil, garlic and grated root ginger then place in a lidded casserole dish. In the same pan, brown the onions, chilli, capsicum and deglaze the pan with the chicken stock, fish and soy sauces then pour it into the casserole. Add star anise, honey and stir in. Bake on a low heat (160°C) and check for tenderness. Check seasoning then remove the chicken and set aside. Thicken the sauce with cornflour mixed with water then return the chicken back to the sauce. Serve on a platter with sliced spring onions sprinkled on top.

#209. Chicken breast with pineapple

Lay the chicken breast in a buttered casserole dish and season. Brush with a barbecue sauce, sprinkle with brown sugar then top with either fresh or canned pineapple pieces. Sliced green capsicum and mint could also be added. Pour in a small amount of chicken stock and bake in the oven till the chicken is cooked. If necessary, thicken the sauce with cornflour and water. Serve on rice.

#210. Crumbed chicken steaks

Cut a skinned and boned chicken breast in half lengthways, place between sheets of baking paper and beat with a rolling pin till uniform thickness is reached. Pass it through flour, egg wash and breadcrumbs then fry in oil till golden brown. Use two of these steaks as you would pieces of bread and place flavourings in the centre such as fried bacon and tomato, cheese, tomato and mayonnaise.

#211. Chicken in Italian seasoning

Place the chicken breasts in a casserole, season and pour over some store-bought Italian dressing. Sprinkle over Italian dry seasoning and lemon juice and bake in the oven till the chicken is cooked. Thicken the sauce with cornflour and water.

#212. Baked chicken à la Grecque

In a mixing bowl, place your selected chicken pieces such as legs or thighs. Add capers, green olives, garlic, sliced capsicums, juice and zest of a lemon and olive oil. Marinate overnight then pour into a baking tin or casserole dish and oven bake. Prepare a drizzle of oil, garlic, vinegar, diced shallot, chopped rosemary and diced feta cheese. When the chicken is cooked, leave to rest and drizzle over the dressing.

#213. Ginger and miso chicken

Poach the skinned and boned chicken pieces in miso stock to which small knobs of root ginger have been added. Poach in the liquid for 25 minutes or until the chicken is cooked then cool quickly and hold in the fridge. Ladle some of the cooking liquor into a small saucepan and reduce to become a sauce then add diced onion and crushed tomatoes. Place the cold chicken through flour, egg wash and breadcrumbs and pan fry in oil, butter, diced root ginger and garlic. Then place in the oven for 10 minutes at 160°C to finish heating the chicken. Taste the sauce liquid and season. Thicken with cornflour and water.

#214. Pistachio-coated chicken

Roughly chop pistachios and mix with panko breadcrumbs. In a mixing bowl pour olive oil, Dijon mustard, honey and mix well. Dip the skinned and boned chicken pieces through the liquid then into the crumb mix. Bake the chicken on an oiled roasting pan till the crumbs are brown and the chicken is cooked through.

#215. Chicken in apricot and ginger sauce

This dish can use any cut of chicken. Fry the pieces in oil, butter and diced root ginger and place in a buttered casserole dish. In the same pan, fry sliced onion and capsicums till soft then add to the chicken. To the frypan add a large knob of butter and brown sugar and more diced root ginger and allow the mixture to caramelise then pour on the apricot liquid from a can of apricot halves. Bring to a simmer, add a pinch of cinnamon, check taste and pour it over the chicken adding the apricots at the same time. Bake in the oven till the chicken is cooked. Remove the chicken and thicken sauce with cornflour and water mixture. Top with crème fraîche and chopped coriander.

#216. Chicken roulade

Lay a chicken breast skin side down on a chopping board then butterfly cut to open the breast out. On the breast, place a layer of fried sliced chorizo then cooked seasoned rice and herbs. Roll up the breast, tie with butcher's twine then wrap in streaky bacon and roast in the oven. Leave to rest before carving.

#217. Chicken pie

In a saucepan sweat off diced onions and garlic, add diced tomato, sliced mushrooms and diced chicken meat and increase heat till the meat and vegetables begin to brown then turn off the heat source. In a jug break eggs, milk, cream and crème fraîche. Place the chicken mix into a casserole dish then pour over the egg mixture and bake in the oven. When the egg mix is set, top the casserole with mashed potato and cheese then bake until brown at 180°C.

#218. Chicken pie No. 2

Poach the chicken in stock that contains chopped onion, celery, parsley, tarragon and seasoning. When cooked, leave to cool then strip off the meat and roughly chop into cubes. In a saucepan, sweat off diced onions, celery, leeks, mixed herbs in butter then add the equivalent amount of flour, stir well then slowly add the chicken cooking liquor till the sauce thickens. While the sauce is cooking, add diced potatoes and sweet potatoes and allow to cook through. Check the sauce for taste and seasoning then add crème fraîche and allow to cool. Spoon the cold mixture into a pie dish, top with flaky pastry, brush with egg wash and bake in the oven at 200°C till cooked.

#219. Chicken tartiflette

In a frypan, brown the chicken thighs, bone in, in garlic butter and oil. When brown, remove the chicken and set aside. Fry diced onions, bacon pieces then add white wine and return the chicken back to the pan. Add in sliced potatoes that have been parboiled first and mix in then bake in the oven for 30 minutes. Pour in cream and top with slices of camembert cheese and return to the oven, cooking for a further 15 minutes. Check for taste and seasoning and serve.

#220. Baked chicken pieces on potatoes and cream sauce

Cut washed potatoes into roughly shaped pieces approximately 25 mm and brown in a frypan with butter, oil and crushed garlic. When brown place in a casserole or baking dish with diced onions and dried mixed herbs. Bake in the oven and in the same frypan brown the chicken pieces till golden brown then add to the potatoes in the oven. When both are cooked, sprinkle over raw spinach leaves and pour over a cream béchamel sauce. Sprinkle over Parmesan cheese and return to the oven for 10 minutes then remove and serve with salad and vegetables.

#221. Cheese-stuffed chicken breast

Lay the chicken breast on a chopping board skin side down, then with a sharp knife cut in half but keep the meat joined so that it is shaped like a butterfly. Spread one half with sun-dried tomato pesto, top with sliced mozzarella, sliced fresh cherry tomato and black olives. Fold the other half back over the filling and secure with toothpicks. Brown the chicken breast on both sides in a frypan in oil and butter then finish off in the oven.

#222. Cranberry and balsamic chicken

Brown the chicken thighs in oil and butter then place in a

casserole dish. In the pan, deglaze with the balsamic vinegar and add the cranberries and sugar if necessary. Allow to simmer then add to the chicken thighs and bake in the oven till the chicken is cooked. Remove the thighs, check seasoning, taste and finish with sour cream.

#223. Chicken puttenesca

Fry the chicken in garlic, oil and butter till golden brown. To the frypan, add capers, diced fresh tomatoes, black olives and a pinch of flaked chilli. Season with pepper and salt and serve on pasta.

#224. Grilled chicken with grilled peaches and pesto

Place the chicken in a hot frypan which contains oil, butter and chopped garlic. Brown both sides then put in the oven to cook through. Meanwhile, slice the peaches in half and remove the stone. Place the peach in the frypan with the chicken, sliced side down. Cook for 3 minutes then turn the peaches over and set the frypan under a grill so that the chicken grills. When cooked, remove the chicken and leave to rest. Top up the centre of the peach half with a spoonful of pesto and serve.

#225. Middle Eastern-style chicken

Prepare a marinade of soy sauce, garlic, olive oil and sumac. Pour into a plastic bag and add boneless chicken pieces, shake well then leave in the fridge for at least 30 minutes if not longer. In a frypan, prepare caramelised onions with sliced onions, butter, oil, brown sugar and dried mixed herbs. Remove the chicken from the marinade and bake in the oven with some of the marinade drizzled over it. Heat Middle East flatbread in the oven then spread with caramelised onions and top with the baked chicken pieces.

#226. Cider-roasted chicken breasts wrapped in bacon

Slice the chicken breast through lengthways but not all the way through. Open out the top piece of the breast and season. Line the chicken base with sliced peeled apple, cinnamon and chopped mint leaves. Then fold back the top and wrap the breast in bacon. Fry in oil and cook the chicken breast through. Pour in cider and allow to reduce. Remove the chicken from the pan then add butter, chopped coriander and thicken the sauce with cornflour.

#227. Crumbed pistachio fried chicken

Flour, egg wash, panko breadcrumbs mixed with chopped pistachios. Prepare a tray of flour, a bowl of beaten eggs with a little milk to dilute and panko breadcrumbs containing chopped pistachio nuts. Dredge the chicken pieces through the seasoned flour, into the egg wash then into the panko crumbs. Fry in a deep fryer or a saucepan of hot oil until nicely browned and cooked through.

#228. Chicken curry

Before starting this dish, soak cashews and almonds in a jug of water just covering them. In a saucepan gently heat oil then add turmeric, cumin, cinnamon, chilli, cloves, coriander, fenugreek and allow the spices to release their oil. Add diced chicken and onion and allow to brown. Using a stick blender blend the cashews and almonds to a paste. Add this to the saucepan and cook the chicken in the sauce. When nearly ready to serve, add coconut milk and chopped coriander leaves. Check seasoning and serve with rice.

#229. Fried chicken with sun-dried tomatoes

Fry the chicken breasts in butter, oil and garlic then add sliced onions, sun-dried tomatoes and mushrooms. Remove the chicken once it is cooked and add flour to the pan. Pour in milk slowly and constantly stir to avoid any lumps. Add cream and check seasoning and spoon over Parmesan cheese.

#230. Sesame chicken No. 2

In a mixing bowl add honey, sesame seeds, soy sauce, crushed garlic, mix then set aside. Whisk egg whites and add cornflour then coat the diced chicken and fry in oil along with a touch of sesame oil. Batch cook until all the chicken is cooked. Return all the chicken to the frypan and add the sesame seed mix and allow to cook through adding small florets of cooked hot broccoli for appearance.

#231. Chicken in tarragon cream sauce

Season and fry the chicken breasts in butter on a medium heat until just cooked through. Set aside and cover to keep warm. In the same frypan, add another knob of butter and allow to warm. To the butter add crushed garlic and dried tarragon. Add in an equivalent amount of flour to butter and stir well. Slowly add in white wine and stir while the sauce thickens. Pour in fresh cream and reduce the heat. Allow the sauce to reduce slightly, check seasoning. Serve the chicken onto the plates and spoon over the sauce.

#232. Chicken in cream lemon sauce

Flour the chicken and fry in oil butter and crushed garlic. When the chicken is cooked add another knob of butter then add chicken stock. Bring to the boil then gently simmer. Pour in fresh cream along with grated Parmesan, Dijon mustard, lemon juice and seasoning. Thicken the sauce by reducing slowly or use cornflour and water.

#233. Chicken tagine

Chicken pieces, diced onion, tomato diced, dried apricots, dates, lemon juice and sliced zest, crushed garlic, cinnamon sticks, turmeric, cumin, ras el hanout, diced root ginger, chicken stock, tomato purée and chopped coriander. Brown the chicken pieces in oil and add to the tagine. In the same frypan, brown the vegetables with the herbs and spices. Deglaze with chicken stock and tomato puree and add all to the tagine then add apricots, dates, cinnamon stick, lemon juice and zest. Serve topped with chopped coriander. If the tagine dish is not available, use a saucepan with lid and keep on a low heat and a gentle simmer.

#234. Balsamic mushrooms and chicken

Chicken breasts, mushrooms, flour, butter, crushed garlic, orange zest, balsamic vinegar, chicken stock, thyme and olive oil. Fry the chicken breasts in a frypan in oil till brown on both sides. Remove the chicken then add butter and whole small button mushrooms, orange zest, garlic and cook the mushrooms through. Add flour and mix well then add balsamic vinegar and chicken stock stirring continuously to prevent lumps from forming. Cook the flour out, check for seasoning then return the chicken back to the pan and add crème fraîche prior to serving.

#235. Chicken breasts stuffed with camembert

Place the skinless chicken breast on a chopping board then slicing from the bottom side of the breast, cut in half without cutting all the way through so that it opens out like a butterfly. Slice a round of camembert into 5 mm wide slices and place on one side. Fold the breast back and hold in place with a toothpick. Using panko breadcrumbs, add to them finely chopped pistachios and mix well. Flour, egg wash and crumb the chicken breast then fry in oil and butter till golden brown.

#236. Chicken pesto roll-ups

Slice a chicken breast in half lengthways and flatten out with a rolling pin. Season the chicken and spread over it some pesto, grated cheese, sliced tomato then roll up and secure with a toothpick. Brown in a frypan in oil and butter then finish off in the oven.

#237. Oven-baked crumbed chicken

This dish uses chicken pieces and is coated in panko breadcrumbs. With the panko breadcrumbs, mix in smoked paprika and cayenne along with seasoning. In a separate bowl soften a couple of knobs of butter and stir in seasoning. Rub the chicken pieces through the butter then into the panko crumbs and pressing hard to ensure a good coating of crumbs. Place on baking paper on a tray and bake in the oven at 190°C for 30 minutes. Check that the chicken is cooked through and leave to rest before serving.

#238. Chicken cordon bleu in puff pastry

Slice open a chicken breast and layer with sliced ham and cheese. Secure with toothpicks and fry in oil and butter till cooked then leave to go cold. Place the chicken on a sheet of puff pastry, wrap and seal the edges with egg wash then coat the whole pastry with egg wash. Bake at 200°C till the pastry is golden brown.

#239. Chicken roll-ups

Cut the chicken breasts in half and flatten out with a rolling pin. Spread basil pesto over the chicken then top with crumbled feta cheese, sliced sun-dried tomatoes, garlic butter and a ham slice. Roll up and secure with toothpicks. Brown in a frypan in oil and butter then finish off in the oven. Could also be topped with a cheese sauce and oven baked with grated cheese on top.

#240. Sweet and sour chicken

Using diced chicken thigh, fry in oil, garlic and root ginger until cooked through and brown. Remove the chicken and in the same pan fry sliced onions and capsicum, carrot matchsticks, chilli flakes and pineapple pieces. Pour in a small amount of chicken stock to which is added Worcestershire sauce, fish sauce, soy and malt vinegar. Reduce slightly, taste the sauce and add brown sugar to give the balance to the sweet and sour taste. Correct seasoning, return the chicken back to the sauce and serve on rice.

#241. Chicken Marsala

In the chicken breast, make a pocket with a very sharp knife and put in there sliced mozzarella and sliced sun-dried tomatoes. Hold in place with toothpicks then fry the breasts in butter and oil till brown and nearly cooked through. Remove the chicken and keep warm then to the pan add sliced onions, garlic, sliced capsicum and mushrooms. Deglaze the pan with Marsala wine and reduce. Check the seasoning, return the chicken to the pan and pour in cream.

Smoked chicken

#242. Smoked chicken strudel

Cut pumpkin and sweet potato into 10 mm cubes and simmer in stock till cooked then drain and cool. In a frypan, fry diced onion in butter, garlic and diced root ginger then quickly add spinach leaves to wilt only and remove from the element. Either filo pastry or puff pastry can be used for this dish. Lay the pastry onto a chopping board and in the case of filo pastry use five sheets and butter between each sheet. Spoon on the pumpkin mix 50 mm from one side. Top with diced smoked chicken pieces, the spinach, cream cheese and sweet chilli sauce. Roll the filling in the pastry and carefully place on a baking sheet. Brush with butter and bake in the oven at 200°C till the pastry is cooked.

#243. Smoked chicken cream pasta

Slice the smoked chicken breast into thin slices and set aside. Prepare a béchamel and add a few knobs of blue cheese to flavour the sauce. In a frypan, fry sliced onions to sweat off but not colour. Cook the pasta (spirals as a choice) in boiling salted water. When the pasta is nearly al dente, add the smoked chicken to the frypan and heat. Pour in the pasta and increase the heat and season mixing the three ingredients together. Pour in some of the béchamel followed by crème fraîche. Top with knobs of blue cheese and serve.

#244. Smoked chicken mac and cheese

Cut the smoked chicken into 10–15 mm cubes and set aside. Prepare a cheese sauce and add a teaspoon of Worcestershire sauce and English mustard. Cook the macaroni in boiling salted water while frying diced onions and bacon in a frypan. When all preparation is complete, mix the macaroni, onions, bacon and sauce. Butter a casserole dish and ladle in macaroni till the casserole is half full. Add cubes of feta and dessertspoons of crème fraîche. Sprinkle through a layer of grated cheese then top up with more macaroni. Top the dish with cubes of sourdough bread that has been fried in butter. Top with grated cheddar and oven bake then grill to brown the cheese.

#245. Smoked chicken quiche

Blind bake shortcrust pastry in a suitable pie dish. Line the pastry base with grated cheddar cheese and sliced red onions. On top place sliced smoked chicken and crumbled feta cheese. Mix together beaten eggs, cream, milk, seasoning, mustard and pour the mixture over the smoked chicken. Bake in the oven until the quiche is cooked. Dip a knife into the baked quiche and it should come out clean when quiche is set.

#246. Smoked chicken tortilla stack

Layer 1: On a baking tray, lay a tortilla and top with relish, sliced smoked chicken and mozzarella. Layer 2: Garlic butter, fried mushrooms, wilted spinach and mozzarella. Layer 3: Tortilla, garlic butter, grated cheese and sesame seeds. Bake in the oven for 15 minutes or until the centre layers are heated. Remove and cut into segments and serve with a salad.

5.

PORK

#	Dish	#	Dish
247	Pork Belly And Black Bean Casserole	283	Sweet And Sour Ribs
248	Roast Pork Belly	284	Roast Pork With Diced Fruit Stuffing
249	Pork Belly Ragout	285	Roast Pork With Rum Stuffing
250	Pork And Milk Casserole	286	Pork Tenderloin Cordon Bleu
251	Pork Chop Casserole	287	Fried Pork Chops With Lemon And Parsley Butter
252	Pulled Pork Casserole	288	Pork Chops With Bacon And Cheese
253	Pork Belly Brine	289	Pork Chops In Honey And Balsamic
254	Apricot. Almond And Vanilla Stuffed Loin Pork	290	Pork Hash Browns
255	Pork Chops In Apple Sauce	291	Pork Wrapped Rice Balls
256	Pan Fried Pork Cutlets With Nut Sauce	292	Pork Wrapped Eggs
257	Pork Ribs Cajun	293	Sausages In BBQ Sauce
258	Pork Belly Orange Sauce	294	Pork Belly Casserole
259	Pork And Peanut Butter Wrap	295	Chorizo Ragout With White Beans
260	Pork Medallions	296	Stir Fried Pork Belly
261	Pork Medallions With Cheese And Leek Topping	297	Pork Chops With Sauerkraut
262	Jerk Pork	298	Pork Ribs In Ginger Ale
263	Roast Pork And Fresh Plums	299	Pork And Lemongrass Fritters
264	Juniper Infused Pork Tenderloin	300	Pork Belly With Hoisin And Marmalade

#247. Pork belly and black bean casserole

Cut the pork into large cubes then fry the pork and chorizo pieces in oil, garlic to brown and seal. Add chopped onions, celery, carrots, black beans and continue to brown. Add tomato paste, cumin, chilli and rosemary then pour in beer, chicken stock and canned tomatoes. Place the pork in an oven dish and bake in the oven for around 2–3 hours. When finishing, add Dijon mustard and sour cream. Serve on rice.

#248. Pork belly

With a paring knife make holes in the skin. In a bowl, pour dry sherry, Chinese five spice, crushed garlic, seasoning and chilli flakes. Rub the mixture into the pork meat, not the skin, and leave to marinate for a few hours but not allowing the liquid on the skin which should be dried with kitchen paper. In the morning, remove from the fridge and place on tinfoil. Fold the tinfoil so that it forms a tray with sides just fitting the piece of pork belly. Again, dry the skin and brush with white vinegar then coat with rock salt which will be removed at the end. Roast for around an hour at 180°C. Scrape off the salt and grill the pork skin, which will blister beautifully.

#249. Pork belly ragout

Cut the belly pork into 25 mm cubes and brown in oil, diced root ginger, turmeric, coriander then turn down the heat, remove the meat and add butter. When the butter has melted add the same amount of flour (roux) and slowly add chicken stock as the sauce thickens. Add diced carrots, grated lemon zest, cannellini beans and return the pork back to the sauce and simmer slowly. Check seasoning and tenderness of the pork then serve.

#250. Pork and milk casserole

Pork cubed, condensed milk, evaporated milk, chillies, brown sugar, cinnamon, allspice, cloves, ginger, pecans, flour, desiccated coconut, marshmallows. Brown the pork with cinnamon and put into a mixing bowl. In the bowl, add chillies, milk, butter, sugar and spices. Spoon the mixture into an ovenproof casserole dish and bake. Prepare a topping of chopped pecans, desiccated coconut, butter and marshmallows and sprinkle over once the pork is cooked. Return back to the oven and bake for a further 5 minutes.

#251. Pork chop casserole

Make a rub out of garlic powder, salt, ground pepper, paprika, onion powder, oregano and thyme. Rub both sides of the pork then fry in a frypan in oil and butter browning both sides. When browned, set aside, add more butter to the pan and sweat off sliced onions, garlic and sliced mushrooms. Pour a little milk into the pan followed by sour cream. Line the base of a casserole dish with sliced potatoes, place the pork chops on top and the sauce over that. Bake in the oven for 30 minutes or until chops are cooked through. Season and serve.

#252. Pulled pork casserole

Mix mashed potato with butter, cream, grated cheese, spring onion and whole kernel corn. Place the potato mixture in a buttered casserole dish and level it out. Top the potato mix with the cooked pulled pork, sauce or gravy and crushed potato chips as a topping. Heat the casserole in the oven till cooked through.

#253. Pork belly brine

75 g sea salt, 190 ml runny honey, 60 g Dijon mustard. Heat the mixture gently then leave to go cold. Place the pork belly in it

for 24 hours. Remove and dry the pork well especially before roasting and making crackling.

#254. Apricot, almond and vanilla stuffed loin of pork

Buy the loin of pork without the rib bones and lay it on a chopping board, skin side down. Prepare a bread stuffing of white crustless bread, diced onions, dried mixed herbs, sage, sliced dried apricots, flaked almonds, vanilla extract, grated lemon zest and juice, eggs to bind and seasoning. Mix well together and lay the stuffing down the centre of the pork. Fold over the loin to encompass the stuffing and secure with butcher's twine. Roast in the oven on a bed of onions and root vegetables till cooked.

#255. Pork chops in apple juice

Put the chops into a Ziploc bag with a cinnamon quill, lemon juice and grated lemon zest then add apple juice. Leave to marinate then dry and fry the chops in oil, butter till golden brown then add sliced apples and apple juice. Thicken the sauce with cornflour, check seasoning and serve.

#256. Pan-fried pork cutlets with nut sauce

Fry the pork cutlets in walnut oil, garlic and brown on both sides, reduce the heat and put a lid on the frypan. When cooked, put the pork to one side, covered with tinfoil, then add two knobs of butter to the frypan and stir to pick up the pan drippings of the pork. Add juice of half a lemon with chopped walnuts and almonds. Simmer then pour in cream and chopped parsley. Return the pork to the sauce, leave for 5 minutes then serve.

#257. Pork ribs Cajun

Simmer ribs in chicken stock and leave to cool. The ribs can either be crumbed or battered and deep fried and Cajun spice can be used in either style. **Cajun sauce**: Fry sliced onions, garlic, chilli and ginger in oil without browning and spoon in two or three teaspoons of Cajun spice then add canned chopped tomatoes, brown sugar and a little olive oil. Simmer slowly and adjust seasoning. When the sauce is cooked, spoon a little on the serving plate and lay the ribs on top. Serve more sauce separately.

#258. Pork belly orange sauce

Put pork in cold water, bring to boil then drain. Mix a marinade/ sauce of orange marmalade, soy, root ginger, star anise, cinnamon, orange juice, Grand Marnier. Roast the pork at 160°C in sauce. Remove pork then add butter to sauce, taste and thicken. Rest the pork before carving and serve with the sauce.

#259. Pork and peanut butter wrap

Prepare a satay-style sauce with peanut butter, chillies, curry powder, garlic, soy and fish sauces, coconut cream, diced root ginger and mix well. Heat slowly in a small saucepan and check on flavour and seasoning. Using either leftover roast pork or pork chops/ribs, prepare and leave to go cold. Spread the wrap with the cold satay sauce, add salad of choice, top with the pork and roll.

#260. Pork medallions

Fry the medallions in oil and garlic then add wine and reduce till caramelisation begins. Add apple segments, sultanas to soften then add cream, mustard and reduce. Check seasoning and serve.

#261. Pork medallions with leek and cheese topping

Fry the pork medallions in butter, oil, crushed garlic and grated ginger till golden brown then set aside and keep warm. In the same pan, add more butter then fry sliced leeks till lightly browned and cooked through. Add a small amount of cheese sauce to the leeks and allow to reduce to keep the mixture thick. Add grated cheese to the sauce then return the pork back to the sauce. Place the pork on a serving plate and spoon over the pan sauce.

#262. Jerk pork

Originates from Jamaica and uses Scotch bonnet chillies, which tend to be exceptionally hot. Cut the pork into large dice 30 x 30 mm. In a food processor, blitz cloves, nutmeg, pimento, ginger, lime juice, Scotch bonnets, spring onions, coriander, runny honey, vinegar and rum. The result will be a paste like thick cream. Pour half of the paste over the pork and mix well so that each piece of pork is well covered. Fry the pork in a frypan in oil and pour in the second half of the paste. It will start to brown and go dry. Pour in a cup of dark rum and allow to burn off leaving only the flavour. The jerk pork will end up being a dryish dish. Serve on rice with dumplings.

#263. Roast pork with fresh plums

Dry the skin of the pork with kitchen paper and if not already scored by the butcher, use a very sharp knife and score the skin in diagonal cuts. Rub in salt then place in a hot oven (200°C) for 10 minutes then reduce to 160°C to slow cook. Halfway through cooking add the fresh whole plums to the roasting pan surrounding the pork. When the pork is cooked remove from the oven and leave to rest. Place the roast tray on an element and apply heat to reduce the liquid in the roasting pan. Add 300 ml port, stirring the bottom of the pan to release all of the drippings from the pork. Remove the plum stones using a slotted spoon then thicken with cornflour and water mixed. Season and serve.

#264. Juniper-infused pork tenderloin

Remove any excess fat and silver skin from the tenderloin. In a mortar and pestle place fennel seeds, chilli flakes, coriander seeds and seasoning. Break the seeds with the pestle then rub the mix into the pork tenderloin. Cook the pork in milk and juniper berries in the oven till cooked through.

#265. Pork medallions

Using the nut of pork cut from the pork chop, beat softly with a rolling pin to thin it out to a uniform thickness. Pass it through flour, egg wash with chopped coriander and parsley in it then repeat. Fry in an oil and butter mix and drain on kitchen paper then leave to rest before serving.

#266. Pork medallions in coffee and Grand Marnier

Use the nut meat from the pork chop. Beat out to even thickness and fry in oil, butter, garlic till just cooked. Leave to rest on kitchen paper. To the same pan, add two shots of short black coffee, 50 ml Grand Marnier, brown sugar and a drop of vanilla. Check the sauce as it reduces. The coffee will make it bitter and the liqueur and sugar will sweeten. Taste for the balance. Add a little fresh orange juice and finely sliced orange zest. Add the pork back to the pan and add a little mascarpone.

#267. Pork medallions with whisky sauce

In a very hot frypan, brown the pork in oil and butter adding slices of streaky bacon to add to the flavour. Before the pork is cooked, remove along with the bacon from the pan and keep warm in the oven. Put diced onion in pan, more butter, sliced garlic and a little chilli. Deglaze the pan with whisky and add a little chicken stock then reduce the liquid. If necessary, thicken with a little cornflour and water.

#268. Roast belly pork casserole

Dice the belly pork with the skin then boil quickly in salted water with spring onions, sliced ginger and garlic for 2 minutes only. Drain the pork, then fry in oil with garlic and ginger. When brown add soy sauce, brown sugar, rice wine and chicken stock. Simmer gently for 20 minutes to cook the pork and reduce the sauce. Check the pork for tenderness, seasoning and serve over noodles.

#269. Roast pork loin

In-between where the skin has been scored, using a sharp paring knife make small holes and place thin slivers of garlic in each hole. Rub the skin with kitchen paper to dry it off. In a food processor put oil, garlic, rosemary and balsamic vinegar then blitz well and pour a little over the pork and massage in. Put the meat in a roasting dish and start in a hot oven to brown the skin then reduce the heat to 160°C. Meanwhile cut small potatoes in half and place in the bowl with the oil mixture. Rub the oil all over the potatoes then place with the pork. Cook till both the potatoes and pork are ready to serve.

#270. Pork chops with brandied caramelised onions

Fry the pork chops in a hot frypan in oil and garlic. When the pork is brown, lower the heat to allow the pork to cook through. In a saucepan, fry sliced onions in oil on a medium heat. Add salt so that the moisture is drawn out of the onions and evaporates. Once the onions begin to brown keep a close eye on them so that they don't burn. Add sliced garlic and brown sugar along with butter. Once the onions are brown add 50 ml brandy and allow to cook out. To the pork chops, add spoonfuls of the caramelised onions then add brandy over the chops and flambé. Pour over cream, bring to a gentle simmer and reduce. Rest the chops for 10 minutes then serve.

#271. Pork medallions with chilli and apricot

In a frypan, fry the pork in oil, crushed garlic and sliced ginger till brown on both sides. Lower the heat and allow the chops to cook through. Add sweet chilli sauce and diced onions then a knob of butter to the pan. When the medallions are cooked, remove and keep warm. Stir the onions to lift any pan drippings then add apricot jam to the pan along with 50 ml stock or brandy and stir again adding a teaspoon of mustard. Taste for seasoning then once the pork is on the serving plate, spoon the sauce over the top.

#272. Pork chops in bacon, onion and mushrooms

Fry the pork chops in a frypan with oil and crushed garlic. As the pork cooks add half slices of streaky bacon. When the chops are cooked remove to a warm place then add diced onions to the pan along with a knob of butter. When the bacon and onions are nearly cooked add the sliced mushrooms and allow to cook through. Return the pork back to the frypan then add pouring cream, simmer gently, season and serve.

#273. Pork Tuscany

Fry the pork in oil, butter and crushed garlic till cooked through and brown on both sides. When cooked, set the pork aside and pour in fresh cream, a little stock, garlic, Italian seasoning and Parmesan cheese then simmer to reduce. Add in sun-dried tomatoes and chopped spinach. Season and serve.

#274. Baked pork chops

Using boneless chops, flatten out slightly with a rolling pin so that they are all of uniform thickness. In a bowl, mix panko breadcrumbs, finely grated Parmesan cheese, chopped garlic, ground black pepper and paprika. Dip the pork in olive oil then into the crumb mix, pressing hard so that the crumb mix holds in place. Put the crumbed pork on a sheet of oiled tinfoil then bake in the oven at 190°C for 20 minutes. Check on the degree of cooking and whether it requires further cooking or remove and leave to rest.

#275. Pork and butter beans

A loin of pork is a good cut of meat for this but shoulder pork could also be used. Dice the pork then place in a large heavy-based saucepan that has oil added and allow the pork to brown all over by stirring. Add crushed garlic, diced root ginger and a large pinch of chilli flakes to the pork while it is frying. Once the pork is brown add butter beans, crushed tomatoes and allow come to the boil. Season then cover with a lid and oven bake. Bake slowly for 90 minutes then add diced fresh apple and cook for another 30 minutes. Check taste and seasoning. If necessary, thicken with cornflour and water, allow to cook out then serve.

#276. Pork and chives

In an oven-friendly frypan, fry the pork chops in oil, garlic, ginger and brown on both sides then put in the oven at 170°C to cook through. When cooked, remove the pork chops and set aside and keep warm. In the same frypan, sweat off sliced onions then add sliced mushrooms. Pour over white wine and reduce then add cream, mustard and simmer gently. Add chopped chives and place the pork back into the pan for 5 minutes then serve.

#277. Pork medallions stuffed with smoked cheese, bacon and parsley

This dish uses two medallions per serve and they are stacked like a sandwich. Fry the pork in a frypan in oil, garlic, diced root ginger and when cooked on both sides set aside and cool in the refrigerator. Prepare a bread stuffing of dried mixed herbs, torn sliced white toast bread, juice of an orange and grated zest, fried bacon pieces and a beaten egg and mix well together. Place a slice of smoked cheese on one of the medallions, top with the stuffing then place the second chop on top and hold in place with toothpicks. Cover with tinfoil and bake in the oven for 10 minutes on 160°C till the stuffing is cooked through then serve.

#278. Pork in red wine

Cut the pork into 3 cm cubes and place in a mixing bowl, cover with red wine and toasted crushed coriander seeds, crushed garlic and segmented red onions. Pour off the red wine, dry the pork, dredge in flour and fry in butter and oil just to brown the pork in batches then place in a casserole dish. In the same frypan, fry diced bacon, garlic then add the red wine to deglaze the pan and add to the casserole. Also pour in passata sauce and bake in the oven for 1 hour. Check on taste and seasoning then serve. Could serve with slices of baguette, toasted and topped with cream cheese, capers and anchovy fillets.

#279. Rolled belly pork

With a very sharp knife remove the skin then slice the pork into thin slices about 5mm thick. Lay out three slices on a chopping board, sprinkle with a little cornflour then cover each slice with another slice. Roll up the pork and hold in place with a toothpick. Fry in a saucepan in oil and garlic till brown all over then into the pan pour a small amount of chicken stock, soy sauce, mirin, diced root ginger and seasoning. Place the pan in an oven for 15 minutes to complete the cooking then leave to rest and serve with a gravy.

#280. Pork chop casserole

Brown the pork chops in a frypan in oil with garlic and root ginger then place into a casserole dish. Brown a sliced onion in the same frypan then add to the chops. Pour in a can of condensed cream of chicken soup along with a little chicken stock and ranch dressing. Bake in the oven for 25 minutes or until the chops are cooked.

#281. Cajun chorizo and prawns

Fry the chorizos in oil and garlic till brown but not cooked all the way through. Add diced onions, capsicum, garlic, Cajun spice, paprika, chilli flakes then remove the chorizo and put aside. Deglaze the pan with the tomatoes, add tomato paste and pour into a casserole dish. Slice the chorizo into large pieces and place in the casserole dish and cook on a low temperature in the oven (160°C). Check seasoning and tenderness of the chorizo. When nearly ready to serve, briefly cook the prawns in oil and garlic then add to the chorizo and continue cooking for 5 minutes. Check seasoning and serve on fettuccine.

#282. Pork and potato casserole

With pork medallions, brown both sides in a frypan in oil and garlic. Meanwhile parboil potatoes in boiling salted water till just cooked then drain and slice into 10 mm thick slices. Line the base of a casserole dish with the sliced potatoes, top with caramelised onions and garlic and sliced celery. Place the pork medallions on top and just cover the potatoes with milk then bake in the oven for 40 minutes. The milk will be absorbed by the potatoes. Top with grated cheese and grill.

#283. Sweet and sour ribs

Brown the ribs in oil and garlic in a frypan then place in a roasting pan. In the same frypan, brown the onion, carrots, then add grated root ginger, capsicums and pineapple rings. Add some of the malt vinegar to the pan, brown sugar, soy sauce, ketchup and water. Pour the sauce over the ribs in the roasting pan and cook in a slow oven for an hour then check for tenderness of the pork and also the sweet/sour taste. Adjust the sweet and sour by using malt vinegar or brown sugar. Remove the ribs when they are cooked and thicken the sauce with cornflour and water. Check seasoning and serve.

#284. Roast pork with dried fruit stuffing

With a shoulder of boned out pork, lay skin side down on a bench. Roughly chop the following and add to a mixing bowl: dried figs, dried apricots, cherries, prunes, candied fruits and dates. Simmer the fruit in a sugar syrup briefly then drain and cool. To the fruit add chopped garlic and rosemary and mix it all with breadcrumbs and seasoning. Place into the pork, roll and tie the pork then roast.

#285. Roast pork with rum stuffing

A leg, shoulder or loin of pork can be used for this dish. Prepare a stuffing by using torn crustless stale bread, sweated onions and garlic, dried mixed herbs, dates, orange juice and sliced zest, beaten egg and approximately half a cup of rum. Mix well and place in the cavity of the pork then tie with butcher's string and roast.

#286. Pork tenderloin cordon bleu

Cut the head off the tenderloin then with a sharp knife cut a slice down the tenderloin so that it is nearly cut in half but opens out like a butterfly. Cover the inside of the pork with slices of ham and cheese then fold the pork back again to form a whole piece. On a chopping board lay slices of streaky bacon side by side then lay the tenderloin on top and fold the bacon over to wrap the pork. Bake in the oven till the pork is cooked.

#287. Fried pork chops with lemon and parsley butter

If desired, remove the skin and some of the fat from the chops. Fry the pork in butter and olive oil till golden brown on both sides. Leave to rest under foil to keep warm while preparing **lemon and parsley butter**: In a bowl, put soft butter, lemon juice, grated lemon zest and chopped parsley. Season and place on cling wrap. Roll to a 35 mm diameter roll and place in the fridge to harden up. Cut off slices and place on top of the pork.

#288. Pork chops with bacon and cheese

Fry the pork chops in a frypan in butter, oil, garlic and allow to brown. While the pork is frying add chopped pieces of bacon then pour in tomato juice and simmer gently to reduce. Add one or two spoons of brown sugar to remove any acidic taste to the sauce. When the pork is cooked, place a slice of cheese on top of each chop then grill.

#289. Pork chops in honey and balsamic

Season the pork then fry in oil and garlic along with chopped bacon pieces. When the chops are brown, put aside then add diced onions to the frypan and reduce the heat. Pour in balsamic vinegar and honey, stir well and reduce the sauce. Check for taste and place the pork back into the pan, heat then serve.

#290. Pork hash browns

Wash the potatoes well but don't peel. Cut them into thin strips ¾ mm squared and 50 mm long and place in a mixing bowl. Add flour, crushed garlic, Parmesan cheese, seasoning and mix well. Combine pork mince with pork sausage meat and mix well adding breadcrumbs, dried mixed herbs and chopped parsley. Mould the pork into thin patties 60 mm in diameter. Place a layer of the straw potatoes onto a piece of baking paper measuring

80 x 80 mm. Top with the pork patty and top with more straw potatoes. Heat 5 mm of vegetable oil in the frypan then place the baking paper into the pan with the aid of an egg slice. As the potatoes on the bottom cook, carefully turn over and cook the other side. Remove the baking paper then place the hash brown on kitchen paper to drain then serve.

#291. Pork-wrapped rice balls

(Similar to Scotch eggs.) Place a soft-boiled egg immediately into ice-cold water to stop it cooking. Prepare a mixture of glutinous rice and flour which will be used to wrap around the egg once it has been peeled. Once the egg has been enveloped in the rice, wrap it in streaky bacon and fry. **Sauce**: Soy, sake, brown sugar and stir well and heat. Baste the balls with the sauce then top with sesame seeds that have been heated in a dry frypan.

#292. Pork-wrapped eggs

Cook the eggs in boiling water for 3 minutes then plunge into ice water. Remove the shell and set aside. Mix pork mince and pork sausage meat together adding dried mixed herbs, breadcrumbs, chopped parsley and a beaten egg. Remove a handful of the pork mixture, roll into a ball then lay it on a chopping board and spread it out using your fingers ensuring there are no thin spots. This meat will cover the boiled egg. Place the cold egg in the pork wrap and fold the meat around it. Use water to seal the join areas and ensure there are no cracks. Run the egg through flour, egg wash, breadcrumbs and brown in a deep fryer. To serve, cut in half and the egg yolk should run over the meat.

#293. Sausages in barbecue sauce

Fry the pork sausages in oil in a frypan till brown all over. In a saucepan put store-bought barbecue sauce, brown sugar, tomato ketchup, malt vinegar, red wine, Dijon mustard, soy sauce and garlic. Heat and reduce the sauce then thicken if necessary with cornflour mixed with water. Cut the sausages into bite-sized pieces, pour over the sauce and cook for 15 minutes then serve.

#294. Pork belly casserole

Remove the skin off the pork belly and cut the meat into large squares 50 x 50 mm. Brown the pork in a frypan in oil with garlic, ginger and diced red onions. Add diced celery, carrot and continue browning the mixture. Pour in chicken stock, runny honey then cook on the element without a lid so that the liquid reduces and becomes thicker. Check for taste and seasoning and serve on rice. It could also be spooned into individual ramekins cold then a puff pastry put over the top and baked.

#295. Chorizo ragout with white beans

In a frypan, fry the chorizo that has been cut into large slices. While it is frying add smoked paprika, diced red onions, garlic and chilli flakes. Once the chorizo is brown and the onions are cooked add canned tomatoes and cannellini beans that have been soaking in water. Place the ragout in a lidded casserole and slow bake to allow the beans to cook through. Check the seasoning and serve.

#296. Stir-fried pork belly

Remove the skin, rub both sides of the pork with a dry mix of Chinese five spice, cinnamon, garlic powder then place in a roasting dish on chopped onions and roast slowly till cooked through. Cool quickly then leave in the fridge overnight. Cut the pork belly into 8 mm slices and leave to marinate in a tray with soy sauce, oil, crushed garlic, Worcestershire sauce, runny honey, orange juice and seasoning. Fry the pork in a wok or frypan in hot oil then hold aside in a lidded casserole. Quickly fry sliced onions, capsicum, broccoli, cauliflower, green beans, crushed garlic and root ginger. Return all back to the wok and pour over some of the marinade then allow to reduce. Serve with soba noodles and plum sauce.

#297. Pork chops with sauerkraut

Fry the pork chops in oil and garlic just to brown then set aside. In a buttered casserole dish, line with sliced potatoes, top with store-bought sauerkraut then place the pork chops on top. In a jug put oil, balsamic vinegar, cider and caraway seeds. Stir and pour it over the pork then top with foil and bake in the oven slowly at 150°C till cooked.

#298. Pork ribs in ginger ale

Place the ribs into a roasting dish then pour in ginger ale, diced root ginger, juice of a fresh orange and orange peel. Cover with a lid or use tinfoil and cook slowly in the oven. When cooked, remove the ribs from the pan and leave to dry. In a saucepan, put soy sauce, ketchup, diced root ginger, brown sugar, garlic, sweet chilli sauce and a little of the ginger ale liquid that the ribs were cooked in. Heat and reduce, if necessary thicken with cornflour and water. Brown the ribs on a barbecue or under the grill in the oven. Baste the ribs with the sauce as they colour then carve the ribs and serve with the sauce.

#299. Pork and lemongrass fritters

With pork mince in a mixing bowl, add finely sliced cabbage, coriander, chilli flakes, chopped lemongrass, grated root of ginger, garlic, breadcrumbs and an egg. Mix the ingredients well, add seasoning then mould the mixture into balls and flatten out. Cook in oil to brown all over then finish in the oven if necessary.

#300. Pork belly with hoisin and marmalade

In a bowl, put marmalade, hoisin sauce, grated ginger, crushed garlic, chilli flakes, brown sugar and a small amount of water to dilute. Score the pork skin then brush the pork with the sauce mix. Roast in the oven and continue basting the pork until cooked. Leave to rest then carve.

#301. Braised pork with prunes

In a frypan, brown the pork piece all over and place in a lidded casserole. To the frypan, add diced onions, grated garlic, cumin, oregano, coriander seeds and heat gently to allow the seeds to release their oil. Pour in chicken stock and a can of chopped tomatoes and bring to a simmer. Pour onto the pork and cook in the oven at 160°C. Towards the end, when the pork is nearly cooked, add prunes and whole almonds and continue to cook for another 30 minutes. Remove the pork to rest and reduce the sauce. Thicken with a roux if required, check seasoning and serve.

#302. Pork crepes

Use fresh pork pieces or offcuts cut into 15 mm size pieces or use cooked roast pork as a means of using up leftovers. In a frypan, fry the diced pork then add diced onion, crushed garlic and grated ginger in oil. When the pork is cooked, remove from the pan and use the same pan to make the crepes. Pour in crepe batter to just cover the base of the frypan. Turn over when the base is brown and cook the other side. Flip out onto a plate, spread with chutney and pork, roll and eat. Vegetables, salads and other meats can also be added to the centre before rolling.

#303. Pork chops in French onion soup

Prepare a French onion soup. Remove any bones from the pork

chops and fry in the frypan in oil, butter, crushed garlic and grated ginger. Brown and cook the chops through then leave to rest. Once the soup is cooked and simmering, place the pork chop in a suitable casserole ramekin, casserole or serving dish. Ladle the French onion soup over the top till it just covers the pork. Top with the grilled cheese croutons, sprinkle with more grated cheddar and grill briefly to brown the cheese then serve.

#304. Pork loin in ginger and orange sauce

Cut the loin into 20 mm thick slices and place in a mixing bowl with crushed garlic, cinnamon, cumin, grated ginger, finely sliced orange rind and seasoning. Drizzle with oil and rub the spices over the meat and leave for 2 hours. Fry the pork in oil and butter till brown on both sides and just cooked then pour in orange juice and two tablespoons of marmalade. Remove the pork, reduce the sauce and thicken with cornflour. Check seasoning and taste. Return the pork to the sauce and allow to sit for 10 minutes then serve. As an added ingredient, Drambuie could also be added at the end to strengthen the orange flavour.

#305. Frikkadels with lime tzatziki

Combine pork mince, diced onions, chopped garlic, seasoning, coriander seed and chopped parsley. Mix well then add a beaten egg and breadcrumbs to form a mouldable mixture. Mould the mince into balls and fry in oil till brown all over. Prepare a tzatziki sauce, adding lime juice and finely grated lime zest.

#306. Cajun pork fingers

Purchase the pork fingers from your butcher, supermarket or cut pork belly into fingers. Either use a Cajun spice mix already prepared or make your own from paprika, cayenne, cumin, garlic powder and cracked black pepper. Rub the pork in olive oil then press into the spice mix so that it is well covered in the Cajun spice. Fry in oil, grated root ginger, crushed garlic. Cook on all sides to brown then serve on top of a Cajun sauce.

#307. Pork cabbage rolls

From the cabbage, retain the whole leaves from the outside of the cabbage that are in excellent condition. Remove the white stalk at the base and blanch the leaves in boiling salted water then cool down immediately in ice water. These leaves will be used to hold the filling. Fry the pork mince in oil, grated root ginger and garlic till brown then add bacon pieces, diced onions, sweet paprika and diced fresh tomatoes. Allow all to cook through then add sliced cabbage and mix well. Into the cooked cabbage mixture add cooked rice, grated cheese, seasoning then again mix well. Lay the cabbage leaves on a chopping board and spoon the mixture into the centre of the leaf then fold into a parcel so that all folds are underneath. Lay the cabbage roll in a buttered casserole dish. Pour over hot brown onion sauce or similar and bake in the oven for 20 minutes then serve.

#308. Peanut pork stir-fry

Pineapple pieces, diced pork, sesame oil, sunflower oil, sliced red capsicums, julienne carrots, sliced bok choy, sliced onions, soy sauce, teriyaki sauce, peanut butter, roasted peanuts, grated root ginger and garlic. Fry the diced pork in both oils and add garlic and ginger. When the pork is brown add vegetables and keep stirring. Pour in the teriyaki and soy sauces along with the peanut butter and roasted chopped peanuts. Season and serve immediately with fried noodles.

#309. Pork and peach kebabs

Trim the pork of skin and fat and dice the pork into 25 mm pieces. Cut the fresh peaches into dice the same size and leave the skin on so that the peach will hold together during cooking. Soak the wooden skewers in water then thread the pork and peaches onto the skewers. Marinate the pork (refer Ziploc marinades) then barbecue or bake in the oven. Serve with ginger apricot sauce.

#310. Roast pork with almonds

Score the skin of the pork roast. Into a mixing bowl, put fresh orange juice, finely sliced orange zest, almond essence along with 200 ml of chicken stock. With a sharp-pointed knife make some holes in the pork between the knife scores and spoon in some of the marinade. At the same time place a slice of garlic and sage in each hole. On the base of the roasting dish place segments of sliced Granny Smith apples with roughly chopped almonds then pour all the orange juice marinade over the pork. Roast the pork in the oven and baste regularly. Prepare crystallised sliced almonds and use them to serve on the pork once the carving has been completed.

#311. Casserole caramel pork

Cut the pork into 20 mm cubed pieces. In a heavy-based saucepan, pour a cup and a half of sugar to a half a cup of water. Allow to reduce and start to colour into caramel. Add diced onions, chilli, chopped garlic, fish sauce and lemon grass. Cook the pork pieces in oil, garlic and ginger till brown then set aside. Add the pork to the caramel sauce and cook slowly for 90 minutes allowing the liquid to reduce. As the liquid evaporates, stir so that the pork does not burn. Add sliced spring onions, chopped chilli and stir in coconut milk. Serve over rice.

#312. Pork tenderloin in puff pastry

A similar take on beef Wellington. Remove the silver skin from the pork tenderloin using a very sharp knife and remove any excess fat. Poke a few knife holes in the pork with a very sharp knife and fill with slithers of garlic. Tie the pork with butcher's twine so that it holds its shape then brown in a frypan till it is sealed, brown all over and partially cooked through. Leave to cool. Prepare a bread stuffing of diced onions, dried mixed herbs, sliced sun-dried tomatoes and prunes. Also make three large crepes to wrap around the pork. Lay the crepes overlapping on a sheet of baking paper, spoon over the stuffing mixture then lie the pork on top. Fold the crepes over to enclose the pork then lay the wrapped pork on a sheet of puff pastry. Enclose the whole package, brush the seam with egg wash and place on a baking sheet join side down. Egg wash the whole pastry then bake at 200°C till golden brown. Serve with a brown onion sauce.

#313. Kahlua and coffee pork

Dice the pork into 25 mm cubes. Pass through flour and fry in oil, diced root ginger and garlic just to brown the pork then place in an oven-friendly casserole. In the same frypan, fry sliced capsicums, sliced chilli, onions then add 100 ml black coffee along with chicken stock. Bake slowly in the oven without a lid so that the liquid can reduce. Adjust the seasoning and when the pork is cooked thicken the sauce if necessary. Just before serving add Kahlua to the sauce and heat gently and stir in.

#314. Brandied peach pork chops

Season the pork chops, fry in oil and diced root ginger. Fry on both sides and when cooked through set aside and keep warm. In the frypan, add a large knob of butter then sliced, skinned fresh peaches. Turn over then pour in 80 ml brandy and carefully light with a match. Allow the flame to die out, add a teaspoon of brown sugar then return the pork to the pan. Reduce the heat and pour in fresh cream, season and serve.

#315. Braised stuffed pork chops

Brown the chops in a frypan on both sides but don't cook through. When brown, set aside into a casserole dish. In the same frypan, brown diced onions, crushed garlic, dried mixed herbs and grated ginger. Place into a mixing bowl and cool then add torn bread slices, orange zest/ juice and chopped parsley. When well mixed, add an egg to bind the ingredients. On the top of each pork chop place a large spoonful of the stuffing and flatten out slightly to cover all the meat area. Pour an onion gravy into the casserole that just comes up to the level of the top of the pork chops then bake slowly in the oven at 160°C for 90 minutes. Serve with mashed potatoes.

#316. Coffee-rubbed pork chops with bourbon sauce

For four pork chops use a tablespoon of fresh, fine grind coffee grounds, finely chopped thyme leaves, cracked pepper and salt. Mix well together. Rub oil on both sides of the chops then apply the rub and massage it into the flesh. Leave in the fridge for an hour. Meanwhile, in a saucepan melt butter then add a finely diced onion, crushed garlic and lightly brown. Pour in half a cup of bourbon, a cup of chicken stock and a teaspoon of instant coffee. Simmer gently and reduce the liquid by half. Reduce heat then pour in cream, stir then check seasoning. Fry the pork chops in oil and butter, rest, then serve with the sauce.

#317. Ham and cabbage fritters

Roughly chop the ham into small pieces and mix with mashed potato. Using leftover roast potatoes also gives this dish a different flavour. Chop cabbage into small pieces and add to the mix. Pour in a little soy sauce, smoked paprika and seasoning. Add beaten egg to make a fritter mix. Fry in oil and butter and brown on both sides. Bacon could also be used in place of ham, taking care not to add too much salt because of the bacon.

6.

VENISON

#318. Venison steak with blueberry sauce

Grill steak to order and rest then deglaze the pan with white wine and blueberries till they mush. Add sugar, orange juice/zest, balsamic vinegar, butter and redcurrant jelly. Reduce the sauce, season and add a knob of butter then serve.

#319. Venison kebabs

Select prime cut of venison and cut into cubes. Marinade the venison in soy, garlic, brown sugar, Worcestershire sauce and grated ginger. Place on metal skewers along with button mushrooms and pieces of courgette. Barbecue the venison kebabs and serve with mushroom sauce.

#320. Grilled venison with cherry and liquorice sauce

Prepare the venison steak by removing any excess fat, silver skin and marinate in red wine and garlic if desired. Grill quickly on barbecue or under a grill. For the sauce, fry onions in a small saucepan till just translucent then add cherries with stone removed, red wine, cherry or red berry jam, chopped liquorice, chicken stock and cracked black pepper. Reduce the sauce, check the seasoning and flavour. Should the sauce need thickening, use cornflour mixed with water to thicken and allow to cook out.

#321. Roast venison wrapped in bacon

Wrap the roast venison in streaky bacon. Lay a sheet of baking paper on a chopping board then lay streaky bacon on the baking paper overlapping each slice side by side. Place the meat at one end, lift the end of the baking paper and tightly roll so that the venison is encased in bacon. Roast slowly at 160°C in the oven till it's just slightly red in the centre. Leave to rest while making a gravy of the pan roast drippings.

#322. Roast venison with blackcurrant sauce

Lay the roast of venison on a bed of root vegetables with rosemary and garlic in the roasting dish. Roast on a slow heat till cooked through. For the blackcurrant sauce, place fresh blackcurrants into a saucepan with a little water and heat. The blackcurrants will break down as the heat is applied. With a stick blender, blend the blackcurrants then add 40 ml crème de cassis and 20 ml balsamic vinegar. Once the venison is cooked, set aside for 20 minutes to rest then serve.

#323. Braised venison

Using a small paring knife, make holes in the venison all over and fill with slivers of garlic. Fry in a frypan till the whole piece is brown all over then place in a braising dish or casserole. In the frypan, brown diced carrots, diced onions, celery and diced pumpkin. When the vegetables are all brown pour in a tin of crushed tomatoes and beef stock. Spoon in fruit chutney, cover with foil and braise slowly at 160°C.

#324. Roast soy honey marinated venison

Prepare a marinade of sliced kiwifruit, soy sauce, honey, sesame oil and peanut butter. Mix together and pour it over the venison. Leave the venison in the marinade overnight and turn it over so that it gets well covered. Place in a hot oven to seal the venison for 15 minutes then reduce the heat to 160°C till cooked.

#325. Roasted marinated venison

Marinate in red wine, oil, garlic, diced onion, peppercorns, cloves and chilli flakes. Leave overnight then dry off on kitchen paper and slow roast.

#326. Grilled venison on potato and sweet potato rosti

Prepare the venison steak and remove any excess fat. Season and rub with oil and prepare to grill. Peel and grate potatoes and/or sweet potatoes, place in a clean tea towel and squeeze out any excess liquid then place in a mixing bowl. To the grated potato add grated onion, garlic, flour, seasoning and beaten egg. Mix well then spoon some of the mixture into a frypan containing hot oil and butter. Brown on both sides then place on baking paper to drain off any excess fat. Place the rosti on the serving plate and top with the grilled venison steak.

#327. Venison schnitzel

Slice the venison into thin slices then flour, egg wash, breadcrumb and fry in an oil/butter mix in a frypan. Place on a serving plate and add capers and lemon segments.

#328. Roast venison

Stud the venison by using a sharp knife to make small holes then adding slivers of garlic and rosemary. On a chopping board lay streaky bacon overlapping each piece. Place the venison at the beginning of the bacon and wrap it around the roast. Roast the venison in the oven.

#329. Venison pie

Fry the cubed venison in oil and garlic till brown and place in a lidded casserole. Then add to it fried onions, garlic, diced celery, carrots, crushed garlic, bacon pieces, dried mixed herbs and juniper berries. Deglaze the pan with a can of crushed tomatoes and red wine and add this mix to the venison along with brown sauce then spoon into an oiled casserole dish. Bake the venison on low for 2 hours and check that the meat is tender. Thicken the sauce with a roux then leave to cool. Top the dish with a sheet of puff pastry, brush with egg wash and bake in the oven at 200°C until the pastry is golden brown.

#330. Braised venison pies

Fry the cubed venison in oil and garlic till brown and place in a lidded casserole. Then add to it fried onions, garlic, diced celery, carrots, crushed garlic and dried mixed herbs. Deglaze the pan with a can of crushed tomatoes and red wine and add this mix to the venison along with brown sauce then pour into a casserole dish. Bake the venison on low for 2 hours and check that the meat is tender. Thicken the sauce with a roux, add in redcurrant jelly then leave to cool. Using individual pie dishes, line with shortcrust pastry and bake blind then leave to cool. Spoon in the cold venison, top with a puff pastry lid, egg wash and bake in the oven at 200°C.

#331. Braised venison

Brown the piece of venison in oil in a frypan with garlic then transfer to a casserole dish in which sliced onions have been placed. To the braising pan add 3 Tbsp red wine vinegar, 3 Tbsp soy sauce, a packet of dry onion soup sprinkled over the top and 400 ml beef stock. Bake in the oven at 160°C for 2 hours then check for tenderness. Check the sauce for taste and thicken with a roux if necessary.

#332. Venison casserole

Dredge the cubed venison through seasoned flour then brown in hot oil, garlic and diced ginger but don't cook through; set aside. To the same frypan add chopped onions, diced carrots, potatoes and diced capsicums. Return the meat to the pan and pour in V8 tomato juice, tomato paste, Worcestershire sauce, beef stock cubes and cook slowly for 90 minutes. Check for tenderness and add seasoning if required.

#333. Venison patties

Venison mince mixed with same amount of lamb, beef or pork mince. As the venison tends to be very lean, the lamb or pork could have a little more fat than usual or add bacon pieces. Heat coriander seeds in a dry frypan for 5 minutes then cool. In a mixing bowl, place the meat, the coriander, allspice, thyme, nutmeg, cloves, Worcestershire sauce, garlic, rolled oats and malt vinegar. Mix well by hand and add seasonings. Mould the meat into patties and place in the fridge to harden up. Fry in oil and garlic.

#334. Venison and peanut stir-fry

Slice the venison into thin slices so that it will fry fast in oil in a wok or frypan with crushed garlic and grated ginger. When cooked, remove and set aside. Fry diced onion, capsicum, chilli and at the end add peanuts. Return the venison to the pan then put in soy sauce, peanut butter, sliced chilli and a half teaspoon of sugar. Thicken with cornflour mixed with water then serve with roasted peanuts and chopped coriander leaves.

#335. Venison steak with blue cheese

Use a thick cut of venison steak and with a very sharp knife, cut a pocket by inserting the pointed end into the steak but keeping the entrance as small as able. Mix blue cheese and cream cheese with crispy bacon pieces and spoon into the pocket. Wrap the steak in streaky bacon and hold in place with toothpicks. Seal quickly in a frypan then finish in the oven. Leave to rest before serving.

#336. Venison ragout

Diced venison, bacon pieces, diced onion, crushed garlic, paprika, chilli, caraway seeds, cloves, juniper berries, thyme, stock, red wine, seasoning. Coat the cubed venison in flour then brown in oil and garlic in a frypan. Once browned transfer to an ovenproof casserole dish. In the same pan fry the bacon pieces, diced onion, and add the paprika, caraway seeds, juniper berries, thyme and chilli. Allow to brown, then pour in red wine and stock to deglaze the pan. Pour the contents of the frypan into the venison and cook on 160°C with a lid or tinfoil on the casserole. When tender, check the sauce for flavour and seasoning and serve.

#337. Venison casserole in bacon and redcurrant jelly

Cube the venison and soak in milk for an hour. Strain off then dry the meat, roll in flour and brown in oil and garlic a few pieces at a time then place in an oven-friendly casserole. In the same frypan, fry diced onions, garlic, diced bacon then add sprigs of thyme, a can of chopped tomatoes, beef stock and redcurrant jelly. Place all into the casserole and slow cook in the oven with the lid on the casserole until the venison is tender. Adjust the seasoning and serve.

#338. Crumbed venison

Using venison schnitzel, bat out to get uniform thickness then run through seasoned flour, egg wash and panko breadcrumbs. Fry the schnitzel in oil and butter till the breadcrumbs are brown. Drain on kitchen paper then serve with garlic butter sauce.

#339. Venison burger patties

Mix venison mince to beef sausage meat 4:1 as this will assist in binding the burgers and give some fat to the venison. To the meat, add breadcrumbs that have been soaked in milk, fried diced onions and garlic, crushed juniper berries and cooked bacon pieces. Bind the mixture with a beaten egg then mould into uniform-size balls and with a meat slice, press down on the balls to create a flat patty. Fry the burger in oil, brown on both sides and cook through to the centre.

#340. Venison schnitzel rolls

Slice the venison into thin steaks and bat out with a rolling pin till uniformly thin. Prepare a stuffing of torn bread pieces, sliced apples, grated carrots, garlic, diced onion, beaten egg, seasoning and blueberries. Place the stuffing on the schnitzel and roll up like a beef olive then secure with toothpicks. Braise in red wine, sliced apple and blueberries.

#341. Venison stroganoff

Slice the venison into finger-size pieces then quickly fry in a frypan in butter and garlic to brown but not to cook through. Place the venison in a casserole dish then in the same pan fry bacon pieces, sliced mushrooms and diced onion. Add flour to absorb the butter along with smoked paprika and tomato paste. Slowly pour in beef stock and thicken the sauce then add this to the casserole dish. Bake slowly in the oven till the venison is cooked. Season then pour in cream and serve. If using grilling steak, make the whole dish in the frypan. If using a braising steak, cut then oven bake.

#342. Venison medallions with plum sauce

Cut the venison medallions and lay them on a tray. Into a measuring jug grate lemon zest, add redcurrant jam, stoneless plums, red wine, chilli flakes and grated ginger. Mix all together then pour it over the venison and hold in the fridge for three hours. Remove the steaks and dry them then grill or barbecue. Heat the marinade and add sugar if necessary, then thicken with arrowroot mixed with water. Allow the steak to rest after cooking, carve and serve the steak and sauce.

#343. Balsamic-glazed venison medallions

In a frypan, fry the venison medallions to the preferred style, for example medium or medium rare. Remove and into the same pan, fry diced onions, crushed garlic, crushed juniper berries, then add balsamic vinegar, stock and reduce. Pour in maple syrup and continue to reduce until a syrupy consistency is achieved. Reduce heat, add pouring cream, season and serve.

#344. Venison casserole in sherry and cumin

Cut the venison into cubes, rub through seasoned flour and brown in oil, garlic and sprinkle in cumin and coriander. Place the browned venison into an oven-friendly casserole dish. In the frypan, fry the diced onions then deglaze the frypan with sherry and stock. Cook in the oven till the meat is tender. Check seasoning and serve.

#345. Venison goulash

Venison cut into 30 mm cubes, bacon, sliced button mushrooms, diced onions, flour, stock, sour cream, paprika, garlic, tomato paste. Cut the venison into 30 mm cubes, dust in flour then quickly fry in oil to seal then place in a casserole dish. Fry bacon, onions, garlic, mushrooms in the same pan, add the paprika then deglaze with stock. Add tomato paste, bring the sauce to a simmer and bake in the oven till the venison is tender. Check seasoning then add sour cream and serve.

#346. Venison casserole in red wine and black peppercorns

Venison, red wine, bay leaves, black peppercorns, onions, carrots, small potatoes, flour, garlic, sour cream and beef stock. Dice the venison, run through seasoned flour and fry in oil in a frypan to seal the meat. Place in a lidded casserole dish. In the same frypan, add, garlic, diced onions, carrots, potatoes cut in half, bay leaves and black peppercorns. Pour in red wine to deglaze the pan and reduce. Bake in the oven at 160°C till the venison is cooked. Check for seasoning, taste then pour in sour cream, heat and serve.

#347. Teriyaki venison

Roast venison, brown sugar, soy sauce, apple cider vinegar, apple juice, garlic, ginger, cornflour. Mix together the brown sugar, soy sauce, apple cider vinegar, apple juice, crushed garlic and grated root ginger. Marinate the venison roast in the mixture overnight then remove and brown the meat in a frypan in oil. Then place in an oven-friendly casserole and pour over the marinade and roast slowly in the oven. When the venison is cooked through, leave to rest. Meanwhile heat the sauce and thicken with a cornflour/water mix. Season and taste.

#348. Braised venison and mushrooms

Brown the whole piece of venison in a frypan in oil and garlic till brown all over then place in a roasting dish that has a lid or use foil. In the same frypan, fry bacon pieces then onions, diced carrots, celery and button mushrooms. Then pour in a can of tomatoes to deglaze the frypan and add beef stock. Pour the deglaze liquid over the venison, add the fresh herbs of thyme, bay leaf and rosemary. Cover the dish and cook in the oven until the venison is ready. Remove the meat and thicken the sauce with a roux. If necessary, add a little sugar to remove any acidic taste of the tomatoes, season and serve.

#349. Roast venison marinated in buttermilk

Place the venison on a chopping board and with a very sharp vegetable knife, push the blade into the venison to make holes so that the buttermilk can get into the meat. Use a bowl that the roast just fits into so that the buttermilk can cover the venison without wasting too much. Pour in the buttermilk and leave for 7 hours then remove from the bowl, wash the meat then treat as a roast. Brown in a frypan till it is sealed all over, then place on a bed of chopped root vegetables with thyme, rosemary and sage sprigs and roast in a slow oven (160°C) till cooked through.

#350. Venison cottage pie

As a method of using up cooked venison, especially roasted venison, chop into small pieces or mince. Add to the mix fried onions, mixed herbs, diced carrots, parsnip and stir in a brown sauce. Pour the minced venison mixture into a pie dish and smooth out. The top is covered with a mashed potato mixture or as an alternative, top with an egg custard and cheese mixture. Bake in the oven till heated through and brown on top. Serve with a fruit chutney.

#351. Venison steak with bourbon sauce

Venison steaks, bourbon, maple syrup, apple cider vinegar, butter, chilli flakes, chopped coriander. Fry the steak in brown butter then set aside. To the frypan, add bourbon, butter, maple syrup, apple cider vinegar and reduce. Whisk in more butter and chilli flakes, reduce heat to the sauce. Season and return steak back to sauce for 3 minutes then serve.

#352. Venison stew with blackberries

Venison cubed, mushrooms, cubed potatoes, diced onion and chopped garlic, tomato paste, oregano, sugar, thyme, rosemary, sage, can of chopped tomatoes, beef stock, blackberries. Dredge the venison cubes in flour and brown in a frypan in oil, garlic and add diced onions. Deglaze the pan with the can of tomatoes then add tomato paste, herbs, potatoes and stock. Place all in a slow cooker and cook for 7 hours on low or cook in a covered casserole dish in the oven on low. Once the meat is cooked add the blackberries, check seasoning and add sugar if the tomato taste is too acidic.

7.

DUCK

#	Dish	#	Dish
353	Duck Breast	371	Braised Duck With Spice
354	Duck Breast Cherises	372	Roast Duck With Ginger And Orange Glaze
355	Duck Breast With Cranberries And Hoisin Sauce	373	Roasted Duck Breast With Cherry Sauce
356	Duck Confit	374	Harissa Duck
357	Filo Stuffed With Duck And Apple	375	Fried Duck With Mushroom Sauce
358	5 Spice Duck Breast	376	Rosemary Duck Breasts And Apricots
359	Honey Roasted Duck Breast With Olive And Mushroom Risotto	377	Roasted Whole Duck
360	Oven Roasted Duck Leg With Honey	378	Roasted Duck Breast With 5 Spice
361	Duck Skewers With Nashi Pear And Soy Glaze	379	Roasted Duck Breast With Bacon And Dates
362	Pan Fried Duck With Mandarin Sauce	380	Roast Duck Breast With Blackcurrant Chilli Sauce
363	Orange And Ginger Braised Duck Breast	381	Duck Breast In Honey Peppercorn Sauce
364	Fried Duck Breast With Raspberry Or Cranberry Sauce	382	Roast Duck Plugged With Orange Zest And Mint
365	Fried Duck Breast In Sherry	383	Roast Duck With Prunes And Juniper Berries
366	Pan Roasted Duck In Marmalade Sauce	384	Seared Duck
367	Roast Duck With Pumpernickel Stuffing	385	Seared Duck Breast With Blood Oranges
368	Roast Duck With Fresh Plums	386	Duck Kebabs Threaded Onto Lemon Grass

#353. Duck breast

Cut through the skin (score it like pork skin) then fry in a frypan with no oil, skin side down. This will render the fat, which will come out into the pan, then turn the duck breast over and brown the other side. Leave to rest, add runny honey, a knob of butter and allspice to pan and baste the duck breast.

#354. Duck breast cherises

Complete as in dish #353. Pour over chicken stock and a little Madeira. In a separate saucepan, pour 50 ml water and a cup of sugar and heat to form a caramel then add stoned cherries and maraschino liqueur and keep warm.

#355. Duck breast with cranberries and hoisin sauce

Heat an oven-friendly pan on an element, score the duck breast, season and place skin side down on the hot pan for two minutes. Turn over and brown the other side then place in the oven and cook the breast for 10 minutes. While the duck breast is in the oven, add fresh cranberries to the same pan. Remove the duck breasts once cooked and set aside to rest. Place the pan back on an element, add a little chicken stock to the cranberries and bring to a boil then reduce heat. Pour in hoisin sauce followed by crème de cassis. Thicken the sauce with cornflour mixed with water, cook out, check seasoning and serve.

#356. Duck confit

Use whole duck legs and thighs. Line casserole with bay leaves and thyme. Place duck legs and thighs in a casserole and cover with rock salt. Leave for 6 hours. Clean off legs and place back in the casserole. Cover with duck fat and cook for 4 hours at 160°C. When cooked, remove from fat, wipe and place in hot oven to crisp skin and bake off the surplus oil.

#357. Filo stuffed with duck and apple

Cook the duck breast as in #353, cut into 10 mm dice then add five spice, cooked diced onions and fresh apple. Using five sheets of filo, brush them with melted butter and place on top of each other. Cut the filo into four squares, place the filling onto the pastry, roll like spring rolls, brush with butter and bake.

#358. Five spice duck breast

Score the skin on the duck breast as in #353 then rub on salt and five spice. Rub in olive oil, thyme. Cook skin side down in a frypan. Top with a weighted lid — use a weight on the lid like a pot of water to press down on the duck. Slice and serve with salad.

#359. Honey-roasted duck breast with olive and mushroom risotto

Score the skin of the duck breast as in #353. Cook skin side down in a dry frypan and let the breast release the duck fat. Drizzle the duck breast with honey. Once the duck breast has been cooked on both sides, return to skin side down, place a lid on the breast and press down with a pot of water as a weight.

Mushroom risotto: Celery, onion, porcini mushrooms, button mushrooms, rosemary and olive oil in blender and blitz, holding back half of the button mushrooms. Fry off in a frypan in olive oil then add arborio rice and coat each grain with the olive oil, adding white wine slowly then chicken stock and stir continually.

Add button mushrooms and straw mushrooms. Finally add butter, Parmesan, lemon juice and chopped parsley.

Mushroom garnish: Fry mushrooms in olive oil, rosemary, garlic and finally add deseeded olives.

#360. Oven-roasted duck leg with honey

In an ovenproof frypan, brown the duck legs in duck fat then oven roast adding a half cup of honey when placing in the oven. Serve it with **Puy lentils**: Cook the lentils in a saucepan in water without any salt, drain and cool quickly. Fry bacon batons in duck fat, diced onions, carrots, thyme, bay leaf, garlic. When cooked, add stock, then the lentils and add in chopped coriander. Check seasoning before serving.

#361. Duck skewers with nashi pear and soy glaze

Five spice, soy sauce, honey. Marinate the duck cubes and skewer with nashi pear. Grill the skewers and coat with glaze while grilling. **Soy glaze**: Simmer soy sauce, honey, five spice and a little demerara sugar till a slightly thicker sauce is formed.

#362. Pan-fried duck with mandarin sauce

Prepare the duck breast as in #353 then marinade in soy sauce, garlic, root ginger and five spice overnight. Dry off with paper towels then fry in a frypan and finish off in the oven. Leave to rest. **Mandarin sauce**: In a heavy-based saucepan, put equal quantities of caster sugar and water and reduce to a light caramel. When it turns to a caramel, remove from the element and add a little cold water, mandarin juice and fish sauce. This will stop further caramelisation. Add mandarin zest, chopped root ginger and two shots of Grand Marnier. Reheat slowly but do not boil.

#363. Orange and ginger braised duck breast

Score the duck breast then seal in a lidded casserole dish, first skin side down then turn over. Remove the duck, drain the duck fat then in the same pan, fry sliced onion, crushed garlic and grated root ginger. Add fresh orange juice, finely sliced orange zest and chicken velouté. Allow the sauce to reduce then return the duck breast back to the pan, lid on and bake in the oven on a low heat (160°C) for 20 minutes. Check that the duck is cooked then leave to rest before carving. Check the sauce for taste and seasoning.

#364. Fried duck breast with raspberry or cranberry sauce

Score the skin of the duck breast and fry skin side down in a dry frypan as in dish #353. Turn after approximately 7 minutes and cook the other side. When nearly cooked add raspberry juice and fresh raspberries to the pan along with some crème de cassis liqueur and let reduce. When the duck is cooked, remove from the pan and rest. Add balsamic vinegar to the pan and reduce. Check the taste and seasoning and pour in a little cream to the sauce. Use cranberries as an alternative to the raspberries.

#365. Fried duck breast in sherry

Prepare the duck breast as in #353. When close to being cooked, reduce the heat and pour in a quality sherry along with a large knob of butter. Remove the duck breast and allow to rest before carving. Add chicken stock to the sherry, reduce and thicken with a beurre manié (equal quantities of soft butter and flour mixed together). Tear off small pieces of beurre manié and add to the hot liquid stirring with a whisk to distribute through the sauce and prevent lumps forming. Finally add a heaped teaspoon of redcurrant jelly.

#366. Pan-roasted duck breast in marmalade sauce

Score the duck breast with a sharp knife and fry skin side down in dry frypan then turn over and fry the other side as in dish #353. To the pan, add orange juice, finely sliced orange zest and brown sugar. Remove the duck breast when it is cooked and leave to rest. Add more orange juice and Cointreau to the pan. Spoon in chunky marmalade and reduce. If necessary, thicken with cornflour and water then check taste and seasoning.

#367. Roast duck with pumpernickel stuffing

Diced onions, slices of pumpernickel, slices of white bread, bacon batons, chopped parsley, thyme, orange juice/sliced zest and an egg. Sweat off the onions, bacon and orange zest in butter. Tear up the bread slices, add the chopped herbs, add the fried onion mix and bind with an egg. Stuff the duck cavity and between the skin and breast meat. Any leftover stuffing can be rolled into balls and cooked in the same roasting dish towards the end of the duck being roasted.

#368. Roast duck with fresh plums

Rub the duck with olive oil, pepper and salt. Into the roasting dish, place peeled red onions that have been quartered and sliced potatoes underneath the duck along with a few fresh plums, squashed garlic corms and thyme. Put into an oven at 200°C for 15 minutes then reduce the heat to 160°C till cooked. Remove the duck when it is cooked and rest covered with tinfoil. Place the roasting pan on the element to reduce the liquid and squash the plums to a pulp. Add Drambuie liqueur to the pan then thicken the gravy with a roux or use cornflour and water.

#369. Roast duck in onion relish

Rub the duck with olive oil, pepper and salt. Into the roasting dish place peeled onions that have been quartered and sliced potatoes underneath the duck along with squashed garlic corms and thyme. Put into an oven at 200°C for 15 minutes then reduce the heat. Remove the duck from the oven and spoon over onion relish and place back into the oven at 160°C till cooked. Leave to rest before carving. **Onion relish**: Sliced onions and root ginger, cooked mashed prunes in red wine and redcurrant jelly. Place in a saucepan and heat adding red wine vinegar and muscovado sugar to balance the taste.

#370. Duck breast with mint and five spice

Place the duck breast fat side up and score as you would a leg of pork as in #353. In a cold frypan, place the fat side down on the frypan and allow the fat to heat and draw away from the duck breast, called rendering the fat. Once the rendering has been completed, pour out the fat then cook the duck breast on both sides but keep it rare in the centre. While it is frying, sprinkle with five spice. Add chicken stock, garlic, a knob of butter and reduce then add chopped mint leaves. Once the duck breast is cooked remove and keep warm. Further reduce the sauce, check for seasoning and taste. Slice the duck breast and plate up then spoon over a little sauce and serve.

#371. Braised duck with spice

Fry the duck legs in a dry frypan slowly to allow the rendering of the fat. In another frypan, sweat off diced onions, garlic, diced root ginger, turmeric, cinnamon, sliced leeks and cumin then add to the duck. Deglaze the vegetable pan with chicken stock and pour all the duck and vegetables into a casserole dish. Slice dried apricots and add to the casserole along with whole dates. In a processor, blitz walnuts to a fine powder then add to the duck and bake the whole dish in the oven. When the duck is cooked, remove the duck, thicken the sauce with a roux, season, taste and serve.

#372. Roast duck with ginger and orange glaze

Rub the duck with olive oil then rub on five spice, orange juice, grated ginger and garlic then leave in the fridge for 2 hours. Roast in the oven when ready. Meanwhile in a small saucepan heat orange juice, grated ginger, honey, brown sugar, soy sauce, star anise and finely sliced orange zest. Allow to reduce to thicken and serve.

#373. Roasted duck breast with cherry sauce

Heat an oven-friendly frypan on an element, score the duck breast and place skin side down into the hot pan for two minutes. Turn over and brown the other side then place in the oven and cook the breast for 15 minutes. Remove the duck and set aside then add a knob of butter and fry diced onions. When transparent pour in a can of whole cherries that have stones removed. Allow to simmer adding star anise and a little brown sugar. Maraschino liqueur could also be added at this point. Check the sauce for taste, seasoning then serve with the carved duck.

#374. Harissa duck

Score the duck breast skin as you would roast pork. Season with pepper, salt and harissa. Place in a dry frypan, skin side down, and allow the fat to render out of the duck. Add a knob of butter to the pan then baste the duck while it is cooking. Cook both sides then leave to rest. The duck can be served with a blackcurrant sauce.

#375. Fried duck with mushroom sauce

Score the duck breast and place skin side down in a cold frypan and place on an element. This will render the fat, releasing it into the frypan, and the skin will become crispy. Turn over and cook the other side leaving the breast rare in the centre. In the meantime, in a saucepan, sweat off diced onions and bacon in butter but do not colour. Add sliced button mushrooms and allow to cook through then add same amount of flour to butter and heat. Pour in milk and cream as the liquid thickens and the flour is cooked out. Bring to a simmer, reduce and season. Spoon the mushroom sauce onto the serving plate and sliced duck breast on top.

#376. Rosemary duck breasts and apricots

Heat an oven-friendly pan on an element, score the duck breast and place skin side down into the hot pan for 2 minutes. Turn over and brown the other side then to the pan add sticks of rosemary, sliced capsicums and a can of drained apricot halves. Add a little of the syrup to the pan then bake in the oven for 20 minutes. Check the duck is cooked then remove from the dish and set aside. Simmer the sauce to reduce and thicken, if necessary, with cornflour and water. Check for seasoning then serve.

#377. Roasted whole duck

Into a mixing bowl put soy sauce, garlic, grated root ginger, honey, sugar, seasoning and mix well. Brush the mixture over the skin of the duck and on the inside. Continue basting while the duck is roasting and again once it is finished.

#378. Roasted duck breast with five spice

Score the duck breast with a very sharp knife and rub over five spice. Place skin side down in a dry frypan and allow the fat to render out of the duck. Once the breast is brown and crispy, turn over, sprinkle with five spice and brown. Place fresh cherries in the pan with the duck then put in the oven to finish cooking. When the duck is still rare in the centre, remove from the oven with the cherries and leave to rest. Add a knob of butter to the pan, melt, add the equivalent amount of flour to make a roux then stir in chicken stock to make the sauce. Allow to simmer to reduce then add 50 ml maraschino liqueur. Return the duck and cherries back to the sauce for 5 minutes, add seasoning, taste and serve.

#379. Roasted duck breast with bacon and dates

Heat an oven-friendly pan on an element, score the duck breast and place skin side down into the hot pan for 2 minutes. Turn over and brown the other side then place in the oven with strips of streaky bacon and dates that have been soaking in a red wine syrup. Roast for 10 minutes and check the duck on degree of cooking completed. Pour in the remainder of the red wine syrup used to soak the dates and leave in the oven for a further 5 minutes. Remove the duck from the pan, reduce the sauce and thicken if necessary, with cornflour and water mix, then add a large knob of butter and seasoning.

#380. Roast duck breast with blackcurrant chilli sauce

Score the duck breast, place skin side down in a roasting pan and heat on an element and cook for 2 minutes. Turn over and brown the other side then place in the oven. At this stage, add fresh blackcurrants to the roasting pan and remove the duck breasts when cooked and set aside. Place the roasting pan on an element, add a little blackcurrant jelly, chilli flakes and chicken stock. Stir well and reduce. Add a large knob of butter and crème de cassis. Reduce further, check seasonings and thicken the sauce with cornflour and water mix.

#381. Duck breast in honey peppercorn sauce

Score the duck breast skin then place skin side down in a cold pan and heat, which will allow the duck to render its fat. It will take around 5 minutes. When the skin is brown and crisp turn over and fry the other side for around 5 minutes. When cooked, remove and set aside and keep warm. To the pan add a knob of butter, chicken stock and honey. Bring to a simmer and stir to lift off the brown caramelised pieces of duck in the pan. Add peppercorns and simmer. Thicken the sauce if required, check the seasoning and spoon the sauce onto the plate. Place thin slices of duck breast on top.

#382. Roast duck plugged with orange zest and mint

Dry the duck with paper towels then using a very sharp vegetable knife plunge holes into the meat 20 times all over. Peel the skin off an orange and slice into very small julienne strips. Wrap the orange piece in a mint leaf then place in the knife cut. Stuff the duck with a wild rice stuffing containing orange juice and zest then roast in the oven. Rest before carving and serve with a pan-made gravy.

#383. Roast duck with prunes and juniper berries

A day before making this dish, soak the prunes in a sugar syrup which could include red wine. Place the duck on a bed of root vegetables, rub with oil, season and sprinkle over chopped thyme and rosemary then roast in the oven at 160°C. After 45 minutes of roasting, place the prunes and crushed juniper berries over the duck and continue roasting. Once the duck is cooked, remove and keep warm under tinfoil. Remove the prunes and roast vegetables from the roasting dish and prepare a gravy from the pan drippings by adding flour, browning then adding chicken stock till it thickens. Season, carve the duck and serve.

#384. Seared duck

Place the scored duck breast, skin side down, in a cold frypan and heat the frypan slowly to render the fat out of the skin. To the frypan, add sage leaves and rosemary and cook for 5 minutes then turn the breast over and give it another 5 minutes. When the duck breast is cooked, remove and keep warm. Pour off most of the duck fat and return the frypan to the element. Pour in chicken stock and add any giblets of the duck if they are available. Reduce by two thirds by simmering, then add cranberry jam. Stir, thicken if required, season and serve. Serve with blueberry chutney.

#385. Seared duck breast with blood oranges

Score the duck breast and place skin side down into the cold frypan and heat slowly to allow the duck fat to render out of the skin. Turn over and brown the other side then place in the oven and cook the breast for approximately 10 minutes. In a frypan, pour caster sugar and allow to caramelise slowly. As it begins to turn brown, reduce the heat and pour in the juice of the blood orange along with a little chicken stock. Allow to reduce then add blood orange segments and finely sliced blood orange zest. Pour the sauce into the duck breast pan to pick up the caramelised duck pieces, top with another knob of butter, orange liquor, heat and reduce then serve.

#386. Duck kebabs threaded onto lemon grass

Debone the duck and cut the meat into approximately 15 mm cubes. Buy lemon grass from the supermarket and trim to thin skewers. Thread the duck meat onto the skewers and marinate in a bowl containing soy sauce, hoisin sauce, grated root ginger, garlic and honey. Leave for two hours then remove and dry the meat. Barbecue or grill the kebabs until the meat is cooked through.

#387. Sesame duck breast with sticky ginger sauce

Score the breast as you would pork skin for crackling. Place in a cold frypan skin side down and place on the cold element then add heat to the frypan. Leave on one side for 5 minutes when the skin should be crisp and brown. Turn over and fry the other side. While the duck is cooking on side one add diced root ginger to the pan. Remove the duck breast and add brown sugar to the frypan and allow it to dissolve. Pour in honey and allow to warm but not to burn. Add chicken stock and reduce till the sauce becomes sticky with the diced ginger in it. Place the duck back in the sauce for 5 minutes then place on the serving platter. Sprinkle with sesame seeds and serve.

8.

ZIPLOC MARINADES

#	Dish	#	Dish
388	Chicken – Honey	395	Duck – Orange Juice
389	Chicken – Sweet Chilli Sauce	396	Chicken – Jamaican
390	Chicken – Coriander	397	Roast Peanut Marinade
391	Chicken – Lemon	398	Dry Rub Marinade
392	Salmon – Butter	399	Wet Rub Marinade
393	Salmon – Wasabi	400	Marinade/Flavouring
394	Potato Fries – Paprika		

These dishes can be stored in a Ziploc bag in the deep freeze and removed when ready to cook. By storing in the marinade, they get the taste into them before freezing. An ideal 'go-to meal' for the working family.

#388. Chicken breast

Honey, soy sauce and garlic.

#389. Chicken breast

Sweet chilli sauce, soy sauce, garlic and brown sugar.

#390. Chicken breast

Coriander, lemon juice, garlic.

#391. Chicken breast

Lemon and ginger.

#392. Salmon slices

Butter, lime juice, soy sauce.

#393. Salmon slices

Butter, wasabi, grated ginger.

#394. Potato fries

Oil, soy sauce, paprika, Italian herbs, pepper and salt. Add all ingredients to the Ziploc bag, shake well then add the potatoes.

#395. Duck breast

Soy sauce, fresh orange juice and zest, brown sugar, cinnamon, star anise, oil and seasoning.

#396. Chicken Jamaican marinade

Thyme, brown sugar, garlic, cinnamon, cayenne, oil, lemon juice and Scotch bonnet chillies. Chop the Scotch bonnet chillies and mix with the rest of the ingredients then add to the Ziploc bag.

#397. Roast peanut marinade

In a roasting dish, dry roast the peanuts and leave to cool. Place in a food processor and blitz to a rough paste. Add garlic, soy, sesame oil, brown sugar, fish sauce, chilli flakes and lime juice. Blitz again to mix all together, season. Add water to thin the marinade down to a pouring liquid. Use with pork, vegetables or barbecue dishes.

#398. Dry rub marinade

Brown sugar, English mustard, oregano, cayenne, paprika, garlic powder and seasoning. Mix well together and massage into the meat or poultry. Leave overnight.

#399. Wet marinade

Ketchup, apple cider vinegar, water, brown sugar, liquid honey, Worcestershire sauce, grated root ginger and seasoning. Add all ingredients to a small saucepan and bring to the boil. Brush onto the meat that has had the dry rub on it then barbecue or bake in the oven.

#400. Marinade/flavouring ingredients

Liquid	Herbs/spices	Sugar/fruit
Oil	Chilli	Marmalade
Soy sauce	Garlic	Tamarillo
Fish sauce	Root ginger	Brown sugar
White wine	Sriracha	Grand Marnier
Red wine	Paprika	Dried apricots
Malt vinegar	Smoked paprika	Dates
Beer	Wasabi	Prunes
Lemon juice	Curry powder	Crème de cassis
Lemon zest	Cinnamon	Tomato ketchup
Orange juice	Coriander	Barbecue sauce
Orange zest	Cardamom	Maraschino liqueur
Apple juice	Cayenne	Preserved lemon
Lime juice	Turmeric	
Lime zest	Cumin	
Worcestershire sauce	Five spice	
Sesame oil	Star anise	
Yoghurt	Harissa paste	
Anchovies	Chipotle	
Honey	Dried mixed herbs	
Coconut milk	Tabasco	
Balsamic vinegar		
Sweet chilli sauce		
Red wine vinegar		

9.

LASAGNE

#	Dish	#	Dish
	MEAT SAUCE	404	Beef Or Chicken Stroganoff Lasagne
A1	Bolognese-Style Sauce #1	405	Fried Lasagne Rolls
A2	Bolognese-Style Sauce #2	406	Beef And Ricotta Pocket Lasagne
A3	Meat-Style Sauce	407	Lasagne Rolls
	BÉCHAMEL/ WHITE SAUCE	408	Cream Of Chicken, Bacon And Mushroom Lasagne
B1	Béchamel	409	Chicken And Bacon Wrap Lasagne
B2	Ricotta Cheese	410	Roast Chicken And Spinach Lasagne
B3	Feta	411	Beef Cannelloni
B4	Mascarpone	412	Chicken Breast Lasagne
	CHEESES	413	Sausage Meat Lasagne
C1	Mozzarella	414	Fried Sausage Lasagne
C2	Blue Cheese	415	Pork And Beef Lasagne
C3	Feta/Ricotta	416	Bacon Lasagne
C4	Haloumi	417	Roast Vegetable Lasagne
	LAYERS	418	Lasagne Dauphinoise
D1	Lasagne Pasta	419	Hasselback Potato Lasagne
D2	French Loaf	420	Lasagne Turnovers
D3	Sweet Potato	421	Roast Cauliflower Lasagne
D4	Butternut Squash	422	Chicken And Bacon Rollup Lasagne
D5	Sliced Aubergine	423	Smoked Chicken And Bacon Lasagne
401	Pork And Veal Lasagne	424	Sausage And Potato Lasagne
402	Butter Chicken Lasagne	425	Chicken Carprese Lasagne

403	Asparagus And Chicken Lasagne

Basic lasagne preparation

Meat sauce

A1. Bolognese style sauce #1

With the selected minced meat (beef, chicken, pork, venison, duck), place into a saucepan, add oil and brown the meat. Add diced onions, garlic, herbs of choice and allow to brown. Then add tomato paste and a tomato-based sauce such as passata. It could be canned tomatoes or pomodoro to infuse the tomato flavour. The sauce needs to be thick enough to stay where it is put and able to be spread out with a spoon.

A2. Bolognese-style sauce #2

Similar preparation to sauce #1 but when using beef or chicken mince, brown in a frypan on top of the stove then place in a baking dish and cook at 180°C and allow to dry out and go brown so that the meat becomes very dry small pieces. When the other ingredients are added to this, the meat will totally absorb the flavours and give a stronger meat flavour.

A3. Meat–style sauce

Select the whole piece of meat you want to use. That could be flank steak, rump steak or any other preferred joint of pork or chicken. Brown the meat in a frypan in oil and garlic then place in a casserole dish. Deglaze the pan with red wine, beef stock, tomato paste and add thyme and sage. Cook very slowly in the oven at 150°C until the beef is able to be pulled apart with two table forks then leave to cool. With the cooking liquor of the beef, thicken and pour it over the beef for inclusion in the lasagne.

Béchamel/white sauce

B1. Béchamel

Equal quantities of butter melted in a saucepan and flour added to the butter. Slowly pour in warm milk as it thickens and allow to simmer gently but not boil. While the sauce is simmering add a whole onion with 3 whole cloves pushed into it.

B2. Ricotta cheese

This is an alternative substitute to béchamel. Mix ricotta with chopped parsley and garlic and season well.

B3. Feta

To either of the above, feta can be added in 10 mm cubed form or crumbled through the sauce and spooned through the lasagne.

B4. Mascarpone

Mascarpone can be used by the tablespoon in any part of the lasagne whether that be in the meat sauce, on the lasagne pasta or on the topping. As the lasagne is cooked, the spoonfuls of mascarpone create little hot spots of explosive cream within the lasagne.

Cheeses

C1. Mozzarella

This is the most common cheese used in lasagne. The choice is over to the person making the lasagne. Mozzarella balls cut into slices can also be used. Either can be used as the topping for the lasagne, which is grilled before serving.

C2. Blue cheese

Can be added as its own component in crumbled form over the meat sauce or over the béchamel/ricotta.

C3. Feta/ricotta

Already mentioned and can be used in any form.

C4. Haloumi

This is another choice, as it can be fried first before assembly.

Layers

The layering between the meat:

D1. Lasagne sheets are usually the number one choice and that can be using fresh pasta sheets or dried pasta.

D2. Slices of toasted garlic baguette is another option.

D3. Fried slices of potatoes or sweet potatoes.

D4. Fried slices of pumpkin or butternut squash.

D5. Grilled slices of aubergine.

Other additives

The alternatives to pasta, in essence, take the name lasagne away from the original dish, but these other options may satisfy medical dietary needs.

E1. Spinach

Defrosted spinach can be used directly as a layer. It needs to be defrosted and dried before adding as a layer. Fresh spinach can be wilted before use and silverbeet can be used as an alternative.

E2. Sun-dried tomatoes

Sun-dried tomatoes can be used as a layer directly into the lasagne. Best to lay them on top of a béchamel sauce.

Assembly

1. Pour or spoon some of the meat sauce directly into the casserole dish so that the base is covered.

2. Add a layer of spinach if it is being used.

3. Spoon over the béchamel or selected option.

4. Top with grated cheese.

5. Add the pasta lasagne sheets and continue the layering.

6. On reaching the top, finish with a layer of béchamel or sliced mozzarella. Sprinkle over grated cheese and bake till cooked through. Approximately 25–30 minutes.

Recipes

#401. Pork and veal lasagne

Select slices or escalopes of pork and veal, bat out so that all are the same thickness then fry in oil and garlic on both sides then leave to cool. Then cut into smaller 50 x 50 mm pieces. In a bowl, mix ricotta cheese with chopped parsley, garlic and grated cheese. Place a layer of pork on the base of a casserole dish, top with the ricotta cheese mix then grated cheese and grated Parmesan. Cover with precooked lasagne ribbons then repeat another layer but substituting veal. When the top of the casserole is reached spoon over ricotta then a thick layer of grated cheese and Parmesan. Top with tinfoil and bake in the oven at 180°C for 20–25 minutes. Remove the foil then place under the grill to brown the top.

#402. Butter chicken lasagne

Cumin, coriander, turmeric, ginger, chilli, cardamom, cinnamon, garam marsala, onion and garlic. In a frypan, pour in oil then add all the spices and heat slowly to allow the natural oils to come out. Add the diced chicken and brown briefly but not to cook through. Spoon the chicken into a casserole dish, add tomato paste along with a little stock then oven bake for 30 minutes at 170°C. When the chicken is cooked remove from the oven and add a large knob of butter, a little coconut cream and cream. Leave the chicken to cool. In a casserole dish, spoon a layer of butter chicken onto the base and spread so that it is well covered. Lay baby spinach over the top and cottage cheese over the spinach. Lay lasagne noodles over the cottage cheese and repeat the layering again. For the final layer over the top of the lasagne noodles, mix cottage cheese and cream cheese with a little cream. Bake till the lasagne is heated then serve.

#403. Asparagus and chicken lasagne

With chicken breasts, remove the skin, cut the breast in half lengthways then bat out so to achieve equal thickness through all the chicken pieces. Fry the chicken in oil, butter and crushed garlic till just cooked through and brown on both sides. Break off the stems off the asparagus and par-poach in a pan of salted water then drain and put into iced water to stop the cooking; drain and dry well. Prepare a béchamel sauce to get ready to assemble. Precook the lasagne ribbon pasta and well before al dente is reached, drain off and cool and dry. On the base of the buttered casserole dish put some of the cooked chicken, spoon in béchamel sauce then add the asparagus, more béchamel sauce then a layer of grated cheese and Parmesan. Top with pasta then complete another layer. Finish with béchamel, top with grated cheese and Parmesan. Cover with foil and bake for 20–25 minutes at 170°C. Remove the foil then grill the top to brown then serve.

404. Beef or chicken stroganoff lasagne

Beef stroganoff is traditionally a Russian classic made with fillet steak which is cut into fingers, fried to point of being rare then mushrooms and cream added and served. Stroganoff has taken a change and now is served with pasta. In this instance, cut the steak or chicken into finger-size pieces and fry in oil, butter and garlic. Remove once cooked and fry diced onions then sliced button mushrooms. If using a casserole grade of meat, add stock, tomato paste and cook slowly on an element until cooked. Leave to cool then add crème fraîche. Once cold, ladle some of the stroganoff onto the base of the casserole dish. Spoon over ricotta cheese then grated cheese and Parmesan. Top with lasagne noodles then repeat the layering. Once the top is reached, spoon over a layer of ricotta followed by grated cheese and Parmesan. Cover with foil and bake 20–25 minutes then remove the foil and grill to brown the top.

#405. Fried lasagne rolls

Cook the lasagne sheets and remove well before al dente, cool and dry. Top one of the sheets with Bolognese sauce followed by béchamel then grated mozzarella and Parmesan. Roll the sheets to form a roll and seal the edges with egg wash to prevent the filling from coming out. Fry the lasagne roll in oil and when cooked lay in a serving dish and top with hot pasta tomato/basil sauce. Serve with freshly grated Parmesan.

#406. Beef and ricotta pocket lasagne

Using sheet lasagne, cook in boiling salted water till just al dente then cool immediately and dry. Rub with oil, cut each sheet in half and lay the two pieces on a chopping board end on end and just overlapping. Prepare a Bolognese sauce and reduce the sauce to keep it quite dry so that it stays in place when spooned onto the pasta. Place a spoonful of Bolognese sauce at one end of the cooked pasta then fold the top right corner over to the left side and hold there. In a mixing bowl, put in ricotta cheese, grated cheese, chopped parsley and mix well. Place a spoon of the ricotta on the pasta and fold back to the right. Continue the folding practice creating the triangle until the end of the pasta is reached. The end product will have the same appearance as a samosa. The folds can be sealed with egg wash then placed in a pomodoro sauce and topped with cheese sauce and baked or rubbed through flour, egg wash, breadcrumbs and deep fried. Serve with a dipping sauce.

#407. Lasagne rolls

Ham, spinach and ricotta mixed. Cook whole sheets of dry pasta and drain immediately when cooked and cool. Rub with oil to stop them sticking. Spoon the mixture onto the sheet lengthways then roll up and place in a buttered casserole dish. Top with pomodoro sauce and cheese sauce. Sprinkle with grated cheese and Parmesan and bake.

#408. Cream of chicken, bacon and mushroom lasagne

Cut the chicken into 25 mm cubes. In a saucepan, sweat off diced onions with thyme, bay leaf, garlic and sage. Add the chicken to colour lightly then just cover with chicken stock and allow to simmer for 15 minutes. Remove from the element and in another saucepan prepare a roux and thicken it with the cooking liquor of the chicken. Return the chicken to the sauce, leave to cool and add mascarpone. In a frypan, fry streaky bacon and whole button mushrooms. Assemble the lasagne by ladling some of the chicken and sauce onto the base of the casserole. Top with slices of bacon and mushrooms, grated cheese and Parmesan. Lay the lasagne sheets over the top then continue to layer. Finish the top with the chicken sauce, grated cheese and Parmesan. Cover with foil, bake at 170°C for 20–25 minutes, grill the top to brown then serve.

#409. Chicken and bacon wrap lasagne

Remove the skin off the chicken breast and cut into half lengthways. Fry the chicken breasts in butter, oil and garlic till brown on both sides and just cooked through. Cool the chicken then wrap each piece in streaky bacon that has been fried in the same pan as the chicken. Lay the wrapped chicken on the base of the casserole and pour in a little béchamel sauce. Top with grated mozzarella and Parmesan. Then spread the lasagne layers over the top. Continue with another layer, finishing off with béchamel on top. Top with sliced truss tomatoes, grated cheese and Parmesan. Bake at 170°C then serve.

#410. Roast chicken and spinach lasagne

An ideal way of using up leftover roast chicken but if none available, roast a chicken and leave to go cold then shred. Make a cheese and tomato pasta sauce and spoon some tomato sauce on the base of a casserole dish then line with shredded chicken. Top with wilted leaf spinach, grated cheese and spoon over the tomato pasta sauce. Using dry lasagne pasta, lay over the top then complete another layer and finish off with pasta sheets on top. Spoon both sauces over the top of the lasagne sheets, top with grated cheese, Parmesan and bake.

#411. Beef cannelloni

Into a mixing bowl add beef mince, sweated off diced bacon, onions, garlic, grated mozzarella, cottage cheese, wilted spinach, breadcrumbs, nutmeg and beaten egg. Fill the cannelloni shells then lay in a casserole dish that has a lining of tomato pasta sauce. When all the cannelloni shells have been filled, top up with the tomato pasta sauce then top that over with a cheese sauce, crumbled feta and grated cheese and Parmesan. Bake till cooked, approximately 20–25 minutes, then serve.

#412. Chicken breast lasagne

Slice the chicken breast in half forming a butterfly cut. Season with salt and pepper then coat with a pasta tomato sauce and ricotta cheese. Top with sliced pepperoni and grated mozzarella then fold the chicken breast back together and secure with toothpicks. On top of the chicken breast coat with the tomato sauce and grated mozzarella. With the chicken breasts in a buttered casserole dish, pour over a béchamel sauce with cheese then mix with the tomato sauce in the casserole. Bake in the oven till the chicken breasts are cooked.

#413. Sausage meat lasagne

In a hot frypan pour in oil then add sausage meat and using wooden spoons break it up into small pieces so that it all browns. When the sausage meat is brown, reduce the heat and add sliced chillies, garlic, brown sauce and simmer. When ready to use in the casserole add crème fraîche. Using a tomato pasta sauce add torn basil, garlic and brown sugar. Layer the sausage meat sauce, lasagne sheets then tomato sauce to the top. Layer the top with grated cheese and bake in the oven.

#414. Fried sausage lasagne

This dish can use an assortment of sausages — pork and chorizo or lamb and chicken — or it can be of just one flavour of sausage. Fry the sausages in a frypan in oil, garlic, thyme and sage. Once browned, turn out onto a plate and leave to go cold. Prepare a béchamel and add a can of chopped tomatoes to the sauce as it thickens. Check seasoning then ladle some of the sauce onto the base of a casserole dish. Lay sliced sausages on top, ladle more sauce over then top with sliced fresh tomatoes, grated mozzarella and Parmesan. Place the cooked lasagne sheets on top then complete another layer. Finish the top with the sauce, grated cheese and Parmesan. Bake at 170°C for 20–25 minutes then grill the top to brown the cheese.

#415. Pork and beef lasagne

Prepare two casseroles of pork and beef. Alternatively, two leftover casserole dishes could be used to use up leftovers or the pork and beef can be stir-fry dishes. Ladle the pork onto the base of the casserole and add cooked florets of broccoli. Top with grated cheese and Parmesan then top with the cooked lasagne sheets. Ladle over the beef casserole, top with sliced tomatoes and basil pesto. Layer on the cheese then the lasagne sheets. Top the lasagne with the beef sauce, cheese then bake and grill.

#416. Bacon lasagne

Line a meatloaf tin with streaky bacon overlapping each slice so that it overlaps on the base of the tin and there is enough hanging over the side of the meatloaf tin to fold back when the lasagne is formed. Onto the bacon spoon a layer of Bolognese sauce, a layer of uncooked lasagne pasta, béchamel sauce, top with grated cheese and layer to the top of the tin. Fold the bacon strips back over and bake in the oven at 160°C for 40 minutes or till cooked.

#417. Roast vegetable lasagne

Roast till just tender a selection of root vegetables such as carrots, parsnip, sweet potato, pumpkin, butternut and also green vegetables such as broccoli, capsicums or Brussels sprouts. To the roasting pan, add crushed garlic, thyme and sage. Leave to cool while preparing a béchamel. Defrost frozen spinach and slice the vegetables into thick slices and lay them on the béchamel sauce which has been poured onto the base of the buttered casserole dish. Pack the root vegetables together and lay the green vegetables on top along with the spinach. A drizzle of basil pesto could be poured over the spinach then top with béchamel, grated cheese and lasagne sheets. Complete a second layer and complete with sauce over the top, grated cheese, bake and grill then serve.

#418. Lasagne dauphinoise

Line the casserole dish with melted butter then overlap slices of potato as the first layer. Spoon over cooked Italian herbed mince, top with grated cheese then pour over enough fresh cream just to cover the potatoes on the base. Complete one or two more layers then top with grated Parmesan cheese and bake.

#419. Hasselback potato lasagne

Wash and peel equal-sized large potatoes then with a sharp knife make slices through the potato but not cutting all the way through. You can place wooden spoons or similar each side of the potato so that the knife does not cut all the way through and it also creates a standard depth. Bake in the oven till the potatoes are cooked and slices open out. Remove, cool the potatoes then place in a casserole dish which the potatoes fit in quite tightly. Place a slice of mozzarella in each slice of the potato then spoon over meat sauce so that the sauce also falls through to the base of the casserole. Spoon over cheese sauce, top with grated cheese and add cubes of feta then bake in the oven till the sauces are hot and the cheese has melted. Grill to brown.

#420. Lasagne turnovers

Prepare a Bolognese sauce and a béchamel sauce. Using a sheet of store-bought puff pastry, lay it on a sheet of baking paper which will be on a baking sheet. Precook lasagne strips keeping them undercooked and dip into cold water immediately to stop them cooking. Don't leave in the water but remove and dry then brush with olive oil. In the centre of the puff pastry, spoon out a length of béchamel sauce, top with Bolognese sauce, grated mozzarella cheese then a layer of cooked lasagne sheet. Continue the layering for two or three layers then fold over both sides of the puff pastry so that they meet over the top of the layering. Seal with egg wash so that the puff pastry forms an oblong parcel. Paint the whole parcel with egg wash and bake in the oven at 200°C till golden brown.

#421. Roast cauliflower lasagne

Make a cut through the centre of the cauliflower then cut slabs of cauliflower 10–15 mm thick off each half until you are left with the two thin side ends. Lay the cauliflower slabs on a flat oiled roasting tray along with capsicums cut into quarters and roast in the oven till three quarters cooked and carrying a brown caramelisation glaze. With a béchamel sauce, pour some into the base of the casserole dish then arrange some of the roasted cauliflower and capsicums in the sauce. Pour more sauce over the top and spoon in dessertspoons of crème fraîche in different parts of the cauliflower and spoonfuls of sun-dried tomato pesto. Cover with grated mozzarella and Parmesan. Top with lasagne sheets then copy another layer again. Top with béchamel, grated cheese, Parmesan and bake for 20 minutes at 170°C then grill to brown the top.

#422. Chicken and bacon roll-up lasagne

This is making individual serves of lasagne. Cook the curly ribbons of lasagne in boiling salted water and remove from the water before they become al dente. Prepare and cut a chicken breast into cubes and fry with bacon. As it cooks, pour in béchamel sauce and allow the chicken and bacon to flavour the sauce. Place the cooked pasta strips on a chopping board and spoon some of the mixture at the beginning of the ribbon and spread. Top with a little grated cheese then roll the ribbon. Into a buttered casserole dish, pour pomodoro sauce then place the roll curly side down into the tomato sauce. Fill the casserole with the rolls, spoon over béchamel, top with cheese and Parmesan and bake in the oven for 20 minutes then grill.

#423. Smoked chicken and bacon lasagne

Cut the smoked chicken into slices. In a frypan, fry bacon strips and sliced onions. In a buttered casserole dish, pour a tomato pasta sauce and place a layer of sliced chicken on top. Then top with cooked bacon and grated cheese. Top with a layer of chicken, cheese sauce, then lasagne sheets. Complete another layer and top the lasagne with grated cheese and bake in the oven at 180°C till cooked.

#424. Sausage and potato (with cream) lasagne

Cook the sausages in a frypan in oil, garlic, thyme and sage then leave to cool. Prepare a mashed potato and when mashing use butter and cream to give a creamy mix. Cut the sausages in half and lay in a buttered casserole. Top with the mashed potato mixture and broken pieces of feta or blue cheese then grated cheese and lasagne sheets. Complete a second layer and top with the mashed potato. Brush with melted butter, grated cheese, Parmesan then bake and grill.

#425. Chicken Caprese lasagne

An ideal way of using leftover chicken which can be roughly chopped and used as is. If using fresh chicken, cut into rough cubes 20–25 mm and brown in a frypan along with garlic and dried mixed herbs. When brown, add sliced onions then chicken stock and cook the chicken through. Thicken the sauce with a roux but only have a minimal sauce to the volume of meat for the lasagne. On the base of the buttered casserole dish lay baby spinach then a layer of cold chicken. Top with slices of tomato, grated mozzarella and torn basil leaves. Top with cheese sauce then the first layer of lasagne pasta. Complete a second layer and finish with cheese sauce over the top of the lasagne. Bake in the oven for 40 minutes at 180°C till the lasagne pasta has cooked. Top with slices of mozzarella and grill in the oven. Garnish with cherry tomato halves, basil leaves and crumbled feta.

10.

MEATLOAF/ MEATBALLS

#	Dish	#	Dish
	MEATLOAF		**MEATBALLS**
426	Pepperoni And Cheddar	443	Meatball Casserole
427	Meatloaf With Bread Stuffing, Bacon And Almonds	444	Meatballs In Tomato And Coconut Sauce
428	Roasted Vegetable Meatloaf	445	Pork Meatballs
429	Coriander Meatloaf	446	Beef Meatballs In Tomato/Paprika Sauce
430	Vegetable Meatloaf	447	Hawaiian Meatballs
431	Indian Meatloaf	448	Meatballs With Lemons And Olives
432	Meatloaf With Sausages And Coated In Mashed Potatoes	449	Meatball Puff Pastry Sandwich
433	Meatloaf With Pizza Topping	450	Middle East Meatballs
434	Rolled Roasted Meatloaf	451	Beef And Pork Meatballs In Gravy
435	Roasted Meatloaf Wellington	452	Meatballs In Potato Skins
436	Baked Alaska Meatloaf	453	Blue Cheese Meatballs
437	Banana Wrapped Meatloaf	454	Meatballs With Apricots, Dates And Almonds
438	Bacon Wrapped Meatloaf	455	Cordon Bleu Meatballs
439	Chicken Meatloaf	456	Beer Can Meatballs
440	Meatloaf With Feta		
441	Meatloaf Patties		
442	Sweet And Sour Meatloaf		

Basic meatloaf

Into a mixing bowl, place the minced beef and sausage meat while soaking sliced bread in milk. Dice an onion and fry in butter with grated garlic and dried mixed herbs then when cold, add to the mince mixture. Add the drained bread/milk along with beaten eggs, tomato paste, chopped parsley, Worcestershire sauce and seasoning. Place the mince into an oiled meatloaf tin, ensuring that it is forced into the corners. Place in a roasting pan and bake in the oven till cooked through. From this basic mixture, many derivatives can be made such as beef/chicken, pork/chicken, duck/chicken.

#426. Pepperoni and cheddar meatloaf

To the basic meatloaf above, cut the pepperoni into 10 mm cubes and mix into the mince mix. Place a layer of the mince in the meatloaf tin then add either grated cheese or sliced cheese. Top the meatloaf with the remaining mix then bake in the oven. When cooked, spread grated cheese over the top and grill to melt and brown the cheese.

#427. Meatloaf with bread stuffing, bacon and almonds

Prepare a stuffing of fresh breadcrumbs, fried onions, fried bacon, dried mixed herbs, crushed garlic, thyme, sage, orange juice, grated orange zest, seasoning and a beaten egg. Mix well together then mix in with the mincemeat along with chopped almonds. Place the meat mix into a meatloaf tin and bake in the oven 170°C till cooked through. Turn out onto a presentation platter while hot and decorate the top with bacon pieces and dry-roasted whole almonds.

#428. Roasted vegetable meatloaf

Roast in the oven a selection of vegetables in oil and garlic. Include green vegetables such as Brussels sprouts, green beans, capsicums or broccoli. The root vegetables will take longer than the greens so start them in the oven first and when all is cooked, leave to cool. Prepare the mincemeat for the meat loaf and place some of the meat into the meatloaf mould to just under halfway.

Top with the cold roasted vegetables then top up the mincemeat. Bake in the oven till cooked then turn out onto presentation plate and serve with a demi-glace sauce.

#429. Coriander meatloaf

Prepare a basic meatloaf and into the mix add coriander seeds, paprika, chopped coriander and grated garlic. Bind the meatloaf with a beaten egg then place into the meatloaf mould and bake in the oven at 170°C till cooked through. Turn out and serve with a fruit chutney and coriander pesto.

#430. Vegetable meatloaf

Prepare the basic meatloaf but before assembling, fry sliced eggplant and mushrooms and leave to cool. Grate courgettes, carrots, sweet potato and pumpkin and mix in with a beef/pork combination. Also mix in whole walnuts and herbs such as thyme and sage. If the mixture is too wet, add fresh breadcrumbs to absorb the liquid. Place some of the meatloaf into its baking dish until half full. Place the cooked eggplant and mushrooms on top then continue with the meat to the top. Bake the meatloaf and turn out when cooked onto a serving platter.

#431. Indian meatloaf

In a mixing bowl, place a 50/50 beef and lamb mix. In a frypan, fry diced onions, crushed garlic, diced root ginger then add turmeric, garam masala, cinnamon, curry powder or a curry paste then add in tomato paste and cook through on a low heat. Allow to go cold then add to the meat along with cooked lentils or rice if desired. Bind with beaten eggs, season then spoon into the meatloaf mould and bake in the oven till cooked through. Turn out onto a serving platter and serve with chutney and naan bread.

#432. Meatloaf with sausages and coated in mashed potato

Prepare the beef mince as in the basic preparation. Select some sausages of choice that will complement the meatloaf then fry in a frypan in oil till cooked through. Place half of the minced beef into the meatloaf tin then line the cold cooked sausages on top. Top up the meatloaf tin with the mixture and bake in the oven till cooked. Leave to cool slightly then carefully turn out onto a baking tray. Prepare mashed potato and mix butter, cream and seasoning into it and ensure no lumps. Using a palette knife or piping bag, spread the mashed potato over the cold meatloaf, briefly bake in the oven to give the potato some colour then serve.

#433. Meatloaf with pizza topping

Prepare the meatloaf and bake in a meatloaf tin till cooked. Turn out onto a baking tray. In a mixing bowl, pour pizza sauce adding grated cheddar cheese and chopped parsley and spoon it over the meatloaf. Top with slices of pepperoni and fresh tomato and grill in the oven till the cheese is brown then serve.

#434. Rolled roasted meatloaf

Beef mince, sliced ham, diced onion, chopped parsley, cooked bacon pieces, grated cheddar cheese, tomato pasta sauce and eggs. In a mixing bowl, put the minced beef along with two slightly beaten eggs and mix well. If the mix is too wet, add breadcrumbs. Turn the mix out onto baking paper and push out to form an oblong 15 mm thick. Top the mince with the pasta sauce, diced onions, ham, bacon, cheddar cheese and chopped parsley. Lift the baking paper from one end and roll the meat and continue till the end of the mince roll is underneath the roll. Carefully place into a roasting tin and bake in the oven till cooked. Add brown sugar to some tomato pasta sauce and spoon it over the roll when it is cooked and grill in the oven till nicely browned.

#435. Roasted meatloaf Wellington

As in dish #434, prepare the meatloaf and shape while it sits on baking paper and on a baking tray. Using the side of your hand, make a V shape approximately 30–40 mm deep along the top of the meatloaf. Fill this with small chunks of cheese then smooth the meat back over the cheese so that it is completely enveloped. Roast the meatloaf until it is cooked through then leave to go completely cold. Using store–bought puff pastry, wrap the whole meatloaf in the pastry and seal the joins with beaten egg wash. Bake in the oven at 200°C till the pastry is cooked. Remove and serve.

#436. Baked Alaska meatloaf

Prepare the meatloaf, place in the meatloaf tin and bake till the meatloaf is cooked through. Turn out the cooked meatloaf onto a serving platter. For the topping, you can use the mashed potato while it is hot and pipe the mashed potato all over the meatloaf, covering top and sides, or with a palette knife smooth the potato all over. Brush with melted butter and bake in a hot oven till the potato browns.

#437. Banana-wrapped meatloaf

Remove the skin from four bananas, cut in half and fry the bananas in oil then place on kitchen paper to drain. In a bowl, mix beef and pork mince along with crushed garlic, sweated onions, dried mixed herbs, seasoning, egg and sliced spring onion. Mix well by hand. Lay the cooked bananas on cling wrap close together then place the mincemeat in a layer over the top of the bananas, the mince layer being approximately 15 mm thick. On top of the mince lay 10 x 10 mm cheese sticks along the centre. Pick up the end of the cling wrap and roll the ingredients so that the bananas enclose the meatloaf. Leave in the cling wrap and place in the fridge for 2 hours. Remove and place in a baking dish, cover with foil and bake in the oven for 45 minutes. Rest, carve and serve.

#438. Bacon-wrapped meatloaf

Prepare the basic meatloaf with any additional ingredients of choice and mix well. Line the meatloaf mould with streaky bacon so that each slice overlaps and the ends hang over each side of the mould. Place the mincemeat into the mould then fold the bacon ends over the meat. Bake in the oven and turn out when cooked onto a baking tray then grill the bacon to crisp it up. Slice and serve.

#439. Chicken meatloaf

In a mixing bowl, place the chicken mince, breadcrumbs, diced sweated onions, garlic, ketchup, Worcestershire sauce, chopped parsley, beaten eggs and mix well by hand. Place on a sheet of cling wrap and flatten out into an oblong sheet then top with sliced cheese. Pull the end of the cling wrap and roll the meatloaf into a roll then place into a buttered casserole dish. Using strips of streaky bacon, criss-cross them over the meatloaf then bake in the oven for 40 minutes. In a saucepan, place ketchup, oil, soy, butter, chilli flakes and brown sugar, heat then thicken and pour it over the meatloaf.

#440. Meatloaf with feta

Use a 50/50 blend of beef and pork mince and place in a bowl. Chop onion, chilli, garlic and mixed herbs then sweat gently in a pan and add to the meat when cold. Finely slice the zest of an orange and add to the mince along with the juice. Cut a 250 g block of feta cheese into 1 cm cubes and add to the mix. Use fresh breadcrumbs then add an egg to bind. Shape into a meatloaf without putting any pressure on the loaf. Halve some carrots and capsicums and begin roasting. Add meatloaf after 10 minutes and cook through. Prepare a sauce tomate and add to the dish then put the meatloaf back into the oven to finish off. Add crumbled feta to the top of the meatloaf, slice and serve.

#441. Meatloaf patties

In a mixing bowl put honey, Dijon mustard, ketchup, soy sauce and stir well together. In another mixing bowl, place the minced beef then add eggs, Dijon mustard, breadcrumbs, grated cheese, some of the honey mixture just prepared, but hold back some to brush the tops before baking, and add seasoning. Make meatballs using wet hands then press down to squash them out to form patties. Brush with the honey mixture and oven bake until cooked. Top with grated cheese and grill briefly.

#442. Sweet and sour meatloaf

Prepare the basic meatloaf and include lumps of fresh pineapple if possible or canned will do. Place the raw meatloaf in the tin and bake till cooked. Turn out onto a serving platter while hot. The sauce can be made prior to cooking the meatloaf. Slice onions, celery, capsicum, diced root ginger, crushed garlic in oil and sweat off in a saucepan. Pour in a can of tomatoes and bring to a simmer. Add any leftover pieces of pineapple and add a small amount of pineapple syrup if canned pineapple is used. Pour in malt vinegar then adjust the sweet and sour taste with brown sugar. Thicken the sauce with cornflour mixed with water, season then pour some of the sauce over the meatloaf and serve.

Meatball preparation

Use whatever mix of mincemeat that suits your taste and that could be beef, pork, lamb, chicken, turkey or a combination of those. Sausage meat in small proportion can also be used as a binding agent and adding fat content. Dice and fry onions in butter to which herbs such as chopped rosemary, thyme, sage or dried mixed herbs can be added. Other spices such as cumin, coriander, curry powder can also be added at this point but leave to go cold before adding to the minced meat. Soak fresh breadcrumbs in milk, squeeze out any excess milk then add to the mince along with an egg which will also help it to bind. Use a large spoon to standardise the amount of mince per meatball then roll the meatballs with wet hands, which prevents the meat from sticking. Continue to prepare the meatballs as per the following dishes.

#443. Meatball casserole

In a mixing bowl, put the minced beef then add sweated off diced onions, garlic, eggs, Dijon mustard, breadcrumbs, grated cheese and seasoning. Use wet hands to make a meatball a little larger than a golf ball. Fry the meatballs in a frypan with oil and garlic just to brown the outside then place in a casserole dish. Pour in a pre-made brown onion sauce and bake in the oven till the meatballs are cooked.

#444. Meatballs in tomato and coconut sauce

Prepare the meatballs as in the basic preparation then fry in oil in a frypan and finish in the oven. In a saucepan, fry sliced onions, Italian herbs, sage and garlic till opaque then pour in pomodoro sauce or similar-type sauce. Add in tomato paste and bring to a simmer. Pour in coconut cream to taste then pour it over the meatballs, cover with a lid and oven bake.

#445. Pork meatballs

Prepare the meatballs as per the basic meatball preparation and brown in a frypan in oil and garlic. When brown, place the meatballs in a casserole dish and into the same frypan cook diced onions and fresh plum halves with stones removed. Add flour to the frypan, reduce heat and thicken the sauce with stock and add plum jam or a suitable berry jam to sweeten the sauce. Pour the sauce over the meatballs and place in the oven at 170°C for 30 minutes or till the meatballs are cooked.

#446. Beef meatballs in tomato/paprika sauce

Fry the prepared meatballs in a frypan just to brown all over then place in an oven-friendly casserole dish. In the same frypan, fry off sliced onions with garlic, paprika then pour in a can of chopped tomatoes and beef stock. Simmer and allow to reduce. Add bay leaves then pour the sauce over the meatballs and bake in the oven at 170°C for 25 minutes. Check the seasoning then serve on fettuccine.

#447. Hawaiian meatballs

Fry pork meatballs in a frypan with chopped garlic till brown then place into an oven-friendly casserole. To the frypan, fry sliced red onions, sliced capsicums, diced fresh tomatoes, cubed pineapple, pineapple juice and coconut milk then pour the sauce over the meatballs. Bake in the oven till cooked, remove the meatballs, thicken the sauce with cornflour and water mixed. Check the seasoning and serve.

#448. Meatballs with lemon and olives

Fry beef meatballs in a frypan in oil and crushed garlic till brown all over then place in a casserole dish. To the frypan, add sliced onions, capsicums, chilli flakes and brown. Pour in a store-bought brown sauce and add sliced lemon zest. Allow to cook for 20–25 minutes in the oven. Add green olives after 15 minutes, continue baking then remove the meatball casserole from the oven, test for taste, seasoning then serve.

#449. Meatball puff pastry sandwich

Prepare meatballs as in the basic preparation method. Using store-bought puff pastry sheets, cut a sheet in half producing two equal-sized pieces. With a second sheet of puff pastry, cut off ribbons 20 mm wide and place around the outside borders of the two halves of puff pastry. Brush the edges with egg wash so that the 20 mm ribbons hold in place. Brush all sheets with the egg wash and bake at 210°C till golden brown and cooked. Line the bottom sheet with meatballs and top with a small amount of the meatball sauce and grated cheese. Lay the second sheet on top and again spoon on the meatballs, sauce and top with cheese. Bake in the oven to heat the meatballs then serve.

#450. Middle East meatballs

In a mortar and pestle grind cumin seed, cardamom seed, garlic then add turmeric and mix well. Spoon this into the basic meatball mincemeat dish using lamb as the prime meat. To the lamb mince also add chopped pistachios. Mould into meatballs then batch fry in oil and garlic and place into a casserole. Pour over a demi-glace style brown sauce flavoured with cumin, turmeric, garlic, cardamom and cook for 25 minutes to finish off the cooking of the meatballs. Serve with flatbreads and plain yoghurt with chopped mint added.

#451. Beef and pork meatballs in gravy

Prepare the meatballs as per the basic preparation plan, fry in a frypan in oil and garlic then once browned, place in an ovenproof casserole dish. In the same frypan, pour 50 ml oil, heat than add flour and stir in. Allow the flour to change colour slowly to brown without burning then pour in beef stock stirring at all times while it thickens. Add garlic, chopped rosemary, bay leaf, thyme and simmer the sauce allowing it to reduce. Check seasoning then pour it over the meatballs and bake in the oven for 20 minutes then serve.

#452. Meatballs in potato skins

Cook the meatballs as in dish #451. Using potatoes or sweet potatoes, wash without peeling then bake in the oven till the flesh is cooked. Allow to cool then cut in half and scoop out the flesh and make mash patties out of the flesh. Leave approximately 8 mm of flesh on the inside of the skin, brush with melted butter and grill to harden the flesh. Place the skin on the serving plate then spoon the meatballs and sauce into the skin and serve.

#453. Blue cheese meatballs

Using the basic preparation of meatballs, divide the mince into equal-size portions then roll to form meatballs. Push your thumb into the meatball to make an indentation, fill with a piece of blue cheese then pull the mince back over the cheese and re-roll so that it is well sealed. Brown the meatballs, place in a casserole then pour in either a pomodoro sauce or gravy and oven bake.

#454. Meatballs with apricots, dates and almonds

Into a mixing bowl place beef mince, torn white bread pieces, mixed herbs, Worcestershire sauce, egg, chopped parsley, Dijon mustard, diced dried apricots, chopped dates and chopped almonds. Mix well and shape into golf ball-size meatballs. Bake in the oven till cooked then serve with an apricot and marmalade purée sauce and flaked almonds on top of the meatballs.

#455. Cordon bleu meatballs

Prepare a meatball mixture to the point of ready to roll them out.

Place the meat on a chopping board and divide the meat into equal-sized portions to enable the meat to be rolled into balls. From a piece of square ham loaf, cut a thin slice then with a block of cheese cut into slices, place a slice on the ham and cut into four equal-size quarters and place on top of each other. Roll the meat into balls, slice in half and place the ham and cheese on one half then join the meat back together again and roll to secure. Fry in a frypan in oil to cooked through or bake in the oven.

#456. Beer can meatballs

Prepare a meatball mix by frying diced onions, crushed garlic, dried mixed herbs, chopped parsley, breadcrumbs and eggs, adding to the mincemeat cold and mixing well. Divide the mince mix into large meatballs and roll to a smooth ball. Using a clean full beer can insert it into the ball leaving it just up from the bottom of the ball. Mound the mince around the base of the beer can and up the side. While the beer can is in situ, wrap streaky bacon around the mince ball at two levels. Carefully pull the beer can out of the mince cup it has made. Into the hole place cold fried onions, chopped fried bacon batons, chopped capsicums and top with grated cheese. Bake in the oven.

11.

PASTA, RICE AND POLENTA

#	Dish	#	Dish
457	Tuna Cannelloni	471	Ravioli With A Mushroom And Walnut Sauce
458	Pork Cannelloni	472	Chicken, Bacon And Pumpkin Cannelloni
459	Chicken, Ricotta And Spinach Cannelloni	473	Tuna Pasta Bake
460	Chicken And Spinach Pasta	474	Penne Vodka
461	Spaghetti With Chorizo And Olives	475	Rice Risotto
462	Chicken Linguine Carbonara	476	Potato Gnocchi With Mushroom Sauce And Feta
463	Roast Gnocchi	477	Rice Burger
464	Prawn And Chorizo Pasta	478	Rice With Saffron
465	Prawns In A Pasta Spiral Cream Sauce	479	Persian Fried Rice
466	Creamed Polenta	480	Smoked Mussel Fettuccini
467	Polenta	481	Spinach And Parmesan Cream Pasta
468	Ravioli With Lemon And Basil Butter	482	Salmon Cannelloni In Lemon Cream Sauce
469	Ravioli With Garlic Butter And Sage	483	Pistachio Couscous
470	Baked Ravioli		

#457. Tuna cannelloni

Use precooked or fresh lasagne sheets. Lay a pasta sheet on a chopping board and spread over it béchamel, drained canned tuna, tomato pasta sauce then grated cheddar cheese. Roll the pasta up to form a cannelloni shell. Place in a casserole dish that has a pasta tomato sauce spread over the base. Fill the casserole with the cannelloni then pour in more pasta tomato sauce and finish with béchamel. Top with grated cheddar cheese and Parmesan and bake in the oven for approximately 20–25 minutes until the pasta is cooked through and the top is grilled to brown the cheese.

#458. Pork cannelloni

To pork mince add sweated diced onions, garlic, dried mixed herbs, breadcrumbs, chopped parsley, beaten egg and crumbled feta. Fill the dry cannelloni shells and lay in a buttered casserole dish that has been covered with tomato, onion and garlic sauce. Top with a cream cheese sauce, sprinkle with grated cheddar cheese and crumbled feta and bake.

#459. Chicken, ricotta and spinach cannelloni

In a mixing bowl, place cooked, pulled-apart chicken adding spinach that has been defrosted or fresh wilted cold and well-drained spinach. To the chicken and spinach add grated cheese, Parmesan, a pinch of nutmeg, chopped garlic, cooked diced onions and ricotta cheese. Mix well then fill dry pasta cannelloni shells or use fresh lasagne sheets and spoon the filling onto the lasagne sheet, roll once, brush the join with egg wash and seal. Cut the cannelloni to equal lengths if using the fresh pasta. Onto the base of the casserole pour a tomato-based pasta sauce, approximately 10 mm, then add the cannelloni. Pour over more tomato sauce and béchamel sauce to create layers of white and orange. Finish off with béchamel and top with grated mozzarella. Bake in the oven for 25 minutes, check that the cannelloni is cooked then grill to brown the top.

#460. Chicken and spinach pasta

Dice the chicken into 25 mm cubes then fry in oil, butter and garlic till brown and cooked through. Set aside to keep warm. In the same pan cook baby spinach in oil with oregano, a tin of crushed tomatoes then add cream and seasonings. Cook the pasta and drain when al dente. Return the chicken to the pan with the spinach, add the pasta and toss. Serve with Parmesan.

#461. Spaghetti with chorizo and olives

In a frypan, cook sliced chorizo and onions in oil and garlic till brown then add pine nuts and black olives. Remove the chorizo mixture and set aside. Cook the spaghetti in boiling salted water and when al dente strain and toss in oil and garlic in the frypan. Add the chorizo mix, sauté together then spoon in sun-dried tomato pesto and cubes of feta. Season and serve with Parmesan.

#462. Chicken linguine carbonara

Flatten the chicken breasts with a rolling pin then fry in oil, garlic and diced bacon till cooked through. Set aside the chicken, bacon then fry sliced onions and mushrooms in the same frypan. In a mixing bowl, add liquid cream and a beaten egg. Cook the linguine in boiling salted water then drain well. Place the pasta into frypan with the onions and mushrooms. Pour the cream and egg mix into the frypan and stir continually while the sauce thickens. Season and spoon the pasta onto the serving plate and top with the chicken. Serve with shaved Parmesan.

#463. Roasted gnocchi

Poach the gnocchi in boiling salted water and as they rise to the top, scoop out with a slotted spoon. Fry the gnocchi in garlic butter till they begin to brown then place in a hot oven for 5 minutes with olive oil added to the pan. Serve the gnocchi over wilted spinach and ricotta cheese and Parmesan. Could also be accompanied by smoked salmon.

#464. Prawn and chorizo pasta

In a frypan, cook sliced chorizo in oil and crushed garlic till brown then add sliced capsicum and onions. Remove the chorizo and vegetables, set aside and keep warm. To the frypan add oil, butter and crushed garlic then place the prawns into the frypan. Sprinkle with Cajun spice and toss briefly. Return the chorizo mix to the frypan, add the cooked pasta and toss well. Spoon in crème fraîche when plated.

#465. Prawns in a cream sauce

In a saucepan, fry prawns quickly adding diced fresh tomatoes, chopped parsley, chopped spring onions, paprika and seasoning. Stir well, reduce heat and add pouring cream then undercooked pasta spirals. Allow the spirals to finish cooking to become al dente then serve the dish topped with Parmesan.

#466. Creamed polenta

Stir cornmeal with chicken stock over low heat until it becomes thick. Add butter, cream and cheese then add seasonings. Great as an accompaniment for roast vegetable salad.

#467. Polenta

Mix together milk and vegetable stock and bring to the boil then stir in polenta. It will thicken and come to a point where it will stick solidly to a wooden spoon. Stir in crushed garlic, oil, grated cheese and Parmesan then pour into a cake tin and let it set then cool in the refrigerator. Remove from the cake tin and cut to desired size then fry in butter till brown. Use as an accompaniment to serve meat and poultry on.

#468. Ravioli with lemon and basil butter

If using store-bought ravioli, place into simmering salted water and when it comes to the top remove from the heat into a bowl and sprinkle over a small amount of olive oil. In a small saucepan, add a knob of butter and heat gently. Add crushed garlic, lemon juice and whole basil leaves. Mix with a wooden spoon till hot. Serve the ravioli in a bowl, spoon over the sauce and grated Parmesan.

#469. Ravioli with garlic butter and sage

Cook the ravioli in salted boiling water then drain well and put straight into a hot frypan that has garlic butter and sage leaves in it. Mix well so that each piece of ravioli is covered in the butter and herbs then add grated Parmesan cheese and serve.

#470. Baked ravioli

Prepare a Bolognese sauce with minced beef, tomato paste, garlic, diced onions and Italian herbs. Poach the ravioli in boiling salted water then drain and lay half in a buttered casserole dish. Spoon over the meat sauce and top with pomodoro sauce and cubes of feta cheese. Repeat the layering, top with grated cheese and Parmesan then bake in the oven till cooked through.

#471. Ravioli with a mushroom and walnut sauce

In a frypan, cook sliced mushrooms, chopped garlic and chopped walnuts in oil till brown then pour in cream and simmer slowly to reduce the cream. Add Parmesan but don't boil. Poach the ravioli in simmering salted water and allow to rise to the top then remove with a slotted spoon. Place the ravioli in a serving dish, spoon over the sauce and serve with freshly grated Parmesan.

As an alternative, button mushrooms can be cooked whole in

butter and garlic and the ravioli served on top of them. Make a walnut sauce of chopped walnuts, marjoram, garlic, olive oil and Parmesan. This sauce is a cold sauce similar to, in preparation terms, chimichurri. Spoon the sauce over the cooked ravioli.

#472. Chicken, bacon and pumpkin cannelloni

Peel and cut the pumpkin into small cubes and par-cook in boiling salted water till just cooked. Fry some bacon pieces in butter and add to the pumpkin. Using leftover chicken, shred it and add to the bowl with the other ingredients. Mix in a cheese sauce and seasoning then spoon into dry cannelloni shells until they are packed with filling. Lay the full cannelloni shells onto tomato pasta sauce and add more sauce around them. Top with more cheese sauce, grated cheese and bake. Serve with Parmesan cheese.

#473. Tuna pasta bake

In a frypan, cook and caramelise sliced onions and garlic then very quickly sear cubed fresh tuna pieces and spoon into a casserole dish. Meanwhile cook spiral pasta in boiling salted water but keeping it quite raw and tough to the bite. Drain quickly and hold in a colander. To the frypan add butter, sliced garlic, roughly chopped capsicum then add same amount of flour as butter, stir well and add milk and stir while it thickens. Add a pinch of chilli flakes and season the sauce. Add the pasta to the sauce and pour it over the tuna. Chop or break feta cheese into small cubes into the casserole, top with grated cheese and bake in the oven for 20 minutes at 170°C till the casserole is brown. Serve with Parmesan.

#474. Penne vodka

In a frypan sweat off sliced onions and crushed garlic. Add pasta sauce then bring to a simmer then add vodka. Cook the penne and toss in a frypan with crushed garlic and pesto. Serve with freshly grated Parmesan cheese.

#475. Rice risotto

In a saucepan, pour oil and sweat off diced onions, carrots, celery without colouring then add the arborio rice or similar-type rice. Allow each grain of rice to get coated in the oil and stir while the rice is absorbing the oil. At this time, add coriander seed and cumin and allow to cook through the rice. Add white wine, stir then slowly add stock as the risotto rice absorbs the liquid. Once all the stock has been absorbed, season and add a large knob of butter and stir in.

#476. Potato gnocchi with mushroom sauce and feta

Buy a good brand gnocchi from your supermarket or if you desire make your own. The gnocchi will be poached in simmering salted water when ready to cook. First, prepare the mushroom sauce by sweating off diced onions and sliced mushrooms in butter. Add a little flour to the saucepan then add milk slowly to thicken the sauce and season. Simmer gently for 10 minutes to cook out the flour then add cream. Poach the gnocchi and as they come to the top of the boiling water, remove to a holding plate until all are cooked. To the mushroom sauce add crumbled feta then serve the gnocchi and spoon over the mushroom-feta sauce.

#477. Rice burger

Any rice can be used but it needs to be dry when cooked therefore arborio rice would be the advantage. Cook the rice using the absorption method so that it holds together when cold. Spoon the rice into greased egg rings and pack so that it is tight fitting then hold in the fridge. Two rice cakes will be used per serving and the filling can be beef, chicken, pork style casserole of any type. The sauce is drizzled over the base rice cake to give flavour while soy and sweet chilli sauce can also be used to add flavour.

#478. Rice with saffron

In a baking dish place the uncooked rice. To the rice add diced red onion, sliced garlic, tomato paste, sun-dried tomatoes then pour in the hot water in which saffron and desiccated coconut has been steeped. Bake in the oven till the rice is cooked.

#479. Persian fried rice

Basmati rice uncooked, butter, oil, cinnamon stick , cardamom pods, garlic, cooked lentils, dates, chopped dill, parsley and coriander. Cook the rice and drain. In a large saucepan melt the butter, add the spices, garlic then the rice, some of the herbs, lentils and the dates. Put on the lid wrapped in a clean tea towel, leave on a low heat and allow crust to form on rice. Tip the rice out onto a serving bowl and sprinkle over the remainder of the chopped herbs.

#480. Smoked mussel fettuccine

In a saucepan, sweat off sliced onions, sliced capsicum, crushed garlic then add smoked mussels and pasta sauce. Simmer gently while fettuccine cooks. Drain the pasta and toss in garlic oil. Add basil pesto to the pasta then pour over the smoked mussel mix. Season and serve.

#481. Spinach and Parmesan cream pasta

Wilt the spinach in very little salted water for a minute, drain and roughly chop. Cook pasta of choice to al dente then drain. Heat a frypan, add butter and the spinach then pour in the pasta and toss. Pour in cream and allow to heat without boiling, add seasoning and top with Parmesan cheese.

#482. Salmon cannelloni in lemon cream sauce

Roughly chop the salmon leaving out the skin and pin bones then place in a mixing bowl. In a frypan, fry diced onion and crushed garlic and add to the mixing bowl when it is cold. Also chop parsley and add to the bowl along with seasoning, lemon juice and grated zest. Tear a small amount of baguette into small 20 mm pieces and add to the salmon along with olive oil and a beaten egg. Once the mix is well mixed together, place the filling into dry cannelloni shells or use cooked ribboned lasagne sheets (San Remo) and create the cannelloni. Prepare a béchamel sauce and add grated lemon zest and juice and once the flour is cooked out add mascarpone. Place the cannelloni into a buttered casserole dish and pour in the cream sauce but hold back some of the cream sauce and add Parmesan and grated cheese. Top the pasta dish and bake in the oven for 40 minutes on 170°C. Grill briefly to brown the top. Serve with a salad and crusty bread.

#483. Pistachio couscous

Place the couscous in a mixing bowl and pour over the same amount of boiling water, stir then cover with a lid and leave for 10 minutes. Meanwhile chop mint, coriander and parsley and set aside. To the couscous add a large knob of butter and stir in with a fork to aerate the couscous. Add chopped pistachios, parsley, coriander and mint, season and, if necessary, add a little virgin olive oil.

12.

TOPPINGS

#	Dish	#	Dish
484	Almond Crusted Fish, Beef Or Chicken	491	Savoury Crouton Crust
485	Blue Cheese, Chilli And Breadcrumb Topping	492	Dukkah Crust
486	French Bread	493	Gremolata Style Topping
487	Crushed Ritz Crackers	494	Herb, Garlic And Cheese Croutons
488	Puff Pastry Wheels	495	Capers, Brown Butter And Breadcrumb Topping
489	Fried Potato Top	496	Rosemary, Orange And Turmeric Crust
490	Scone Topping	497	Greek Yoghurt, Grated Cheese And Beaten Eggs

#484. Almond-crusted fish, chicken or beef

To a mixing bowl, spoon in flaked almonds, panko breadcrumbs, grated lemon rind, chopped parsley and oil. Melt butter and drizzle it through the panko mix but don't mix to a paste. Keep the mix to crumbs. Use to spread over fish, chicken or beef dishes.

#485. Blue cheese, chilli and breadcrumb topping

In a frypan, fry breadcrumbs in butter along with freshly sliced chilli slices. The bread to be used should be stale bread and grated on a tri-grater so that the crumbs are quite large. Once brown, leave to go cold then mix with crumbled blue cheese and mix together. Sprinkle it over meat dishes, grilled steak, fish or vegetables dishes.

#486. Baguette slices

Cut the baguette on an angle then spread with garlic butter on both sides. When putting on top of a soup or casserole, place close together and put the dish under the grill. Sprinkle with grated cheddar and continue cooking. The top could also be sprinkled with pieces of blue cheese, feta or sesame seeds.

#487. Crushed Ritz crackers

The amount of Ritz crackers required will depend on the size of the casserole dish being used. However, take one or two sleeves of Ritz crackers, place between a clean tea towel and hit gently with a rolling pin to create pieces of the crackers. To the crackers add grated cheese, chopped parsley and melted butter. Spoon the crackers over the casserole or fish dishes to create a 5 mm minimum topping. Place the casserole back in the oven to heat the topping.

#488. Puff pastry wheels

Similar to cheese palmiers. Lay the sheet of puff pastry on the bench and spread with grated cheese. Roll the pastry up from one end into a roll then cut into 15 mm wide strips. Lay them on baking paper on a baking sheet, brush with egg wash then bake in the oven at 200°C till cooked. Leave to go cold then place on a casserole dish that could use a topping. Other things could also be added to the filling, such as fruit chutney, mustard, tomato ketchup.

#489. Fried potato top

In a saucepan, boil potatoes till they are just cooked. Drain and roughly chop into 25 mm pieces. Heat oil, butter in a frypan and fry the potato pieces till they are nicely browned. Add chopped rosemary to the potatoes and cook with them. When cooked, spoon the potatoes over the pie or casserole then oven bake.

#490. Scone topping

An ideal means of using up scones over a meat or poultry casserole. Cut the scones in half and butter generously. When the casserole is cooked place the scones sliced side down onto the meat, poultry or vegetables, sprinkle over grated cheese and oven bake for 10 minutes and grill for 2 minutes.

#491. Savoury crouton crust

Cut bread into 20 mm cubes and fry in butter and oil till brown all over then leave to cool. In a dry frypan, heat whole almonds till brown but not burning. Into a mortar and pestle place chopped parsley, garlic, almonds, cloves, olive oil, the croutons and crush till it is all mixed together. Add to any savoury dish at the end of cooking. It will flavour and thicken the dish.

#492. Dukkah crust

Chopped pistachios, chopped hazelnuts, sesame seeds, coriander, cumin. Mix all ingredients together and use over meat, fish or vegetable dishes.

#493. Gremolata-style topping

In a bowl, mix butter, dates, walnuts, ginger, lemon zest/juice and chopped parsley. Fry breadcrumbs in the butter then chop the other ingredients and mix into the breadcrumbs in the pan. Spoon over the meat or chicken once served.

#494. Herb, garlic and cheese croutons

In a mixing bowl, place soft butter, crushed garlic, dried mixed herbs, chopped parsley, grated cheddar and seasoning. Mix well then slice sourdough bread into slices and toast. Spread the mix over the toasted sourdough and grill. When cool cut the croutons into 20 x 20 mm squares and place on the top of casseroles, soups, salads or any other items that are suitable for its use.

#495. Capers, brown butter and breadcrumb topping

Mix together panko breadcrumbs, cracked black pepper, capers, chopped parsley in brown butter to a heavy crumb mix. Spoon over meat, fish or vegetable dishes.

#496. Rosemary, orange and turmeric crust

Mix panko breadcrumbs with grated orange zest, grated fresh turmeric root or powdered turmeric and fresh orange juice. To the mixture, rub in soft butter then place the crust on a casserole-type dish then bake and eat.

#497. Greek yoghurt, grated cheese and beaten eggs

To Greek yoghurt add grated cheese then mix in beaten eggs. This topping can be used on top of shepherd's pie, lasagne, or other pasta dishes.

13.

FISH

#	Dish	#	Dish
498	Baked Stuffed Blue Cod	516	Goujon Of Fish Tempura
499	Baked Whole Snapper Fillet	517	Grilled Tuna
500	Flounder With Seafood Stuffing	518	Rolled Sole Fillets
501	Crumbed Flounder	519	Filo Fish Packets
502	Tuna And Macaroni Casserole	520	Almond Crusted Snapper Fillets
503	Tuna And Avocado Cakes	521	Seafood Thermidor
504	Tuna Bake With Cashews	522	Fish Casserole
505	Fried Tuna And Soba Noodles	523	Fish Cakes
506	Vodka And Tonic Battered Fish	524	Fish Fillets With Lentils
507	Crumbed Fish With Brown Butter, Capers And Lemon	525	Fish Tagine
508	Roasted King Fish	526	Seared Tuna With Grapefruit And Avocado Salsa
509	Baked Fish Pie	527	Sole Gratin
510	Curried Fish	528	Peanut Crumbed Fish Fillets With Fried Banana
511	Snapper With Curry Rub	529	Fried Snapper With Walnut Stuffing
512	Sole With Caper Cream Sauce	530	Olive Crusted Fish Fillet
513	Crumbed Sole Fillets With Flaked Almonds	531	Fried Snapper With Scallops
514	Fried Snapper Pesto	532	Fillet Of Snapper With Black Olives, Tomatoes And Capers
515	Fried Fish Fillet With Tomato And Garlic Sauce	533	Snapper With Tomatoes, Capers And Lemon Grass

#498. Baked stuffed blue cod

Using skinned and boned fillets of cod, season the cod with pepper and salt. Prepare a stuffing of fresh breadcrumbs, anchovy fillets, diced fried onions, chopped parsley, lemon juice and zest and seasoning. Mix well together and bind with a beaten egg. Spread the stuffing over one fillet, top with the second fillet and tie with string. Place on baking paper, brush with a mix of oil and butter then bake in the oven at 190°C.

#499. Baked whole snapper fillet

Leave the skin on but remove the bones. Lay it on a buttered piece of tinfoil with the sides turned up so that the liquid cannot escape. In a bowl, mix diced root ginger, crushed garlic, tomato juice, oil, molasses, chopped chilli and coriander. Stir well, season the fillet then pour over the liquid and bake in the oven till the snapper is just cooked. Sprinkle with chopped spring onions and serve.

#500. Flounder with seafood stuffing

Remove the skins from both sides of the flounder but leave the head and tail on. On the top side, run a sharp knife along the backbone and follow the bones down one side towards the fins. Do the same with the other side so that the fillets fold back but are still attached to the fish. Rub the fish with oil, season and bake in the oven until cooked. As soon as it is cooked, remove from the oven and with the same sharp knife, lift out the backbone which will freely come away. In a separate frypan, fry prawns, scallops and 10 mm cubes of diced salmon in butter. Any other seafood can also be used such as octopus or mussels. When cooked, place the seafood in the centre of the flounder, brush with butter and sprinkle over a little lemon juice then briefly grill and serve.

#501. Crumbed flounder

Follow the same procedure as in #500 but this time remove the head. Fold the fillets back then rub the flounder through flour, egg wash and breadcrumbs, ensuring that it is well coated in crumbs. Deep fry the flounder till golden brown, remove the backbone and place slices of beurre maître d'hôtel in the centre. It will melt into the flounder flesh.

#502. Tuna and macaroni casserole

Prepare a cheese sauce while cooking the pasta in boiling salted water. In a frypan, fry diced onions, crushed garlic, chilli flakes then leave to cool. To the cheese sauce add the onion mixture, seasoning, diced tomatoes and mix well. Spoon the cooked macaroni into a casserole dish and add the tuna. It can be canned tuna or fresh tuna diced. Mix in the cheese sauce along with more grated cheese and add spoonfuls of crème fraîche and keeping them as whole as possible. When the macaroni is baked, these crème fraîche ponds will heat and create a small pocket of sauce in the area. Bake in the oven for 20–30 minutes, top with grated cheese and Parmesan, grill and serve.

#503. Tuna and avocado cakes

In a mixing bowl, put the avocado flesh, cold mashed potato then add drained tinned tuna. Mix in diced onions, crushed garlic, breadcrumbs, chopped coriander, grated cheese and an egg. Shape the mix into cakes then place in the fridge to harden up. Dip the cakes through flour, egg wash, breadcrumbs then fry in butter and oil till golden brown on both sides.

#504. Tuna bake with cashews

In a dry frypan, heat the cashews and allow to brown but not burn then set aside. When cool, place in a food processor and blitz but hold some whole cashews back for a garnish. Prepare a béchamel sauce and spoon the blitzed cashews into the sauce along with chopped parsley. Fry onions and garlic in a frypan in butter till opaque and add to a mixing bowl. Add a drained can of tuna to the mixing bowl. Cook penne pasta in boiling salted water, drain and mix with the tuna. Pour over the béchamel sauce, mix well and pour into a casserole dish. Top with grated cheese and bake in the oven.

#505. Fried tuna and soba noodles

Cut the tuna into cubes and marinate in hoisin sauce, soy, brown sugar and a few drops of sesame oil. In a frypan or wok if available, quickly fry florets of broccoli, baton carrots, sliced red onion, diced tomato flesh in garlic and grated ginger then place in saucepan with a lid to keep warm. In the same pan, fry the tuna with some of the marinade once the tuna is brown but not cooked through. Add to the vegetables. Cook soba noodles in boiling salted water, drain then toss the noodles through the wok. Return the tuna and vegetables to the pan then serve.

#506. Vodka and tonic battered fish

Dried yeast, tonic water, flour, vodka, apple cider vinegar, sugar, salt. Sieve the flour into a bowl, make a small well in the centre then mix yeast, sugar and a few millilitres of warm water and put into the well in the flour then leave for it to bubble. Pour in tonic water, cider and vodka and mix to a batter and leave to bubble. It is now ready to use. Put fish through seasoned flour, into batter and deep fry.

#507. Crumbed fish with brown butter, capers and lemon

Use skinned and boned fillets. Dip through flour, egg wash and sourdough breadcrumbs that have been combined with grated lemon zest. Then fry in butter and oil and add lemon juice while frying. When just cooked, place on the serving plate, spoon over brown butter and add capers and thinly sliced lemon slices.

#508. Roasted kingfish

Briefly fry the kingfish in butter on an element on both sides then finish cooking in the oven. When removing from the oven, add a knob of butter, capers and lemon juice. Baste the fish with the sauce before serving. Serve with basil béarnaise sauce and fried lemon zest.

#509. Baked fish pie

In a heavy-based saucepan, fry sliced leeks, diced onions and garlic in butter. When the leeks and onions are opaque, add the same amount of flour (roux). Pour in milk slowly and allow to thicken but don't allow the sauce to become too thin. Cut a strong-flaked fish such as snapper into large 5 x 5 cm pieces . Pour some of the sauce into a buttered casserole and add the fish pieces then top with more sauce. In another saucepan, boil potatoes till they are just cooked. Drain and roughly chop into 25 mm pieces. Heat oil then add butter to a frypan and fry the potato pieces till they are nicely browned. Add chopped rosemary to the potatoes and cook with them. When cooked, spoon the potatoes over the fish pie then oven bake. The pie is ready to serve.

#510. Curried fish

Strong-flaked fish, chopped onions, crushed garlic, grated ginger, turmeric, cumin, garam masala, cinnamon, mustard seeds, cardamom seeds, chilli, coconut milk, juice of a lemon and chopped parsley. Fry the onions slowly in a saucepan in oil adding the garlic, ginger, turmeric, cumin, garam masala, cinnamon, mustard seeds, cardamom and chilli. Add a can of crushed tomatoes and coconut milk. Dredge the fish through flour, fry then place in the sauce and very gently simmer. Correct seasoning and serve on rice and with poppadoms.

#511. Snapper with curry rub

In a bowl, add curry powder, turmeric, cumin, garlic and grated root ginger and stir well. Cut the snapper fillet into portion size then dip both sides into the rub. Fry in oil to nicely brown on both sides. When cooked, add sliced chilli if desired and coconut cream. Heat, season and serve on rice.

#512. Sole with caper cream sauce

Fry the sole fillets in butter and lightly brown on both sides. Add a spoonful of capers and pour in a little cream. Season and serve.

#513. Crumbed sole fillets with flaked almonds

Remove the skin and the fillets from the sole and trim the edges. Run the fillets through seasoned flour, egg wash and breadcrumbs to which flaked almonds have been added. Fry the sole in olive oil and butter till brown on both sides.

#514. Fried snapper pesto

With skinned and boned snapper, cut into serving-size portions, dredge through flour, dip into beaten egg and fry in oil, butter and crushed garlic. Fry both sides till golden brown then place on the serving plate. Place a few spoonfuls of basil pesto along the top of the fish with lemon segments.

#515. Fried fish fillet

Using a fish fillet that has a strong flake and holds together well, put it through flour then coat one side in egg white and flaked almonds. Fry the coated side first then turn over and complete the frying process. Serve on a bed of puréed butternut. Cook butternut pieces in stock then reduce, thicken then add cream. Make a sauce with sliced onions, garlic and tomatoes.

#516. Goujons of fish tempura

Goujon is a term given to a cut of fish which is shaped the size of a little finger. Prepare a tempura batter by mixing flour, cornflour, salt and very cold soda water in a bowl and mix well. Place the goujons of fish into flour then into the batter quickly and deep fry each piece individually. Don't overload the fryer so that they stick together or cool the fryer temperature quickly. Cook until brown then serve with tartare sauce.

#517. Grilled tuna

Prepare a rub of grated root ginger, ground black pepper and oil then rub over the tuna. Make a glaze from sugar, water, rice vinegar, soy sauce, grated ginger and wasabi. Heat the ingredients in a saucepan and thicken with arrowroot. Brush it over the tuna while it is on the grill.

#518. Rolled sole fillets

Trim four fillets of the sole and place on a chopping board. Prepare a stuffing of breadcrumbs, diced sweated onions, diced mussels, chopped prawns and the trimmings from the fillets. Mix together and bind with an egg. Season the sole fillets then place a tablespoon of stuffing at the narrow end and roll the fillet then hold in place with a toothpick. Place in a buttered casserole dish and cook in the oven till the fillet is just cooked. In a saucepan, boil fish stock and reduce then add cream, chopped parsley then pour it over the sole and serve.

#519. Filo fish packets

With melted butter, paint four sheets of the filo and place on top of each other. Cut the sheets in half. In a bowl, mix tomato segments, whole kernel sweetcorn, chickpeas and black olives. Mix well and season then spoon some of the mixture into the middle of each half of the filo pastry. Top with a portion of white fish then fold over the filo pastry to form a packet. Brush with melted butter and bake in the oven.

#520. Almond-crusted snapper fillets

Chop flaked almonds and put into a mixing bowl along with panko breadcrumbs and chopped parsley. Cut the snapper fillet to portion size then dredge the fillet through flour, egg wash and the almond crumb mix. Fry in a mix of oil and butter on both sides till golden brown.

#521. Seafood Thermidor

In a large heavy-based saucepan, sweat off diced shallots, sliced garlic in butter. Poach the cut fish portions in fish stock, onions, parsley stalks and a little lemon juice. Then cook shrimps, crab, scallops, mussels and crayfish if available. Undercook all the fish and cool quickly, keeping the cooking liquid aside. In the saucepan, melt butter then add the same amount of flour to make a roux for the velouté then pour in some of the poaching liquid, milk and crème fraîche. Place two egg yolks in a small bowl, pour a little of the hot sauce into the bowl, stir quickly then pour back into the sauce and continue stirring. Cook the flour out then check seasoning and add a little English mustard. Put the fish and sauce together and serve out of either a crayfish half shell or a scallop shell. Coat the top with grated mozzarella and Parmesan and grill.

#522. Fish casserole

In a frypan, fry diced red onion, garlic, zucchini along with cumin, coriander and curry powder. Add in cooked lentils, top with fish stock and allow to simmer gently and reduce. Add in coconut milk, diced fresh tomato, fresh coriander and add seasoning. To the casserole add sliced fish portions and allow to cook then serve.

#523. Fish cakes

Use a strong-flaked fish like blue cod. Place in a roasting tin and bake in the oven in oil along with sliced onions then allow to cool. Flake the cold fish then mix with mashed potato, chopped cooked prawns, chopped cooked mussels and parsley. Combine all ingredients then spoon in chopped garlic and mayonnaise and with wet hands mould the mix into cakes. Place in the fridge to harden then dip through panko breadcrumbs and fry in butter and oil till nicely browned on both sides. Serve with a tomato salsa.

#524. Fish fillet with lentils

In a saucepan, lightly fry sliced red onions, garlic, sliced zucchini, cumin, coriander, curry powder, chillies and tamarind. Add lentils and stock and leave to simmer till the lentils are cooked then add toasted desiccated coconut threads. Pour in coconut milk and add diced fresh tomato flesh. Pour the lentil mix into a frypan then add the sliced fish fillets and spinach leaves. Cook gently till the fish is cooked then serve with lemon segments and chopped coriander.

#525. Fish tagine

This dish requires fish fillets that are of firm flake texture. In a saucepan pour some oil, heat gently then add turmeric, cumin, diced onions, crushed garlic and root ginger. Add diced pumpkin, sweet potato and potatoes that have been peeled and roughly chopped into 30 mm pieces and allow to brown. Pour in a can of crushed tomatoes, dates, the juice of a lemon and the zest which has been finely sliced. Top the liquid with fish or chicken stock till the vegetables are only just covered and allow to simmer gently. Cook until the root vegetables are cooked then top the vegetables with the pieces of fish and put the lid on the saucepan. The liquid should only just simmer so that the fish does not break up. Remove the saucepan from the heat, lift off the fish and place the vegetables on a serving dish, top with the fish and garnish with flaked almonds and chopped coriander leaves.

#526. Seared tuna with grapefruit and avocado salsa

Prepare the grapefruit by separating the segments and set aside. At the same time, juice a grapefruit for part of the dressing. Also segment the avocado into similar-size segments. Place both sets of segments on a platter, sprinkle over chilli flakes and sliced red onions. For the dressing, pour the grapefruit juice and lime juice into a bowl with balsamic vinegar then add virgin olive oil. Stir well then drizzle over the salsa. Smear the tuna steak with olive oil and sear on a hot frypan or a hot griddle plate. Serve on a platter with lemon segment and capers.

#527. Sole gratin

With the filleted sole, take the four fillets, fold in half and in a small frypan, poach the fish in fish stock and lemon juice. Make a roux of butter and flour then thicken with the cooking liquor used to cook the fish. Allow the sauce to simmer and reduce then pour in cream and grated cheese. Place the sole into a casserole that has a little of the sauce on the base. Pour over more of the sauce, top with grated cheese then bake for 5 minutes and grill to brown the top.

#528. Peanut-crumbed fish fillets with fried banana

Cut the skinless and boneless fillet of fish into portions. On a tray mix flour, chopped roasted peanuts and breadcrumbs then mix well. Place the fillets on the crumb tray and press down well then fry the fish in oil and brown on both sides. While the fish portions are frying, remove the skin from a banana, cut lengthwise then in half and fry each quarter in the same frypan.

#529. Fried snapper with walnut topping

Slice the skinned and boned snapper into portions then dip through seasoned flour and fry in oil, lemon juice and butter till brown on both sides but just undercooked. While the fish is frying, in a new pan prepare the walnut crumb topping below. When the fish is plated up, sprinkle the topping over the fish fillet.

Walnut crumb topping: Chopped walnuts and garlic, grated fresh breadcrumbs, finely sliced lemon zest, butter. Mix all the ingredients together in a mixing bowl then fry in butter and oil till it just begins browning then remove from the heat.

#530. Olive-crusted fish fillet

Green olives, chopped parsley, basil, white sliced crustless bread, Parmesan, lemon zest and juice, olive oil and a strong-flaked white fish. Tear the bread and place into a mixing bowl along with chopped green olives and the rest of the ingredients. Add seasoning and mix well then spread over the fish fillet approximately 10 mm thick. Bake the fish in the oven till cooked.

#531. Fried snapper with scallops

Using skinned and boned snapper, cut into portion size required. Dip through seasoned flour then fry in butter and oil in a hot frypan. Don't overcook the fish, leaving it just cooked in the centre. When all the fish is cooked, place on kitchen paper to dry up some of the oil. Immediately fry the scallops in the same pan in butter, cooking each side for 90 seconds then removing from the frypan. Plate up the snapper and top with scallops.

#532. Fillet of snapper with black olives, tomatoes and capers

Using skinned and boned fish fillets, cut the fillet into portion size. Lay the fish portions on the bottom of a buttered casserole dish and season. Slice a large tomato and place two or three slices of tomato on each portion then top with capers and sliced black olives. Place two or three teaspoons of butter on each fillet and bake in the oven till the fish is cooked.

#533. Snapper with tomatoes, capers and lemon grass

As in dish #532, use skinned, boned and portioned fish pieces. Lay in a buttered casserole dish and season. Sprinkle over cinnamon, finely chopped tops of lemon grass, then sliced tomatoes and capers. Top with butter and oven bake till the fish is cooked. Serve with lemon segments.

14.

SALMON

#	Dish	#	Dish
534	Salmon In Pastry	553	Pan Fried Salmon With Honey, Orange Sauce
535	Almond And Herb Crusted Salmon	554	Salmon Loaf
536	Salmon And Leek Pie	555	Smoked Salmon Mille Feuille
537	Salmon In Bourbon	556	Baked Salmon On Nori
538	Grilled Salmon With Bourbon Butter And Brown Sugar Glaze	557	Salmon In Orange Sauce
539	Grilled Salmon With A Scallop And Prawn Sauce	558	Baked Salmon With Spinach
540	Salmon, Tuna And Olive Cannelloni	559	Pernod Salmon
541	Seared Salmon Fillet	560	Apricot And Ginger Glazed Salmon
542	Grilled Salmon With Strawberry Salsa	561	Salmon And Tuna Kebabs
543	Thai Fillet Of Salmon	562	Baked Salmon With Cream Lemon Sauce
544	Salmon Fillet Wellington	563	Baked Salmon Tartare
545	Salmon With Brown Butter Sauce	564	Slow Roasted Salmon Fillet
546	Salmon And Tuna With A Caper, Lemon Sauce	565	Poached Salmon In Whisky
547	Miso Baked Salmon	566	Salmon In Whisky Cream Sauce
548	Fried Salmon Cubes	567	Salon Tartare
549	Salmon With Tomatoes	568	Salmon Loaf
550	Salmon Kedgeree Cakes	569	Salmon Cannelloni With Lemon Cream Sauce
551	Salmon Burgers	570	Smoked Salmon Terrine

#534. Salmon in pastry

Prepare a buttery scone mix and roll out to an oblong. Flake the salmon and add one cup of béchamel to three cups of salmon along with, lemon juice and zest, chopped parsley and grated cheddar. Place the salmon in the centre of the pastry and spread out lengthways. Fold the pastry over the filling with both sides meeting top middle. Make slits in the top, brush the pastry with milk and bake at 200°C for around 30 minutes. When cooked, cool then decorate the top with smoked salmon slices.

#535. Almond and herb crusted salmon

Use stale breadcrumbs and mix with chopped parsley, Parmesan, thyme, garlic, chopped almonds and seasoning. Rub the salmon with oil then spread the crumb mix over the salmon and oven bake till the salmon is cooked. Serve with a butter sauce.

#536. Salmon and leek pie

Cut the leek across the stem into 15 mm thickness and place in a bowl of water to rid any dirt. Remove the skin and pin bones from the salmon and cut into chunks approximately 30 mm square. In a large-based saucepan, melt butter and add the drained washed leeks then add the same amount of flour as butter to form a roux. Pour in milk as the sauce thickens, season and add sliced lemon zest, lemon juice and chopped dill. Pour some of the leeks into a casserole dish, top with the salmon pieces, spoonfuls of crème fraîche and pour more leeks over the top. Using a baguette for croutons, cut into 10 mm wide slices, toast and spread with garlic butter. Place these croutons on top of the leek and salmon and bake in the oven till the salmon is cooked, approximately 20 minutes. Top with grated cheese and grill to brown the cheese then serve. A puff pastry top would also suit the dish.

#537. Salmon in bourbon

Buy a piece of skinned and boned salmon. Mix bourbon, soy sauce, diced root ginger, chilli flakes, crushed garlic and sesame oil. Place the salmon in the marinade and leave in the refrigerator overnight. Oven bake or barbecue and brush with the marinade while cooking.

#538. Grilled salmon with bourbon butter and brown sugar glaze

Remove the pin bones and cut the salmon across the fillet at 40 mm wide pieces. In a small saucepan, melt butter and add muscovado sugar and stir to combine on a medium heat. Stir in bourbon until completely mixed in and allow to reduce. Place the salmon in a roasting dish, spoon over the glaze then grill or barbecue the salmon. Continue basting the salmon while grilling and spoon over some of the sauce when serving.

#539. Grilled salmon with a scallop and prawn sauce

As in dish #538, prepare the salmon the same way. In a frypan, melt butter once the pan is hot and sear the scallops on both sides then in the same pan quickly toss the prawn meat so that it just colours. Remove both the scallops and prawns and add flour to the frypan then add milk slowly to make the sauce. Stir continuously so that the sauce doesn't go lumpy. Pour cream into the sauce, check seasoning and add lemon juice and grated lemon zest. When the salmon is grilled, place the scallops and prawns into the sauce and simmer for 5 minutes, then place the salmon on the serving plate and spoon over the scallop and prawn sauce.

#540. Salmon, tuna and olive cannelloni

This dish can be made with either fresh or canned salmon and tuna. Place the cut salmon and tuna pieces into a mixing bowl then add defrosted dried spinach, grated lemon zest and juice, sliced olives, chopped coriander, Parmesan, ricotta and a beaten egg. Mix well then fill the dry cannelloni shells and place into a casserole dish that has pomodoro sauce lining the base. Once the casserole dish is fully lined, pour over more sauce then for the last third use béchamel sauce. Spread grated mozzarella on top and bake in the oven at 180°C for 20–25 minutes then grill the top to brown.

#541. Seared salmon fillet

Keep the skin on but remove the pin bones. Rub both sides with oil and seasoning then place in a hot frypan or hotplate skin side up for 3–4 minutes. Turn over and give another 3 minutes. The centre of the salmon should be raw with the heat lines from both sides of the fillet closing in on the centre. Prepare fettucine by boiling in salted water till al dente then drain. While the fettuccine is cooking, fry diced onions in a frypan and add diced fresh tomato flesh then top with roughly chopped smoked mussels. Pour in the fettuccine, toss well to mix all ingredients together, season then place on a serving platter. Using a fish slice, carefully place the salmon fillet on top.

#542. Grilled salmon with strawberry salsa

In a bowl, mix soy sauce, garlic, runny honey and oil then brush it over the salmon. Grill the salmon, brushing the sauce mix over it at regular intervals. Prepare a salsa of fresh strawberries, diced avocado on rocket with a vinaigrette dressing.

#543. Thai fillet of salmon

Line a roasting tray with tinfoil, spray with oil and turn up the edges of the foil so it retains all liquid. Line the base with freshly sliced pineapple, slices of lemon and a sprinkling of chilli flakes. Lay the fillet on the pineapple. In a mixing bowl put hoisin sauce, sliced bird's eye chilli, sweet chilli sauce, diced root ginger, crushed lemon grass and rice vinegar. Mix well then spoon the sauce over the salmon and bake in the oven. When nearly cooked, grill in the oven for a minute to give it colour. Serve with a green salad.

#544. Salmon fillet Wellington

With a whole skinned and boned salmon fillet, place the fillet on the puff pastry (store-bought) with 20 mm free all round. In a frypan, quickly fry prawns till they are cooked then place in a bowl. Break an egg into a bowl with a small amount of milk then dip in some whole sliced crustless white bread to absorb the egg. Add to the prawns. Sweat off diced onions in butter till translucent, add chopped parsley and mix all together in the mixing bowl along with seasoning. Lay the bread mix on top of the salmon and smooth out then lay cold wilted spinach on top of the bread stuffing. Egg wash the edges of the bottom piece of pastry then place the second piece of pastry on top. Trim the pastry around the salmon, brush with egg wash and bake at 200°C till golden brown and the salmon is just still pink in the centre. Serve with hollandaise sauce.

#545. Salmon with brown butter sauce

Cut a slice of salmon off the fillet 50 mm wide leaving the skin on but remove the bones. Make a brown butter by placing 100 g butter in a heavy-based saucepan and placing on an element. Slowly it will melt then the salt content will start to brown the butter. Be careful not to brown too fast or it will burn. When nicely browned, add lime juice and grated zest along with honey. Brush it over the salmon then grill or bake. Keep brushing during the grilling process.

#546. Salmon and tuna with a caper lemon sauce

A can of tuna and a slice of fresh salmon skinless and boneless. In a mixing bowl mix oil, capers, crushed garlic, lemon juice, grated lemon zest and seasoning. Cook pasta of choice to al dente stage and drain. Cut the salmon into 20 mm cubes and fry in oil. When nearly cooked add the can of tuna to heat it up then add to the pasta. Pour the oil sauce over the pasta, mix well and serve.

#547. Miso baked salmon

Mix miso and mirin to form a paste then spoon over a darne of salmon. Continue spooning over the miso for 30 minutes then bake the salmon in the oven. In a fish broth, put slices of fresh ginger and cook soba noodles. Drain the noodles and place on a plate with the salmon on top. Top with grated carrot and daikon and serve with wasabi.

#548. Fried salmon cubes

Cut the salmon into 30 mm cubes then roll in flour and deep fry or fry in oil in a frypan. Serve in a salad or serve on rice with a soy, garlic, honey dressing and wasabi.

#549. Salmon with tomatoes

In a saucepan with butter and oil, sweat off diced onions with fresh tarragon, basil, chopped garlic then add diced tomato flesh and heat through. Leave to cool then add balsamic vinegar and lemon juice. Check for seasoning. Place the salmon on a baking tray and bake. When nearly cooked, spoon over the sauce for the final three minutes and serve.

#550. Salmon kedgeree cakes

Prepare a kedgeree and leave to go cold overnight. If it is very thick and well stuck together that is great, otherwise mix in dry breadcrumbs or flour. If very dry add a beaten egg to help it bind. Divide the mixture up into equal quantities and roll into balls a little larger than a golf ball. Press down on the ball to flatten it out into a cake. Coat with flour, egg wash and breadcrumb then fry in butter and oil mix till golden brown on both sides. Drain on kitchen paper then serve with a salad or vegetables. **Kedgeree**: Dice onion and fry in a frypan with curry powder, chopped chilli, then add rice, seasoning and stock. Bring to a simmer till the rice is cooked, meanwhile flake the smoked fish. Once the rice is cooked, add a knob of butter, chopped parsley, the flaked smoked fish and wedges of hardboiled egg.

#551. Salmon burgers

Skinned and boned salmon, smoked salmon, potatoes, diced onion, spring onions, milk, lemon juice and zest, egg yolk, breadcrumbs, parsley, cream cheese. Gently simmer the fresh salmon in milk, remove and break into chunks and allow to cool quickly. Mix the cold salmon, smoked salmon, sliced spring onions and diced onion, lemon juice and finely sliced lemon zest, chopped parsley and cream cheese in a bowl. Season then mix by hand and add enough mashed potato to make a firm mix. Shape the potato mix into balls then flatten to the size of the burger buns. Hold in the fridge to firm then dredge through flour, egg wash and breadcrumbs. Fry in oil and butter and serve with lemon wedges or make a full burger using buns, salad vegetables, mayonnaise.

#552. Pan-fried salmon on chilli and corn salsa

Buy a darne of salmon from the supermarket or fishmonger. In a bowl, mix maple syrup, chilli flakes, oil, balsamic vinegar and brush it over the flesh of the fish then top with pepper and salt. On the skin side, with a very sharp knife make cuts through the skin approximately 4 mm deep. Fry the salmon flesh side down in oil and butter for 4 minutes, spooning the cooking liquor over the salmon while it is cooking then turn over and cook for another 3–4 minutes. The salmon should just about be cooked through and the skin should be crispy. Prepare a salsa of whole kernel corn mixed with diced red onions, sliced chilli and diced red capsicum. Drizzle a little of the salmon dressing over the salsa. Serve a lemon caper dressing with the salmon.

#553. Pan-fried salmon with honey orange sauce

Prepare and cook the salmon as in dish #552 and fry in oil and butter, spooning the cooking liquor over the salmon as it is cooking. When cooked, remove the salmon, add another knob of butter and pour in orange juice, liquid honey, cinnamon and grated orange zest. Simmer gently so that the honey doesn't burn. As the sauce thickens, remove from the heat and spoon the sauce over the salmon once it is plated.

#554. Salmon loaf

Butter the sides and base of a meatloaf tin then carefully line the tin with four sheets of filo pastry that have been buttered between each sheet. On the base of the tin line it with skinned and boned fresh salmon. On top of the salmon, lay sliced onions then small pieces of parboiled broccoli, carrot batons and smoked capsicum pieces. Fold the filo pastry back over the pie filling, brush with butter and bake in the oven at 190°C for 20 minutes. Take care when turning the pie out of the mould that you don't get burnt from the steam.

#555. Smoked salmon mille-feuille

Bake three oblongs of puff pastry 150 x 80 mm after poking with a fork and brushing with egg wash. When cooked place on a wire rack and leave to cool. Place the first sheet of pastry on a serving platter. In a mixing bowl, shred the smoked salmon then add sliced sun-dried tomatoes, cubed feta cheese and chopped parsley. Prepare a cheese sauce keeping it quite thick then adding ricotta cheese to the sauce and mixing well. Spoon some of the sauce into the salmon and fold in then spread over the base pastry. Add a second sheet of the cooked pastry and continue spreading the smoked salmon until all three sheets are covered. Use sliced tomatoes on top, drizzle with balsamic vinegar and add chopped spring onions.

#556. Baked salmon on nori

Brush four sheets of filo pastry and place on top of each other. In the centre of the filo place double sheets of nori, which the skinned and boned salmon pieces will sit on. The salmon should be cut from the fillet 50 mm wide. Drizzle over teriyaki sauce, brown sugar and oil then fold up the filo to form a package with the seam over the top. Bake in the oven on 200°C till golden brown then serve immediately.

#557. Salmon in orange sauce

Prepare the sauce by pouring fresh orange juice into a mixing bowl and adding finely sliced orange zest, soy sauce, crushed garlic, sesame oil, Sriracha and seasoning. Mix well then pour it over salmon steaks in a casserole dish and leave in the fridge to marinate for 2 hours. Either fry the salmon in a frypan in oil or bake it in the oven in the casserole. Either way, brush the salmon while it is cooking. When cooked, leave to rest then heat what is left of the marinade, thicken with cornflour and water and spoon it over the salmon while it is on the serving plate. Top with sesame seeds.

#558. Baked salmon with spinach

Wilt the spinach in minimal water and salt, drain then blitz in a food processor and add a drizzle of cream and seasoning then leave to go cold. Using four sheets of filo, butter each and place on top of each other. Place a slice of boneless salmon at the beginning of the filo, spoon over the spinach and top with chopped walnuts. Fold the filo and salmon over to form a package, fold in the sides then continue to roll to form a package. Butter the filo, sprinkle with sesame seeds and bake in the oven.

#559. Pernod salmon

Using a darne of salmon, cut two or three slices through the skin with a sharp knife, season both sides and fry in a mixture of oil and butter. The cuts allow cooking liquor and the heat to enter and present crispy skin. When cooked, remove the salmon and rest and add sliced red onions to the frypan. As they become transparent add in sliced button mushrooms and cook through. Pour in Pernod and allow to reduce slowly then pour in cream. Season and thicken if necessary. Return the salmon to the pan for 3 minutes then serve.

#560. Apricot and ginger glazed salmon

Grate root ginger into a mixing bowl and add two spoonfuls of apricot jam and a drizzle of soy sauce and olive oil. Mix well and brush it over the salmon. Bake the salmon in the oven and continually baste with the sauce while it is cooking.

#561. Salmon and tuna kebabs

Using the head of the fillet of salmon, cut into cubes of 25 mm and cut tuna into the same-size cubes. Soak the wooden skewers in water then thread the salmon and tuna onto the skewer as alternative cubes. If desired they can be marinated in a soy sauce-based marinade or grilled as they are. Could also be barbecued.

#562. Baked salmon with cream lemon sauce

A fillet of salmon can be used for this dish or salmon steaks. Drizzle a baking tray with oil, place the salmon on the tray and bake so that the salmon is just cooked in the centre. In a small mixing bowl, put sour cream then add a touch of Tabasco sauce, lemon juice and Dijon mustard. Mix well and spoon it over the salmon when serving. As an alternative sauce, prepare a béchamel and add grated lemon zest, sour cream, Dijon mustard and Tabasco if a hot spice sauce is desired. Season well and serve.

#563. Baked salmon tartare

Egg, salmon fillet, lemon juice, Tabasco, chopped shallots, caper, gherkins and chopped chives or parsley. Boil the egg and when cool, grate and set aside. Bake the salmon fillet in the oven and when the centre is not quite cooked, remove from the oven, cool then flake the flesh into large pieces. In a bowl, whisk the lemon juice, Tabasco, anchovy fillets and whisk in oil till it emulsifies as you would when making an egg mayonnaise with egg yolks and oil. Chop the capers and cornichons and mix in the chopped chives/parsley. Place the flaked salmon on a serving plate, sprinkle over the caper and grated egg mixture then drizzle over the dressing.

#564. Slow-roasted salmon fillet

Rub the salmon fillet with a mixture of olive oil, lime juice, brown sugar, chopped basil, rosemary and seasoning. Place the whole fillet skin side down on oiled baking paper and bake in the oven at 160°C until cooked through.

#565. Poached salmon in whisky

Poach the salmon in fish stock, parsley stalks, lemon zest, diced onions and whisky. **Whisky sauce**: Prepare the sauce the same as hollandaise sauce but add whisky and some of the cooking liquid at the end.

#566. Salmon in whisky cream sauce

Spread the salmon piece with a mix of honey, Dijon mustard and cracked pepper then fry in a butter and oil mix in a frypan. When cooked, remove to a serving plate and keep warm. Into the pan pour whisky and reduce the liquor. Reduce the pan heat and pour in cream with chopped dill. Stir gently and don't boil then spoon it over the salmon.

#567. Salmon tartare

Cut an avocado into 10 mm dice and coat with lemon juice. Cut very fresh salmon into similar-sized pieces and the same with fresh mango. Place a pastry cutter ring on a serving plate and put the avocado on the base. Next layer is the salmon then top with the mango cubes. Place in the fridge and allow to set for 30 minutes then carefully remove the pastry ring and sprinkle with a balsamic dressing.

#568. Salmon loaf

Poach the skinned and boned salmon in fish stock then cool quickly. Tear the salmon into flakes and place in a mixing bowl. Add 250 gms apple sauce, breadcrumbs, crushed garlic, crumbled feta, an egg to bind and chopped parsley. Mix the ingredients then spoon into a meatloaf tin and bake in the oven at 170°C for 20–30 minutes.

#569. Salmon cannelloni with lemon cream sauce

In a mixing bowl, place small pieces of salmon, either fresh or canned. Then add diced shallots, chopped parsley, torn bread pieces, seasoning, finely sliced lemon zest and Italian herbs. Mix well and spoon into dry cannelloni shells. Lay in a casserole dish and pour over pomodoro sauce then a béchamel sauce that has finely sliced lemon zest, lemon juice, diced feta and cream added. Top with grated cheese and bake in the oven for 25 minutes, then serve.

#570. Smoked salmon terrine

Using a terrine casserole, line it with cling wrap and drape the cling wrap over the sides. Cover the base of the terrine with smoked salmon slices then complete around all sides with the smoked salmon slices also hanging over the side of the casserole. Prepare a mix of mashed avocado, finely sliced lemon zest and juice, diced fresh tomato flesh, chopped parsley, crushed garlic and cooked prawns. Push down on the filling so that it is forced into all corners of the casserole then fold back the overhanging slices of salmon. Line the top with more salmon slices so that it is totally covered, fold back the cling wrap and place a flat tray with a weight on it so that it puts pressure on the terrine. Leave in the fridge for 24 hours then turn out onto a serving platter, decorate and serve with crackers.

#571. Salmon en croute

Buy a side of salmon skinned and boned. Lay a sheet of baking paper on a flat aluminium baking tray then place a sheet of puff pastry on the baking paper. Lay the salmon on top and brush with sun-dried tomato pesto. Put another sheet of puff pastry over the top and seal the edges with egg wash. Trim off any excess pastry, brush the top with egg wash and bake in the oven at 200°C till golden brown. **Sauce:** Simmer cream and add sun-dried tomato pesto and torn basil. If there are any leftover pieces of salmon, chop and put in the sauce and if available chopped cooked prawns could also be added. Season and reduce.

15.

SEAFOOD

#	Dish	#	Dish
572	Steamed Mussels With Chorizo And Green Olives	588	Prawns In Honey, Lime And Sesame
573	Stuffed Mussels	589	Prawns In Coconut Curry
574	Mussels And Salmon With Sweet And Sour Sauce	590	Crumbed Sesame Prawns
575	Steamed Mussels In Coconut Curry Sauce	591	Battered Prawns
576	Baked Cajun Seafood	592	Bloody Mary Prawns
577	Prawn Balls	593	Garlic Mussels
578	Curried Prawns And Coconut Cream	594	Breaded Mussels On Skewers
579	Scallops And Mussels In A Cream Sauce	595	Mussels In White Wine And Olives
580	Scallops Mornay	596	Salt And Pepper Squid
581	Prawn And Scallop Potatoes	597	Oyster Stew
582	Scallops With Miso	598	Thai Seafood Curry
583	Scallops, Lobster And Mussels	599	Prawns In A Basket
584	Seafood Casserole	600	Seafood Strudel
585	Prawns In Garlic And Cream Sauce	601	Broiled Scallops' Bourbon
586	Garlic King Prawns And Scallops In Cream Sauce	602	Scallops And Prawns In Vodka And Lime Butter Sauce
587	Prawn And Spinach Alfredo		

#572. Steamed mussels with chorizo and green olives

In a frypan sweat off diced chorizo in butter till it begins to brown and releases some of its oils, then add diced onions, green olives, garlic and chilli. Meanwhile, place the fresh mussels in 4 mm white wine, fish stock, parsley and diced fresh tomatoes and boil the liquid to steam open the mussels. Discard any mussels that don't open. Remove half the shell from each mussel plus the beard and place on a serving platter. Spoon over the chorizo mixture and serve with crusty bread.

#573. Stuffed mussels

Steam the fresh mussels in white wine, fish stock, parsley stalks and lemon peel until the shells are open then remove from the shell. When cool remove the beard and set the mussel aside. In a bowl, mix breadcrumbs, soft butter, olive oil, grated cheese, chopped parsley, finely sliced lemon zest and oregano. Mix well then force the stuffing into the mussel. Lay them on a buttered casserole dish and bake in the oven. Serve with hollandaise sauce and crusty bread.

#574. Mussels and salmon with sweet and sour sauce

Cook the mussels in a saucepan with a tight-fitting lid in 3 mm water, white wine, parsley stalks and bay leaf. When the shells are open, remove the mussel meat, beard and leave to cool. Bake the salmon in the oven. In a small saucepan, fry sliced onions, crushed garlic, chilli, sliced capsicum and pineapple pieces till they have sweated down then add malt vinegar and brown sugar to achieve a sweet and sour taste. Maple syrup can also be used to adjust the flavour. Season and thicken with cornflour mixed with a little water to form a paste. Place the salmon on the plate and put the mussels around it. Spoon over the sweet and sour sauce.

#575. Steamed mussels in coconut curry sauce

Mussels, grated lemongrass, mussel stock, coconut milk, Thai curry paste, fish sauce, sugar, chopped spring onions. Steam open the fresh mussels and hold back some of the cooking liquor. Remove one of the shells so that the mussel is still anchored into a half shell. At the same time remove the beard. Into a saucepan put the curry paste onto warmed oil and heat gently. Add coconut milk, fish sauce, sugar, lemon grass and a little of the mussel stock. Bring to a simmer and reduce slightly, check seasoning then add mussels in half shells.

#576. Baked Cajun seafood

Decide what type of seafood is going to be used in this dish — fillet of fish, prawns, mussels, scallops, squid, lobster or whatever else is desired. In this instance, the fillet of fish and mussels will take a little longer than the prawns and scallops. Rub oil over the seafood followed by the Cajun spice then place the fish and mussels in a roasting dish and cook at 190°C in the oven. Add the scallops and prawns at the very end and they will take around 2 minutes.

As an alternative, you could place the seafood in a casserole dish and pour over a Cajun sauce which consists of a tomato-based pasta sauce containing garlic, basil, oil, Cajun spice, tomato paste, brown sugar and olive oil blended in a food processor. Briefly sauté the seafood then pour the sauce over the seafood, add tablespoons of crème fraîche atop the sauce and bake in the oven.

#577. Prawn balls

Remove the tails, shell and heads from the frozen prawns then place in milk and simmer gently. In another saucepan, sweat off onions and garlic then add flour. Use the prawn milk to flavour the béchamel but keeping the mixture very thick and allowing the flour to cook out. Add grated cheddar cheese, prawn meat, seasonings and leave to cool. When cold, mould into balls around the size of golf balls then flour, egg wash and breadcrumb and deep fry.

#578. Curried prawns and coconut cream

Buy a curry paste from the supermarket checking the heat of the curry is to your satisfaction. In a saucepan, gently fry some of the paste with crushed garlic and additional chopped root ginger. Add a small amount of water to liquefy the paste to a sauce then add a small can of coconut cream. Simmer gently and stir well. In a frypan, quickly fry the prawns in oil then add some of the sauce. Lastly spoon in mango chutney, season and serve on rice.

#579. Scallops and mussels in a cream sauce

With scallops and mussels that have already been removed from their shells, fry the mussel meat in butter and grated garlic till heated through then remove. Fry the scallops in the same pan but searing them very quickly so that they are just brown on the outside but still raw in the centre. Keep the mussels and scallops aside then into the frypan add a knob of butter and once melted add the same amount of flour as butter. Stir then add milk to make the sauce. Keep stirring and don't allow the sauce to go lumpy. As it thickens, stir in cream and finish off with crème fraîche and chopped parsley. Check seasoning, plate the mussels and scallops back in scallop shells with the scallops on top. Spoon over the sauce and grill briefly.

#580. Scallops mornay

Prepare a cheese sauce and finish with cream. In a frypan, wilt fresh spinach in very little water and butter then drain well. In a small frypan, toss the scallops in hot clarified butter till they are brown on the outside but only just cooked in the centre. Deglaze the frypan with white wine and reduce then pour in the cheese sauce to pick up the flavour of the fried scallops. Place the spinach on a plate, top with the scallops then spoon over a little of the cheese sauce.

#581. Prawn and scallop potatoes

Using large potatoes, slice 2mm off the top of the unpeeled potato and the same on the bottom so that the potato sits evenly. Cut out another 5 mm of raw potato from the centre but leaving the skin on and put a knob of butter in its place. Bake the potato till cooked then scoop out the centre. Fry prawns in hot oil and remove then add butter and fry the scallops very quickly and remove. Deglaze the pan with white wine and reduce. Add a little flour then fish stock and lemon juice/sliced zest. Check the taste and seasoning then put the prawns and scallops back in the sauce, add chopped parsley then spoon into the potato skins and serve with crème fraîche on top.

#582. Scallops with miso

In a saucepan, put mirin and miso that has been diluted with hot water. Add crushed garlic, grated root ginger, soy sauce and bring to a simmer. In a frypan, quickly fry the scallops till just cooked then place three back into a scallop shell. To the sauce add a knob of butter and thicken with cornflour and water. Check seasoning then spoon it over the scallops and sprinkle over sliced spring onions.

#583. Scallops, lobster and mussels

In a heavy frypan, fry the freshly opened mussel meat in oil and butter till cooked. Remove and set aside and in the same pan add a knob of butter, increase the heat and quickly fry the sliced lobster then the scallops. Set all the seafood to one side and keep warm. Again, in the same pan fry diced shallots and grated lemon zest, add white wine and reduce. Pour in fresh cream, a knob of butter, simmer gently and return the seafood to the pan to reheat, season and serve.

#584. Seafood casserole

Mussels, salmon, prawns, scallops, diced onions, capsicum, garlic, chopped parsley, Worcestershire sauce, Parmesan, mayonnaise, cooked bacon pieces. Sauté the onions and diced capsicums, add garlic and when transparent add béchamel sauce then the seafood, cheese, mayonnaise and bacon. Top with cheese and bake.

#585. Prawns in garlic cream sauce

Fry headless prawns without shells in butter with garlic and chilli flakes, add white wine, reduce then add mascarpone. Serve with pasta.

#586. Garlic king prawns and scallops in cream sauce

Remove the head, shell and devein the prawns. Heat butter in a frypan with a touch of oil and add sliced garlic. Quickly fry the prawns and scallops till they begin to change colour then spoon in a small amount of béchamel sauce and pouring cream. With a red capsicum, cut into pieces and quickly fry. Serve the prawns and scallops on the capsicums and spaghetti.

#587. Prawn and spinach Alfredo

In a very hot frypan, add oil and garlic then fry the prawns quickly and toss in the pan while frying. Remove the prawns and in the same pan fry onion, garlic, bacon pieces till brown then add baby spinach leaves and wilt. Pour in fresh cream with grated Parmesan and heat. Add cooked fettuccine noodles then place the prawns back into the pan. Turn over by tossing in the pan, season and serve.

#588. Prawns in honey, lime and sesame

In a mixing bowl beat eggs, soy sauce, crushed garlic and malt vinegar and add the prawns to marinate for 30 minutes. Flour, egg wash and breadcrumb the prawns and bake in the oven in a buttered dish. In a saucepan, melt butter then add soy sauce, honey, lime juice, sesame seeds and thicken with cornflour and water. Season the sauce then pour it over the baked prawns.

#589. Prawns in coconut curry

With shelled and deveined prawns, set aside in garlic, ginger and coconut oil. In a saucepan, fry diced onions, capsicums, grated ginger and garlic in coconut oil just to sweat off then add the spices cumin, fenugreek, cardamom seeds, cinnamon, turmeric and reduce the heat to allow the spices to release their oils. Add fresh diced tomatoes and chicken stock, bring to a simmer then check for taste and seasoning. Fry the prawns in coconut oil very quickly then add to the sauce with coconut milk. Simmer for 4 minutes then turn off the heat. Serve over rice and add chutney and naan bread. As a garnish, fry a few king prawns in their shell and plate over the curry sauce on the serving plate.

#590. Crumbed sesame prawns

Using prawns that have been deveined and without shell, dry on kitchen paper then put through seasoned flour, egg wash and then into white sesame seeds ensuring they are well coated. Fry the prawns in vegetable oil that has a few drops of sesame oil added for flavour. Serve with rice and an avocado salsa.

#591. Battered prawns

Buy prawns that have been shelled and deveined. Put through flour then a frying batter and straight into a deep fryer. Don't overload the fryer and keep them separate while frying so that they don't stick together. Serve on rice with a sweet chilli sauce.

#592. Bloody Mary prawns

Using a quality tomato juice, pour into a mixing bowl with vodka then add a dash of Worcestershire sauce, crushed garlic, Tabasco to taste, finely chopped celery and celery salt. Cook the prawns very quickly by frying in butter then set aside and cool and hold in the fridge. Mix the prawns with the sauce and taste for seasoning. Serve either in a shot glass with an aperitif fork or on a flat-based teaspoon. They could also be served in wide-mouthed champagne glasses.

#593. Garlic mussels

In a large saucepan, heat butter and add diced onion, 10 cloves garlic, celery and chopped tomatoes till opaque. Add white wine, stock, sugar, parsley and seasonings. Add mussels, top the saucepan with a lid and steam the mussels open. Throw away any mussels that don't open. Add chopped parsley, coriander and dill stalks. Spoon the mussels into a serving platter and serve with a warm baguette.

#594. Breaded mussels on skewers

Place the unopened mussels into a large saucepan with 5 mm of water, diced onion, celery, bay leaf, garlic and put a lid on the saucepan. Take the mussels out of the saucepan when they are cooked (when the shells open). Remove from the shell, removing the beard at the same time, and leave to cool. Put the mussels through flour, egg wash and panko breadcrumbs and fry in oil and butter till golden brown. Place on kitchen paper to drain then thread four mussels onto a wooden skewer and place on a presentation platter. **Sauce**: Make a sauce from diced onions, two or three diced mussels, fish stock, Tabasco, lemon juice and zest.

Bring to the boil, simmer and season and thicken with cornflour mixed with water. **Note**: If the fresh mussels do not open while being steamed, throw them away as they are dead.

#595. Mussels in white wine and olives

Steam open the mussels as in the dish #594, remove from the shell and remove the beard. In a saucepan, heat butter and garlic on a medium heat adding diced onions and diced fresh tomato flesh. Add in the mussels, white wine and simmer gently. Don't overcook the mussels and remove from the saucepan with a slotted spoon. Thicken the sauce with a roux, season and add green olives to the sauce. Place the mussels back into a half shell, spoon over the sauce and serve.

#596. Salt and pepper squid

Prepare a crumb mix of peppercorns, sea salt, five spice and chilli flakes. Mix well together in a mortar and pestle then place in a bowl. Put the cut squid through a dip of flour, egg wash and the salt and pepper mix then fry in hot deep oil. Drain on kitchen paper and serve with a yoghurt spiced dish.

#597. Oyster stew

Fresh oysters, butter, pinch chilli flakes, garlic, paprika, salt and pepper, milk, chopped parsley. Heat the butter and sweat off the onions and garlic. Add paprika, seasoning and chilli. Drain the oysters of their liquid and set aside. Add the milk to the onions along with parsley and oyster liquor. Simmer very gently, add fresh oysters till the edges start curling then remove and serve.

#598. Thai seafood curry

Cut a fillet of fish into small portions with no skin or bones. Take some prawns, removing the tails, some freshly cooked mussels and a can of whole sardines. In a saucepan, pour coconut oil adding diced onions, red curry paste, diced root ginger, crushed garlic, lime juice, fish sauce, brown sugar, salt, sliced capsicum, grated carrot and water. When the liquid is simmering add the seafood and raw spinach. Season and top with chopped peanuts and coriander.

599. Prawns in a basket

Wash and peel starchy potatoes then cut roughly into batons 5 x 5 mm. Dry the batons in a dry cloth or kitchen paper then place on a tray. Dust with flour and seasoning then place in a fine metal sieve that has a bowl-shaped base. Push the potatoes in with a slotted metal spoon then place the whole thing into hot fat in a saucepan pushing down on the potatoes so that they stick together. Beware that the fat does not spill over the edge of the pot and catch fire on the stove if not using a deep fryer. When the basket is brown, remove from the fat and leave to cool slightly then sit on a plate. Fry the prawns in a frypan in oil, butter, garlic, root ginger and soy sauce so that they are just coloured. Sprinkle with seasoning and lemon juice, spoon into the potato basket and serve.

#600. Seafood strudel

In a frypan, fry in butter prawns, chopped mussels, skinless boneless white fish, squid rings, salmon pieces or any other combination of seafood. Place the seafood in a mixing bowl and add sweated off diced onions, chopped garlic, chopped parsley then add cold cheese sauce which has sliced lemon zest included. Season well and add cream but keep the sauce thick. Using four sheets of filo pastry, place a sheet on baking paper which is on a baking sheet. Butter each sheet and layer on each other. Spoon the cold seafood mixture in a line on the filo pastry to create the filling, sprinkle with grated cheddar cheese then roll the filo to form a tube of seafood in filo. Brush with melted butter, top with sesame seeds and bake in the oven at 190°C till brown. Serve with hollandaise sauce.

#601. Broiled scallops in bourbon

Wrap scallops in a slice of streaky bacon and skewer. Marinate the skewer in bourbon, maple syrup and Dijon mustard. Cook the scallops on a barbecue or under the grill but don't overcook. Sprinkle with finely sliced spring onions.

#602. Scallops and prawns in vodka and lime butter sauce

Soften the butter in a mixing bowl then add crushed garlic, chopped parsley, fresh lime juice, grated lime zest and vodka. Mix well then spoon onto cling wrap, roll into a tube shape 40 mm diameter and store in the fridge. Cook the scallops and prawns in the vodka butter ensuring that the scallops are undercooked. Remove from the pan and keep warm. To the same pan, add chopped bacon pieces and diced onions. When cooked add fresh spinach leaves and stir till wilted then add a spoonful of honey and more vodka butter. Return the scallops and prawns to the pan, season and serve.

16.

SHEET PAN MEALS

Sheet pan meals are cooked on a lipped baking/roasting tray. The meat, poultry or fish pieces are cooked on the tray with the vegetables. In the case of root vegetables, the potatoes, sweet potatoes, parsnips or pumpkin need to be parboiled first then added to the tray. Meat/chicken can be browned first in a frypan then added to the tray along with garlic corms, rosemary, oil and whatever spices are called for, for example Cajun. The vegetables need to be turned over regularly to stop them burning and the meat needs to be brushed with oil or marinade where appropriate. Soy, Worcestershire, hoisin can also be added for flavour.

Where using a large array of vegetables, once cooked they can be arranged line by line to co-ordinate colours of the food on the tray against the protein.

Sheet pan meals can be ideal as a quick preparation meal for after work as all is cooked on one tray, or it's another means of preparing a family meal where everybody helps themselves off the pan.

Because there is such a large variety of meat and vegetables that can be mixed on the tray, co-ordinating how long they will take to cook and when they are going to be added to the tray is the main objective so that every item is ready to serve at the same time.

#603. Sheet pan beef and broccoli

In a mixing bowl put soy sauce, oyster sauce, crushed garlic, chilli flakes, sesame oil and cornflour. Mix well then spoon over steak that is on the baking sheet. Bake in the oven but keep it rare. Slice the steak into thin ribbons and place back onto the baking sheet. In the same mixing bowl, put vegetable stock, brown sugar, soy sauce, hoisin, oyster sauce and cornflour and mix well. Place the precooked broccoli florets around the steak then pour the sauce over the broccoli and steak then oven bake.

#604. Baked sausages with vegetables

On a lipped baking tray, cook the sausages with diced pumpkin, sweet potatoes, carrots, red onion segments, broccoli florets, cauliflower florets, cubed potatoes and mushrooms.

#605. Sheet pan fish portions

Portions of fish such as snapper cut to portion size and baked on the tray once the vegetables are nearly cooked. The fish needs to be one of strong flesh to hold it all together while cooking. Asparagus, red onion segments and baton carrots suit this dish well.

#606. Sheet pan salmon with asparagus and mushrooms

Cut the salmon into 40 mm wide pieces, brush with a soy, hoisin, garlic, ginger, oil, sesame oil and honey marinade then bake with vegetables such as asparagus and mushrooms with a dressing.

#607. Sheet pan salmon with Brussels sprouts and green beans

Cut the salmon fillet into 40 mm wide slices. Drizzle with maple syrup then pack with a crust of breadcrumbs mixed with melted butter, chopped parsley, mustard and Parmesan cheese. Bake the salmon with baked Brussels sprouts, green beans, red onions halves and any other vegetables of choice.

#608. Sheet pan salmon or tuna with capsicums and red onion

Sprinkle the salmon with olive oil, seasoning and garlic. On the sheet pan, include sliced pieces of capsicum and segments of red onion.

#609. Sheet pan salmon or tuna with beans, asparagus and cherry tomatoes

Dress the salmon with oil, seasoning, garlic and bake in the oven. Top and tail the beans, remove the hard root end of the asparagus and place on the sheet pan with the cherry tomatoes. Drizzle the vegetables with oil and seasoning. Bake till cooked.

#610. Sheet pan snapper with cabbage steaks

With a large round cabbage, remove the outside leaves then cut through the centre of the cabbage. Cut a 10 mm slice from the inside so that some of the hard root is part of the slice. This slice can then be cut in half if the cabbage is large but ensure both halves have part of the root holding them together. Cut as many slices as required per number of diners. Place the cabbage slices in a buttered roasting pan. Sprinkle over grated garlic and ginger then drizzle with oil and soy sauce. Cut the snapper fillets into portion-size pieces and hold aside. Bake the cabbage steaks in the oven at 190°C for 5 minutes then place the snapper portions on top, season and back in the oven for 5 minutes or until the snapper is almost cooked through. Remove and serve.

#611. Sheet pan pork

Using pork chops or medallions, marinate in oil, garlic, soy, root ginger, oregano and balsamic vinegar. Prepare the vegetables using chunky capsicum, zucchini, diced sweet potato, baton carrots, sliced garlic bulbs and oil. The sweet potato and carrots will take the longest to cook so start them first then the pork then follow with the rest of the vegetables

#612. Sheet pan pork tenderloin with red cabbage and apple

Prepare the pork tenderloin by removing any excess fat and silver skin. Stud the pork with ginger and garlic pieces by inserting a very sharp vegetable knife through the meat and inserting the ginger and garlic. Rub the pork with oil, add seasoning then place in a roasting dish and cook at a high heat of 210°C for 5 minutes to brown and seal the pork. Remove from the oven and place red cabbage slices into the same pan along with sliced apple segments, whole dates, cherry tomatoes and 50 ml malt vinegar. Put it back in the oven at 190°C until the pork is cooked through. Remove and let the pork rest before carving and serving.

#613. Sheet pan Cajun chicken with courgettes and capsicums

Drizzle the chicken with oil then sprinkle with Cajun spice and seasoning, place on the baking sheet and put in the oven at 190°C. Peel and cut a sweet potato into dice, parboil then add to the chicken in the oven along with crushed garlic. Prepare yellow and green courgettes by cutting into rings, roughly chop a capsicum and quarter a red onion. When the chicken is nearly ready to be removed from the oven, add the vegetables and cook through turning with an egg slice while cooking.

#614. Sheet pan fried chicken with broccoli and cauliflower

Using chicken breasts, place between cling wrap and beat with a rolling pin to create a uniform thickness of the chicken. Dip through flour, egg wash and breadcrumbs then fry in oil and butter mix till just browned on both sides. Place the chicken on a sheet pan along with blanched broccoli and cauliflower. Oven bake the chicken and vegetables. Let the chicken rest before serving.

#615. Sheet pan chicken with sweet potato and green beans

Bat out the chicken breast so that it is the same thickness throughout. Peel and slice the sweet potatoes into 7 mm slices and place on an oiled baking tray. Other root vegetables may also be added as an alternative choice. Bake in the oven at 180°C until getting soft then add the seasoned chicken and green beans, drizzling with oil and grated garlic. As the items cook through, remove and keep warm then serve.

#616. Sheet pan chicken panzanella with zucchini and cherry tomatoes

This dish can use whole chicken pieces or diced chicken. In a large mixing bowl put olive oil, crushed garlic, rosemary, thyme, lemon juice and zest and chilli flakes. Place the chicken in the bowl, mix well and leave for 3 hours. Remove the chicken from the marinade, place in a roasting pan and bake in the oven at 200°C. With ciabatta bread, tear into 30 mm size pieces and after 20 minutes of the chicken cooking, remove the tray, stir the chicken so that it browns all over, add the bread pieces which have been dipped through the chicken marinade and allow them to bake and brown also. As the bread browns, place cherry tomatoes on the tray along with zucchini pieces and bake till all pieces are cooked. Remove and serve.

#617. Bacon-wrapped chicken breast with red onion rings, roast potatoes

Slice the chicken breast into a butterfly form then place a slice of smoked cheese in the centre and fold the breast back to shape. On a bench lay out streaky bacon, slightly overlapping each slice.

Place the chicken breast on the end and roll so that the breast is totally covered by the bacon. Place the chicken on the oiled sheet pan with roast potatoes that have been cut and parboiled. Add sliced red onion rings after 15 minutes to cook with the chicken. Oven bake then serve the whole pan.

#618. Sheet pan hamburger roast with sauté potatoes and sweet potatoes

Prepare the hamburgers from a mixture of beef mince, sausage meat, cooked onions, garlic, breadcrumbs, dried mixed herbs and a beaten egg. Shape into burger patties and place onto the sheet pan. Around the burgers, place red onion cut into quarters, blanched diced potatoes and sweet potatoes, pieces of sweetcorn and streaky bacon slices. Using hamburger buns, the sheet pan ingredients can be used to make traditional burgers or plate and serve as a meal with buns.

#619. Sheet pan foiled chicken with roasted root vegetables

Using chicken breasts, wrap each breast in a piece of foil that has olive oil added along with crushed garlic, sun-dried tomatoes, sliced onion and capsicum on the base. Place the foil breasts on the baking sheet and add root vegetables to bake at the same time. Allow the chicken to rest after cooking and beware when opening the foil because of escaping steam, which can cause burns.

#620. Sheet pan steak wraps with capsicum and tomatoes

Slice green, red and yellow capsicums into strips. Place in a bowl with oil, garlic, chilli flakes and seasoning. Spread out onto a sheet pan and bake in the oven for 10 minutes at 200°C. In a very hot frypan in a little oil, brown the steak (rump or sirloin) on both sides then add to the sheet pan. When steak is cooked to the desired degree, remove and rest. Slice the steaks into 10 mm wide pieces and place them back onto the sheet pan. Serve with store-bought wraps, aioli mayonnaise, sliced tomatoes and avocado. Serve a side salad separately.

#621. Sheet pan pork medallions with potatoes and bean mix

Gently bat out the medallions with a rolling pin to make all the pork pieces the same thickness. Peel the potatoes and use a ball cutter available in most supermarkets to cut out potato balls. Place the balls in cold salted water and bring to the boil. Drain and place in a roasting tin in oil and butter and roll them around while baking to ensure that they all brown. Place the medallions onto the baking tray and turn over after 4 minutes then add the mix of top-and-tailed butter and green beans.

#622. Sheet pan pork chops with apple wedges

Cut small potatoes into quarters then place on the sheet pan with sliced onions, garlic and oil. Also add chopped parsnip the same size as the potatoes. In a frypan, very quickly brown the chops in oil then add to the sheet pan and turn over during their cooking. Also, with the pork, peel and wedge some apples and place on the same tray. When all the items are nearly cooked, spoon on frozen mixed vegetables and cook through.

#623. Sheet pan sweet and sour pork

Cut the pork into 25 mm size pieces and place in a bowl with soy, minced root ginger and garlic. Cut red and green capsicums into 30 mm size pieces after deseeding, cut pineapple the same size, top and tail whole green beans, dice onions then spread all pork and vegetables on a roasting pan. Drizzle with oil, more root ginger and bake in the oven. Spoon over some of the pork marinade while the pork is cooking. In a saucepan, put pineapple juice, chopped tomatoes, garlic, ginger and malt vinegar. Add brown sugar to get the sweet and sour taste and adjust accordingly. Thicken the sauce with cornflour mixed with a little water. When the meat and vegetables are cooked, spoon onto fried rice along with the sauce.

#624. Orange pork medallions, sweet potatoes and pineapple

With a sharp knife or potato peeler, remove the zest from an orange and get rid of the white pith. Then finely slice the zest and set aside. Squeeze the oranges for the juice and mix in canned pineapple juice. Place the pork medallions in a bowl, pour over a little of the juice, diced root ginger, garlic and allow to marinate. Peel and slice the sweet potatoes into 7 mm slices and place on the pan. Start the sweet potato in the oven and then add the pork. Once the pork is nearly ready, add pineapple to the tray. Pour over the juice mix, add knobs of butter, cover with tinfoil then bake in the oven at 160°C for 15 minutes. Check on the completeness of the pork and sweet potato, remove the foil and grill briefly to brown the top.

#625. Sheet pan steak with broccoli and courgette

Remove the florets from the broccoli and parboil in boiling salted water then cool immediately in iced water. Cut a courgette into half lengthways then half again to get four quarters. Heat the oven to 210°C. Rub the steak with oil and drizzle the vegetables with the oil. Add cherry tomatoes to the other vegetables, place all on the roasting dish, season and place in the oven. Turn the vegetables over while they are roasting to ensure even colour. Turn the steak once and remove when the desired degree of cooking is reached. Leave the steak to rest then cut a third of the steak into slices and present on the plate with the other two thirds still to be cut by those consuming the meal.

#626. Sheet pan chicken with diced pumpkin and Brussels sprouts

Place the chicken breasts under greaseproof paper and gently beat with a rolling pin to achieve uniform thickness. Rub with oil and season with pepper and salt. Peel and dice pumpkin into 15 mm size pieces, prepare Brussels sprouts ready for roasting and cut a red onion into quarters. Place all the vegetables on the roasting tray and drizzle with oil and chopped rosemary. Place the chicken on the pan and roast in the oven at 170°C till cooked. The chicken and vegetables may be ready at different times, so remove each item when cooked and set aside.

#627. Sheet pan prawns with tomatoes and asparagus

Prawns cook very quickly so the vegetables will need to be cooked first. Slice capsicums of different colours and cut into 30 mm size pieces. Halve tomatoes, remove some of the internal flesh and drizzle in oil and seasoning. Cut asparagus into 40 mm length pieces and rub all the vegetables with oil. Place on the roasting tray and cook at 190°C, turning as they cook so they don't burn. When nearly cooked, place the prawns on the tray. They should be cooked within 5 minutes. Remove and place the prawns and vegetables on dinner plates and serve with lime quarters.

#628. Sheet pan bacon-wrapped stuffed chicken breast with root vegetables

Stuff chicken breast with sliced smoked cheese then wrap in streaky bacon. Brown in frypan then place on baking sheet. Courgettes, carrot pieces, parsnips, sweet potatoes can be included on the tray.

#629. Sheet pan chicken and vegetables

On the tray put thick baton carrots and diced chicken breasts approximately 20 mm cubes. Bake at 190°C. While they are baking, parboil the broccoli and green beans then add to the tray. In a mixing bowl, place sesame oil, brown sugar, soy and oyster sauce, diced ginger, crushed garlic, hoisin sauce and sesame seeds. Mix well, remove the tray from the oven and pour the liquid over the ingredients cooking on the tray. Turning the vegetables and chicken, add the sliced mushrooms and return to the oven. Cook until the vegetables and chicken are cooked then serve.

#630. Sheet pan sausages with cauliflower and broccoli

Select the vegetables desired and prepare ready to roast. Select small potatoes, parboil then roast. Cut cauliflower into florets, parboil then into iced water, then diced sweet potatoes or broccoli. Rub the vegetables with oil and place on the roasting tray with garlic. Place the sausages on the tray but do not prick them before or during cooking. Cook in the oven at 170°C, turning the ingredients while cooking.

#631. Sheet pan sausages and chorizo with red onion segments

Wash small potatoes, sweet potatoes and carrots. Cut the potatoes in half and cut the sweet potato and carrot to a similar size. Parboil the root vegetables for 5 minutes then drain and place on an oiled sheet pan then put into the oven at 170°C. After 10 minutes add the chorizo and sausages along with large red onion segments. When the sausages and potatoes are nearly cooked, add asparagus spears and cook out. When removing from the oven ensure all ingredients are cooked. If not, remove those that are and continue with the rest of the ingredients.

#632. Sheet pan pesto chicken and vegetables No. 1

In a bowl, mix basil pesto, Dijon mustard, chilli flakes, chopped garlic and olive oil. Dice a large potato into 20 mm cubes and cut carrots and pumpkin the same size. Parboil in salted water for 5 minutes, drain then place in the pesto bowl and mix well. Place on the sheet pan and bake in the oven. Add diced chicken to the pesto then broccoli and place on the sheet pan. Remove from the oven once the chicken and potatoes are cooked. Serve with a balsamic vinaigrette.

#633. Sheet pan pesto chicken and vegetables No. 2

Use vegetables of choice but also the vegetables in dish #632 can be used. Parboil then arrange on a sheet pan. Coat with a little olive oil, crushed garlic, oregano, thyme and basil then bake in the oven for 20 minutes. Meanwhile remove the skin and bones from chicken thighs if not already done. On the inside of the chicken thigh smear the meat with a sun-dried tomato butter which contains a pinch of chilli flakes. Take the roast vegetables out of the oven and place the chicken on top, which will allow the chicken flavours to drift through the vegetables. Bake till the chicken thighs are cooked through, spooning the flavoured butter over the chicken.

#634. Sheet pan Cajun chicken and potato wedges

In a mixing bowl put honey, soy sauce, garlic powder, butter, olive oil, Cajun seasoning, Italian seasoning and lime juice and mix well. Heat on a low heat until warm. Cool then place the chicken breasts in the marinade for two hours. Place on a lipped, oiled oven dish and bake in the oven. Add prepared potato wedges and bake with vegetables of choice, for example asparagus, beans, broccoli.

#635. Sheet pan honey sesame tofu with green beans

Cut the tofu into 20–25 mm cubes and marinate in soy, chilli flakes, apple cider vinegar, brown sugar, oyster sauce and a few drops of sesame oil. Place the tofu on an oiled baking tray along with the top-and-tailed green beans. Turn the tofu over while cooking and drizzle with the marinade. Pour the marinade into a saucepan, simmer and thicken with arrowroot. When the tofu is brown, remove along with the beans and place on a serving plate. Spoon over the sauce and sprinkle with sesame seeds.

#636. Sheet pan meatballs with chickpeas

Prepare meatballs and make them 30 mm in diameter. Place in a roasting tray that has a lip, spread with a little oil then cook the meatballs in the oven at 180°C, turning while they are cooking so that they brown all over. After 10 minutes add to the tray canned chickpeas and courgettes and continue cooking. When the meatballs are nearly cooked, add cherry tomatoes, season the tray then serve.

17.

FOIL
COOKING

#	Dish	#	Dish
637	Salmon, Broccoli, Tomatoes And Courgettes	645	Sausages, Potatoes, Beans And Bacon
638	Salmon Crusted With Parmesan And Crumbs	646	Sausage And Rice Foil
639	Snapper With Sweet Potatoes And Bok Choy	647	Chicken Breast With Broccoli
640	Seafood Parcels	648	Chicken And Rice
641	Fish, Mussels And Prawns	649	Chicken And Asparagus
642	Garlic Prawns, Beans And Potatoes	650	Chilli Lime Chicken
643	Sausages And Mushrooms	651	Chicken Breast With Vegetables
644	Sausages With Potatoes, Asparagus, Cherry Tomatoes		

Foil cooking involves using foil or parchment paper to cook the meal on an individual basis. Because the foil is sealed it creates a steam effect hence cooking the ingredients inside. There are two discussions to be had about which side of the foil is to be used.

a. Place the food on the dull side of the foil, which has been oiled or spread with butter. When the package is sealed the shiny side of the foil will attract the heat and cook the inside ingredients.

b. Place the food on the shiny side, which has been oiled or buttered, so that the dull side is on the outer. It is then said that the dull side of the foil will attract the heat and not deflect it as the shiny side will.

In effect, go with what you feel comfortable with.

When placing fish, chicken, meat or prawns in the foil they are best placed on a vegetable base such as sliced blanched potatoes, sliced onions or courgettes or a mixture of all. This will prevent the protein from taking all the heat and burning. To create the steam, if no liquid has been called for, put in 50 ml water or stock to start the steam process.

A couple of small knife holes need to be cut into the foil on top to allow steam to escape so the package does not blow apart.

When assembling the package, have the sides of the foil turned upwards so that vegetable liquid does not escape, for example tomato juice if using tomatoes. It also makes it easier to seal. Collect both sides of the tinfoil and turn over to entwine and make the seal. Wind it down but leave 10 mm between the food and the top of the seal, then put in two knife holes.

When opening the foil after cooking, beware that the steam in the package can cause severe steam burns. Keep your face well away. Place a tea towel over the package and open slowly.

Rice, couscous, pasta and polenta are also ideal bases to put on the base of the foil and on which to place the meat, poultry or fish. In some instances, the protein will be better fried first before packing in the foil. This will give it better colour and taste.

#637. Salmon, broccoli, tomatoes and courgettes

On the baking paper which is on the tinfoil, lay broccoli florets, tomato segments, sliced red onions and sliced courgettes. Drizzle with oil, grated root ginger and crushed garlic then place the salmon on top which has also been rubbed with oil and seasoned. Over the top of the salmon, bring the two edges of the foil together and fold them into a tight seal. Place two knife holes in the top then place in a roasting tin and in the oven at 170°C for 20 minutes or until cooked through.

#638. Salmon crusted with Parmesan and crumbs

Place the baking paper on the foil and spread with whole kernel corn, top-and-tailed green beans with sliced tomatoes. Lay the salmon on the vegetables, drizzle with oil then top with a mix of grated Parmesan and fresh breadcrumbs that has been mixed together with soft butter and seasoning. Spoon over melted butter, fold and bake in the oven.

#639. Snapper with sweet potatoes and bok choy

Peel and parboil sweet potatoes then slice into 5 mm thick slices. Lay them on the baking paper, top with sliced red onions and bok choy. Grate root ginger over the vegetables and drizzle with oil and soy sauce. Place the snapper on top, fold, season and bake.

#640. Seafood parcels

Cut the fish into portion size pieces leaving the skin on which will hold the fillet together. Scales should have been removed. On a sheet of foil, place a piece of buttered baking paper. In a mortar and pestle smash the lemongrass along with crushed garlic, grated root ginger, chopped fresh chilli, parsley, oil to make a paste. Lay the selection of seafood — fish, mussel meat, prawns, oysters, scallops — on the baking paper, fold and bake in the oven. Serve with hollandaise sauce.

#641. Fish, mussels and prawns

Place a piece of baking paper on a sheet of foil and sprinkle with oil. Into a mortar and pestle add chopped lemongrass, garlic, grated ginger, chopped chilli and crush to a paste then add some olive oil. On the baking paper place green vegetables such as bok choy, silverbeet, green beans or similar. Place the fish fillet, raw mussels and prawns on top and spoon over the paste. Season then wrap the foil into a parcel with the seams being uppermost. Bake in the oven and beware when opening the foil that the steam will be exceptionally hot.

#642. Garlic prawns, beans and potatoes

Boil a few potatoes till just cooked then drain and cut into thick slices while warm. Spread garlic butter onto the foil then place the potato slices on the garlic butter. Top with the prawns then spread top-and-tailed beans over the top. Drizzle with oil and add garlic butter, season then fold the foil and bake in the oven for 20 minutes. Check that all is cooked, season then serve.

#643. Sausages and mushrooms

Rub the baking paper with butter then add sliced onions and mushrooms that have stalks removed. Drizzle over melted butter and top with the sausages. Bake in the oven for 20 minutes then open the foil and grill to brown the sausages.

#644. Sausages with potatoes, asparagus and cherry tomatoes

Using small potatoes, cut in half, parboil till al dente then place on a baking sheet/foil with the sausages and oil. Both the potatoes and sausages will require turning during cooking. Add the cherry tomatoes to the tray after 10 minutes. During the process they will become very soft but still be in their skin. Add the asparagus with 10 minutes to go, season the tray of food and serve.

#645. Sausages, potatoes, beans and bacon

Buy small potatoes, cut in half and parboil in a saucepan of water, while at the same time browning the sausages in a frypan in oil. Lay the sheet of foil on the bench and when the potatoes are almost cooked, drain and place in the middle of the foil. Place the sausages on top of the potatoes, line the sides with green beans that have been top and tailed then lay fried streaky bacon over the top. Drizzle with a little oil and add a knob of butter. Fold the foil to complete the envelope, place in a roasting dish and bake at 180°C for 25 minutes. Check that it is all cooked then serve.

#646. Sausage and rice foil

Place a sheet of foil on the bench and brush with oil. Add chopped celery, onion, red capsicum, garlic and ginger. Top with sliced sausage for which chorizo would be a good choice because of the spices. Add cooked rice, knobs of butter and a little stock to keep it moist, seal and bake.

#647. Chicken breast with broccoli

Brown the chicken breasts briefly in a frypan in butter and garlic then cool. Place the chicken on the foil along with broccoli florets. Add a knob of butter and ranch dressing. Seal and bake in the oven till cooked.

#648. Chicken and rice

On a sheet of buttered baking paper which is on foil, spoon on cooked rice. Place a flattened chicken breast on top with whole mushrooms between the rice and the chicken. Add small broccoli florets and peas. Spoon over a drizzle of chicken stock, season, wrap and bake. On the same tray, add seasoned diced potatoes, chicken stock and oil wrapped in foil and bake.

#649. Chicken and asparagus

Brown the chicken in a frypan on both sides then place the chicken on thin slices of cooked potato and season. Place trimmed asparagus alongside with fresh tomato slices, sliced lemon zest, lemon slices and seasoning. Seal and bake.

#650. Chilli lime chicken

Place the foil on a chopping board and line the base with slices of onion then slices of lime on top. Place the chicken thighs on the lime and drizzle with olive oil, lime juice, chopped coriander, crushed garlic, runny honey, chilli and grated lime zest. Wrap the chicken in the foil and oven bake.

#651. Chicken breast with vegetables

Cut out the square of foil then drizzle over olive oil. Cut baby potatoes into half then half again and lay them on the foil. Cut an onion the same way then add small pieces of carrot and celery. In a bowl, mix Dijon mustard, oil, crushed garlic, thyme and rosemary then finely sliced lemon zest. Place the chicken breast on the vegetables and brush with the Dijon mix, season the breast with pepper and salt then fold the foil to envelope the food making a small steam hole in the top of the foil. Bake in the oven at 190°C for 30 minutes or till cooked then serve.

18.

VEGETABLES

#	Dish	#	Dish
652	Asparagus Spears	705	Baked Crisp Courgette Rings
653	Asparagus Wrapped In Streaky Bacon	706	Courgettes Baked
654	Asparagus Wrapped In Prosciutto	707	Grilled Courgettes On Flat Bread
655	Asparagus In Cream Sauce	708	Parmesan Crusted Zucchini
656	Asparagus With Olive And Orange Butter	709	Baked Zucchini
657	Broccoli Casserole	710	Rolled Courgettes With Carrot And Celery
658	Roasted Broccoli With Flaked Almonds	711	Courgette Pizza Slices
659	Green Beans In Mushroom Sauce With Bacon On Top	712	Braised Leeks
660	Green Beans With Cherry Tomatoes And Feta	713	Mushrooms In Bourbon
661	Green Beans With Chopped Walnuts, Lemon And Chilli	714	Balsamic Soy Mushrooms
662	Garlic And Ginger Beans	715	Crumbed Deep Fried Mushrooms
663	Green Beans Wrapped In Bacon	716	Caprese Portobello Mushroom
664	Minted Green Beans	717	Roasted Garlic Button Mushrooms
665	Beetroot Wrapped In Foil	718	Mushroom Filled With Wild Rice And Mashed Potato
666	Beetroot With Orange And Ginger	719	Mushrooms Stuffed With Spinach
667	Roasted Beetroot In Balsamic And Brown Sugar	720	Mushrooms On A Rosti Base
668	Lemon, Rosemary And Sage Beetroot	721	Stuffed Mushrooms With Crabmeat And Cheese

#652. Asparagus spears

Cut or break off the root end of the spears then roll them in olive oil that has paprika and chopped parsley added. Roll through panko crumbs then bake in the oven till golden brown.

#653. Asparagus wrapped in streaky bacon and puff pastry

Cut a sheet of store-bought puff pastry into strips 20 mm wide and use streaky bacon. Break off the base of the asparagus and spiral wrap with the streaky bacon. Then spiral wrap with the puff pastry but leaving gaps between each spiral. Brush with egg wash and bake in the oven.

#654. Asparagus wrapped in prosciutto

Break off the root end of the asparagus spears then wrap each spear in thinly sliced prosciutto. Fry in very little oil and turn on all sides till the prosciutto is brown. Serve as an entrée or as a side. Also serve with basil pesto.

#655. Asparagus in cream sauce

Trim the base of the asparagus and poach in simmering salted water. Prepare a béchamel sauce using white wine as part of the liquor to thin down the roux. Add Dijon mustard, check seasoning and add cream. Place the drained asparagus on a serving dish and coat the bottom half of the asparagus with the sauce.

#656. Asparagus with olive and orange butter

Trim the root end of the asparagus so that all are of the same length. Either poach the asparagus in simmering salted water or barbecue till tender. Place soft butter into a mixing bowl and squeeze in orange juice, finely sliced orange zest and black olive halves. Mix well, season then serve it over the asparagus when on the dinner plate.

#657. Broccoli casserole

Cut the broccoli into florets and blanch in boiling salted water then drain and refresh under cold water immediately. In a mixing bowl, put a can of mushroom soup, diced onions and garlic, chopped tomatoes, mayonnaise and eggs. Mix well together and pour it over the florets which are in a buttered casserole dish. Top with grated cheddar cheese then crushed crackers and bake in the oven. Serve as a side dish.

#658. Roasted broccoli with flaked almonds

Trim the broccoli into florets and parboil for 2 minutes, drain then place in a roasting dish with oil and cook in the oven at 180°C. After 5 minutes, sprinkle over flaked almonds and continue cooking. Chilli flakes could also be sprinkled over the broccoli at the same time.

#659. Green beans in mushroom sauce with bacon on top

Top and tail the beans and maintain the length of each bean. In a saucepan, add a large knob of butter and cook bacon that has been cut into batons. Add sliced mushrooms and fry. Remove the bacon and mushrooms then add the same amount of flour as butter then slowly pour in milk. Allow the sauce to simmer gently, season and set aside. Cook the beans in boiling salted water to a point of still being crunchy, drain, pour over the mushroom sauce and serve.

#660. Green beans with cherry tomatoes and feta

Top and tail the beans and cook quickly in boiling salted water till only just cooked. Drain then toss in the saucepan with butter and seasoning and cherry tomatoes. Spoon onto a serving dish, crumble over feta cheese and drizzle with olive oil.

#661. Green beans with chopped walnuts, lemon and chilli

Top and tail the whole beans and cook quickly in boiling salted water till just cooked then drain and refresh in cold water to keep their colour. In a frypan, brown fresh breadcrumbs with garlic, chopped walnuts, lemon zest and a pinch of chilli flakes. Toss well together then spoon it over the beans and serve.

#662. Garlic and ginger beans

Top and tail the beans and keep the same length. Quickly boil in salted water till still underdone. Meanwhile grate garlic and root ginger and place in a frypan that has butter melted in it. Drain the beans, add them to the frypan with the garlic and ginger, toss until each bean is coated with the butter mixture, season then serve.

#663. Green beans wrapped in bacon

Top and tail the fresh green beans. Cook quickly in boiling salted water then plunge into iced water to stop the cooking process. Wrap five stems of beans in streaky bacon and bake in the oven. Place on a serving plate and drizzle with balsamic vinegar.

#664. Minted green beans

Top and tail the beans but leave whole. Place into boiling salted water containing mint leaves. Cook quickly but don't overcook and leave them with a snap in them. Drain well and quickly flush under cold water. Place into a frypan with butter and more sliced mint, toss and serve.

#665. Beetroot wrapped in foil

Tear off a piece of tinfoil and lay it on the bench. Smear with olive oil, wash the beetroot and place in the centre of the foil. Envelop the beet in the foil, place in a roasting pan and slow roast till the beetroot is cooked through.

#666. Beetroot with orange and ginger

Cook beetroot in simmering salted water or in a pressure cooker. When the beetroot is cooked, the skin will just pull away from the flesh. Cut the beetroot into 20 mm sized dice and toss in a frypan with butter, grated root ginger and orange juice with sliced orange zest. Remove the beetroot and thicken the sauce with cornflour and water mixed. Season and serve.

#667. Roasted beetroot in balsamic and brown sugar

Cover the beetroot in cold water, bring to the boil and add salt. Simmer slowly until cooked and the skin will peel off easily. Cut the beetroot in half through the stem and root. Then cut each half into three segments. Into a saucepan put balsamic vinegar and brown sugar and allow to simmer and thicken till it becomes syrupy. Place the beetroot segments into the pot, stir then leave to cool. Serve when ready.

#668. Lemon, rosemary and sage beetroot

Bring to the boil from cold salted water and simmer till the skin is able to fall away from the beet. Skin, top and tail the beetroot, cut into quarters and place in a roasting pan with olive oil, lemon peel, rosemary and sage then roast at 180°C. As the beetroot is already cooked, it only requires 10 minutes to pick up the lemon and herb flavour.

#669. Beetroot, caramelised onions and feta

Prepare the caramelised onions by slicing the onions and slowly frying them in oil until they begin to take colour. Add sliced garlic, dried mixed herbs and continue cooking so they continue to colour. Add a large knob of butter and brown sugar, lower the heat. Small whole onions can also be added by simmering first then caramelising in butter and brown sugar and added to the sliced onions once they have finished cooking. Roast or boil the beetroot till cooked, cool then remove the skin and cut into wedges. Place the onions on a serving platter, segments of beetroot over the top then cubes of feta cheese.

#670. Beetroot and bacon in foil

Cut off the tops, wrap the beetroot in streaky bacon and place on foil that has been buttered. Add oil, thyme leaves, a little balsamic vinegar and honey. Wrap and bake.

#671. Brussels sprouts with cream, Dijon and citrus sauce

Peel off the outside leaves of the sprouts, make a knife cut in the stem and cook in boiling salted water till just cooked. Like pasta, they should be al dente. In a small saucepan, pour in cream and heat adding Dijon mustard, grated lemon zest and grated mozzarella. When the Brussels sprouts are cooked, drain well, place in the serving dish and pour over the sauce.

#672. Skewered Brussels sprouts and bacon

Remove the outer leaves of the sprouts, cut a slice in the root then briefly cook for 2 minutes in boiling salted water then plunge into iced water to stop the cooking instantly. With three sprouts, skewer one then skewer a piece of streaky bacon at one end. Fold the bacon over one side of the Brussels sprout skewer then add another sprout, fold the bacon round and so on. Spoon oil and butter over the skewers then bake in the oven until both the bacon and the Brussels sprouts are cooked.

#673. Brussels sprouts in a bacon and cream sauce

Remove the outside leaves and cut a slice in the root so that it will cook at the same rate as the sprout. Cook the Brussels sprouts in boiling salted water but don't overcook and allow them to go mushy. In a separate saucepan, prepare a béchamel, while in a frypan cook bacon pieces and allow them to caramelise. Add the Brussels sprouts to the frypan along with a knob of butter, stir well to lift the caramelised pieces on the bottom of the pan then pour over some béchamel and serve.

#674. Brussels sprouts with blueberry balsamic and pecan nuts

Remove the outside leaves of the Brussels sprouts, cut a slice in the stem and cook in boiling salted water until just cooked, then drain well. While the sprouts are cooking, dry fry pecan nuts in a frypan till they start to brown then turn out onto a chopping board and roughly chop. Return the drained Brussels sprouts to the saucepan, drizzle with blueberry balsamic vinegar then spoon onto a serving platter. Sprinkle with the chopped pecan nuts.

#675. Brussels sprouts topped with bacon and breadcrumbs

Remove the outer leaves of the Brussels sprouts, make a knife cut in the stem and cook in boiling salted water. When cooked, drain well and place on a serving platter. While the sprouts are cooking, cut streaky bacon into small batons and fry in butter till cooked and caramelised. Add in breadcrumbs and continue frying until brown. Spoon the breadcrumb mix over the Brussels sprouts and serve.

#676. Bacon and Brussels sprouts skewered

Cook bacon in butter in the frypan. Ideal for this dish is bacon pieces that are chunky and can be cut to size. Parboil the Brussels sprouts in boiling salted water then cool instantly in iced water. Thread the bacon and Brussels sprouts onto wooden skewers with cherry tomatoes in between and black olives at each end. Brush with garlic butter and grill in the oven.

#677. Roast butternut with orange and strawberry sauce

Peel and deseed the butternut then cut into small pieces 40 mm in size approximately. Roast in vegetable oil, grated garlic and ginger, juice of half an orange and add sage and rosemary to the pan. Roast until the butternut is cooked through. Meanwhile, into a small saucepan pour fresh orange juice, grated orange zest, fresh strawberries and simmer. Once the fruit breaks down, spoon in strawberry jam and reduce to thicken the sauce. Check for taste then plate the butternut and drizzle the sauce over it.

#678. Stuffed butternut squash

Cut the butternut squash in half lengthways then remove all the pith and seeds. Prepare a bread stuffing using sliced onions and mushrooms, spinach, garlic, grated cheddar cheese, garlic and a little béchamel to bind. Spoon the stuffing into each half then place the two halves back together again and tie with butcher's twine. Bake in the oven until the squash is cooked through, remove from the oven and cut into rings to serve.

#679. Roasted butternut squash

Remove the skin and seeds and cut to pieces of the same size. Pour vegetable oil into a roasting tin and roast the squash. Add bacon pieces with the squash while it is cooking and when the squash is cooked, drizzle with runny honey and chopped pecans. Put back in the oven for 5 minutes then remove and place on a serving plate.

#680. Sliced baked butternut

Cut the butternut in half lengthways then remove the pith and seeds. Cut slices off one half 20 mm wide and roast in the oven in oil and butter with the other half which is also deseeded and peeled. Cut a slice off the base of the whole half butternut so that it sits on a serving plate evenly. Turn over during cooking so that both sides brown. When cooked place the whole butternut half onto a serving plate and top with pieces of butternut, crusted bacon pieces, chopped parsley and spoonfuls of sour cream.

#681. Braised red cabbage with apple and caraway seeds

Slice the cabbage into 10 mm wide slices and place in a thick-based saucepan with 3 mm of water. Add diced, peeled apple and half a teaspoon of caraway leaves then place the saucepan on a very hot element with a lid on the saucepan. Allow to boil quickly for 3 minutes, test the cabbage then drain off the water. Add a knob of butter and seasoning then place the lid back on the cabbage and leave till it is time to serve. The cabbage should have a bite to it.

#682. Roast cabbage with date sauce

Slice the cabbage into 15 mm thick slices including the stalk so that it holds together. Roast in a hot oven in oil, butter, garlic and ginger till just cooked. Serve immediately with a **date sauce**: Soak dates in a sugar syrup then when soft, remove and roughly chop. Add lemon juice and sliced zest to the dates.

#683. Red cabbage balsamic

Slice the red cabbage into 10 mm strips. Into a saucepan, fry off sliced red onions, diced root ginger and apple segments in butter then add the red cabbage with 50 ml water and place a lid on. Remove the lid and allow the liquid to escape but don't overcook the cabbage. It should still retain some bite. Drain in a colander, place on serving tray and drizzle with balsamic vinegar.

#684. Harissa and maple roasted carrots

In a bowl, mix oil, orange juice, harissa paste, crushed garlic, grated ginger, coriander powder with pepper and salt then put the small baby carrots into the mixture for 30 minutes. Roast the carrots in the oven till cooked, reduce the heat and pour in maple syrup. Roast for another 5 minutes then serve.

#685. Roast carrots with cumin yoghurt

Buy small carrots and if available, buy multi colours. Leave a little of the tops on, about 30 mm, and roast in the oven in oil, garlic and cumin seeds. Baste while roasting till cooked. Meanwhile mix plain yoghurt with cumin powder to serve with the carrots.

#686. Carrots baked on coffee beans

Peel carrots and mix in a bowl with oil and garlic. In a frypan, place whole coffee beans and oven bake slowly. Place carrots on top and cook slowly. Throw away the beans after use.

#687. Garlic butter roasted carrots

Use either small specialty carrots (purple, yellow, orange) or large carrots cut into quarters. Roast in oil and butter and keep turning through the cooking process. When cooked, place on serving tray, add slices of garlic butter and turn them through it.

#688. Barbecued carrots with dressing

Slice the carrots lengthways and barbecue if possible to leave grill marks. If not, fry the carrots till golden brown then place on the serving tray. Prepare a dressing of olive oil, malt vinegar, garlic, orange juice and zest.

#689. Mashed carrot in tomato case

Peel and cut the carrots into similar-size pieces then boil them until soft and cooked through. Drain well then place the saucepan back on the element to allow any excess water to evaporate. Mash the carrots, add butter, season well and add any herbs if desired. Cut off the top of a tomato and remove the seeds and flesh. Stuff the tomato with the carrot mash and top with mascarpone cheese.

#690. Garlic cauliflower mash

In a food processor, blitz the cooked florets then drizzle in roasted mashed garlic, seasoning and cream.

#691. Roast cauliflower with a caramel sauce

Cut the cauliflower into slabs by removing all greenery then sitting it on a chopping board, head up, and cutting through the centre. Cut off 15 mm cauliflower steaks from each half until only a small end piece is left. Place the slabs in a roasting dish with oil, butter and thyme. Roast in a hot oven (190°C), turning over during the roasting process. Place on a serving platter and keep warm. In a frypan, slowly melt white sugar until it goes to a syrup and starts turning brown. Add a large knob of butter, reduce the heat but don't stir the pan at any time. Just shake and swirl the pan to allow the butter and sugar to mix. Pour in a small amount of cream then stir to incorporate. Place the cauliflower on the dinner plate and drizzle over the caramel sauce.

#692. Roast cauliflower

Cut the cauliflower into florets and place in a Ziploc bag. Add oil, crushed garlic, salt, panko breadcrumbs and grated Parmesan cheese, shake well then roast the cauliflower in the oven with oil.

#693. Roast cauliflower pieces with Parmesan

Remove the florets from the cauliflower stalk, trim either side of the stem then cut it in half. Place on an oiled roasting tray, add a knob of butter then roast in the oven for 10 minutes at 180°C. Check and sprinkle over grated Parmesan cheese and return to the oven to complete cooking.

#694. Sesame cauliflower

Cut the cauliflower into florets and cook al dente in boiling salted water. Drain well. Meanwhile, into a small saucepan put soy sauce, sesame oil, runny honey and demerara sugar. Reduce till it thickens and becomes sticky and remove from the heat. Arrange the cauliflower on a serving platter, pour over the sauce and sprinkle with sesame seeds.

#695. Cauliflower steaks

Remove the base leaves then cut through the middle of the cauliflower. Using one half, make a cut through 10–15 mm wide to form a whole cauliflower steak. Fry the cauliflower in a frypan in oil, root ginger and garlic and brown on both sides. Drizzle the cauliflower with harissa paste then bake in the oven till cooked. Place on the serving platter and sprinkle with sliced almonds.

#696. Herb crusted cauliflower steak

Cut the cauliflower as in dish #695, then fry in the frypan on both sides till it is nicely browned and place on a baking tray. In a mixing bowl, place freshly made breadcrumbs, diced fried onions, grated cheese, chopped parsley, coriander and dried mixed herbs. Add an egg to bind the mix, spread it over the cauliflower and bake in the oven till cooked then serve.

#697. Cauliflower with bacon, capers and capsicum

Cut the cauliflower into florets and cook in boiling salted water till just cooked but slightly al dente. In a frypan, fry roughly chopped capsicum and bacon pieces in butter till cooked. Arrange the cauliflower on a serving plate, spoon over the bacon mix and top with a spoonful of capers.

#698. Cauliflower fritters

Cook the cauliflower pieces in boiling salted water then roughly mash the cauliflower but leaving it lumpy so that the cauliflower can be identified in the fritters. Mix with chopped parsley, crushed garlic and mint. Prepare a batter and pour it over the cauliflower, stirring well. Cook spoonfuls of the fritter mix in a frypan in oil and butter till brown on both sides.

#699. Thai cauliflower steaks and peanut sauce

Cut the cauliflower from the top, through the stalk, forming 15 mm wide steaks. Cook the cauliflower steaks in a frypan or bake in an oven tray. Place the cauliflower steaks on a serving dish, pour over peanut sauce and top with dry pan-fried peanuts. Serve with rice.

Peanut sauce: Stalk lemongrass, sesame oil, grated root ginger, chilli paste, brown sugar, soy and fish sauces, crushed garlic, spring onions, peanut butter mixed with a little warm water. Beat the lemongrass with the back of a knife then mix all ingredients and heat gently in a saucepan.

#700. Cauliflower casserole

Cut the cauliflower into florets and cook in boiling salted water, then mash with a potato masher. Add in eggs, grated cheese, diced sweated onion and garlic and seasoning. Spoon the cauliflower mix into a buttered casserole dish, top with melted butter and grated cheese then bake in the oven.

#701. Grilled courgettes with tapenade

Top and tail the courgettes then slice into thick slices of 10 mm thick lengthways. Brush both sides with oil then quickly grill till nearly cooked. Spread each slice of courgette with tapenade then grill till cooked and serve immediately.

#702. Crisp courgettes

Slice the courgettes into rings 7 mm thick and place on a sheet of oiled baking paper which is on a baking tray. Put a spoonful of grated cheese on each piece and top with a pinch of chilli flakes. Bake in the oven till golden brown on top and crisp. They can also be served as a savoury dish with drinks. Serve with a tomato salsa dip.

#703. Courgette and potato cylinders

Grate cooked potato and raw courgette and mix in roughly chopped capsicum. Add to a mixing bowl then add seasoning, grated garlic, flour and beaten egg. Mould into small cylinders 40 x 15 mm and bake in the oven on a greased oven tray.

#704. Filled courgettes

This dish needs large-diameter courgettes. Slice off both ends then every 5 mm make a slice in the courgette. Into each slice place a filling, for example salami, tomato segments, sun-dried tomato slices, sliced red capsicum or whatever your choice may be. Brush the courgette with butter and bake in the oven till cooked.

#705. Baked crisp courgette rings

Slice the courgette into rings and place on an oiled tray. Drizzle with oil and a pinch of chilli flakes then bake in the oven till the courgettes go brown and crisp.

#706. Courgettes baked

Slice the courgettes into rings and line the bottom of a buttered casserole dish with them. Top with a layer of sliced red onions and tomatoes. Add another layer of courgettes and a second layer of onions and tomatoes finishing with courgettes on top. Drizzle with soy and melted butter then bake.

#707. Grilled courgettes on flat bread

Top and tail the courgettes then cut into batons 60 x 10 x 10 mm approximately and place in a mixing bowl. To the bowl pour in olive oil, sliced red onions, grated garlic and ginger. Allow to mix well then place on a grill rack and grill in the oven, turning while cooking to brown the baton courgettes all over. When cooked, lay out on a piece of flat bread, and top with chopped coriander, crumbled feta and an olive oil dressing.

#708. Parmesan crusted zucchini

Cut both ends off the courgette then cut into batons approximately 40 x 10 mm. Dip through breadcrumbs that have grated Parmesan and chopped parsley added to it. Place on greased baking paper and bake in the oven till golden brown.

#709. Baked zucchini

Top and tail the courgettes, cut in half lengthways and place in a roasting dish with olive oil, garlic, thyme and sage. Place into a hot oven and turn over during the roasting process. When soft and cooked, pour over a small amount of pomodoro sauce, grated cheese and put back in the oven to reheat then serve.

#710. Rolled courgettes with carrot and celery

Top and tail the courgette then using a very sharp knife or a vegetable peeler that cuts 4 mm slices, slice the courgette. Cut a carrot and celery stick into 50 x 5 mm sticks. Lay the courgette onto a board, spread with a pasta tomato sauce then lay four or five sticks of carrot and celery on the courgette, season and roll up. Lay them in a casserole dish and bake in the oven till cooked.

#711. Courgette pizza slices

Top and tail the courgette then slice into 5–7 mm slices lengthways. Fry or barbecue the strips on both sides then place on a baking sheet. Spoon on a pizza sauce covering the whole of the courgette slice then add black olive halves. Top with grated cheese and grill in the oven.

#712. Braised leeks

Remove the green top from the leeks then wash well to remove any soil or sand. Brown the leeks in a frypan in oil and butter then place into a casserole dish. Deglaze the frypan with chicken stock then add to the leeks. Add crushed garlic, thyme and rosemary to the liquid then bake in the oven without a lid so that the cooking liquid can reduce. When cooked, remove the leeks to a serving dish and thicken some of the stock to pour over the leeks when serving. Top with crushed walnuts.

#713. Mushrooms in bourbon

Cook the mushrooms in an oil, garlic and butter mix in a frypan. When they are cooked, remove from the frypan then pour in half a cup of bourbon, flame then reduce. Add mustard, half a cup of cream and seasoning. Return the mushrooms back to the sauce then serve.

#714. Balsamic soy mushrooms

Button mushrooms, balsamic vinegar, soy sauce, garlic, thyme, seasoning, oil. Mix all the ingredients in a bowl, place in a baking dish and roast in the oven.

#715. Crumbed deep-fried mushrooms

Dip the button mushrooms through flour, egg wash and breadcrumbs and deep fry.

#716. Caprese portobello mushrooms

Remove the stalks then fry the mushrooms in oil, butter and garlic on both sides. Lay the mushrooms on a tray skin side down. Place small pieces of mozzarella cheese, cherry tomato halves and torn basil on top. Grill when ready to serve then drizzle with a balsamic and oil dressing.

#717. Roasted garlic button mushrooms

In a roasting pan, melt butter on an element and add whole smashed garlic corms that have the skin removed. As the pan heats, add the button mushrooms then place in the oven at 190°C. Shake the roasting pan and turn over the mushrooms during the roasting process. The mushrooms will absorb the butter then release some of it once they are cooked. Shake over seasoning then serve.

#718. Mushrooms filled with wild rice and mashed potato

Fry portobello mushrooms in butter on both sides then leave to cool. In a bowl, mix mashed potatoes with cooked wild rice, diced onions and garlic. Spoon the mixture onto the inside of the mushroom, top with a small knob of butter and bake.

#719. Mushrooms stuffed with spinach

With portobello mushrooms, fry both sides in a frypan in garlic butter then place on a baking tray skin side down. Prepare a stuffing from frozen spinach that has been defrosted and pressed into a chinois/sieve to get rid of all excess water. Toss the spinach in the same frypan as the mushrooms and add butter, cinnamon, nutmeg and seasoning. If the spinach is still too wet, add breadcrumbs to absorb the liquid. Spoon onto the mushroom, top with crumbled feta and bake until cooked.

#720. Mushrooms on rosti base

Remove the stalks from the portobello mushrooms and fry in a frypan in butter, olive and grated garlic. Fry on both sides then set aside and keep warm. Grate the potatoes on a coarse grater into a clean tea towel to remove all the liquid. Place the potato into a mixing bowl and add beaten egg with milk, seasoning, garlic and mix well. Spoon the potato mixture in large spoonfuls into hot butter and oil in a frypan and turn over once brown on the base side. Place onto kitchen paper to drain then onto a serving plate. Top with the mushrooms and serve.

#721. Stuffed mushrooms with crabmeat and cheese

Use portobello mushrooms. Brush with garlic butter and grill briefly. Into a mixing bowl, put a can of drained crab meat, mix in cream cheese and chopped parsley. Spoon the mixture onto the mushrooms, top with grated cheese and grill.

#722. Red onion and chilli marmalade

Slice the red onions and place into a large saucepan with oil, garlic and salt and cook on a medium heat. Stir to stop the onions sticking to the base of the saucepan, evaporate the liquid and allow the onions to brown. Add white sugar to caramelise the onions then add chilli flakes, chunky marmalade and again reduce. Season and serve.

#723. Parmesan onions

Peel the onion then cut into 15 mm thick rings. Remove two or three of the centre rings and place the onion on an oiled casserole dish. Into the centre of the onion ring spoon a little béchamel sauce and place in the deep freeze to harden up. Top with grated cheddar cheese and Parmesan cheese then bake until the onion rings are soft.

#724. Baked onion rings

Peel and slice the onions 20 mm thick. Place into an oiled roasting dish, keeping all the onion rings within the main diameter ring together, then bake in the oven at 180°C till they begin to brown. Remove the dish from the oven and pour over a mixture of cream cheese, cream, garlic and chopped parsley which has been beaten together. Keep the liquid below the level of the onion rings. Put the dish back into the oven and cook slowly so that the rings don't break up.

#725. Caramelised onion tarte Tatin

Select small pickling-size onions that are around the same circumference. Peel the onions and par-cook in boiling water then add butter and brown sugar to the saucepan to caramelise them. In another saucepan, caramelise sliced onions in water and brown sugar caramel adding dried mixed herbs and garlic to the mix. Add knobs of butter then add the whole baby onions to the sliced onion mix. There needs to be enough small onions to fit tightly into the oven-friendly frypan when the pastry is added. Pour the sliced onion mix into an oven-friendly frypan while still hot and top with a sheet of store-bought puff pastry, pushing the pastry down the inside of the frypan. Paint with egg wash and place the pan in the oven at 200°C. (When placing the pastry over the onions, it is necessary to complete this very quickly.) When the pastry is cooked, remove from the oven, place a serving plate over the frypan and turn the frypan over so that the pastry now becomes the bottom of the dish. Be careful on turning over the dish that you do not get splashed with hot caramelised sugar.

#726. Roast caramelised parsnips

Peel and cut the parsnip into even-sized pieces. Roast the parsnip in oil and garlic. When cooked, add balsamic vinegar, brown sugar and butter to the roasting pan and place on an element to heat the sauce and colour the parsnips.

#727. Fried parsnips

Peel and cut the parsnips into equal-size pieces. Cook in boiling water till just cooked. Fry in butter and oil to brown on all sides and add chopped nuts. While frying, sprinkle over brown sugar and lemon juice. Toss then serve.

#728. Roast tandoori pumpkin

Peel, slice the pumpkin and remove the seeds. Cut the pumpkin into small pieces, add to a store-bought tandoori paste which is mixed with plain yoghurt and combine till totally covered. Roast the pumpkin in the oven until soft and nicely browned, as well as some cashew nuts. Place the pumpkin on a serving platter, spoon over the roasted cashew nuts and top with chopped coriander leaves. Serve with rice and naan bread if this is a main vegetarian dish.

#729. Pumpkin fritters

Mashed pumpkin, flour, eggs, baking powder, sugar, lemon juice and cinnamon. Keep the mashed pumpkin in a dryish state then add eggs, baking powder, sugar, lemon juice and cinnamon. If the mix is too wet, add dry breadcrumbs or more flour. Mould into balls then flatten and fry in butter and oil. Drain on kitchen paper. Canned chickpeas could also be added to give texture to the fritters.

#730. Pumpkin stuffed with rice

Cut a pumpkin through the stem and separate the two halves. Take one half and cut out a piece of skin from the side which will form a base for the pumpkin to sit on. Remove all the pith and seeds and season the inside. In a saucepan, cook a mix of wild rice/rice 1:2 in salted water till cooked. To the cooked rice add sweated off diced onions, diced capsicum and ginger, crushed garlic, sliced celery, diced tomato flesh, chopped parsley and seasoning. Spoon the rice into the cavity of the pumpkin, drizzle with melted butter and olive oil then cover with tinfoil and bake slowly in the oven at 160°C till the pumpkin is cooked. Slice into sections and serve.

#731. Pea, pesto, spinach, cheese rice cakes

Grease muffin tins and line with baking paper. In a large saucepan add oil along with spring onions, diced onions, smoked red peppers and diced courgette. Add arborio rice then chicken stock slowly allowing it to cook out, adding lemon zest and juice and butter to keep it creamy. Whisk cream and eggs together and pour it over the rice adding Parmesan and cheddar cheese. Quickly mix in the spinach then spoon the mixture into the muffin tins and bake around 30 minutes until they are cooked. Serve with meat or fish dishes.

#732. Pea salsa

Add chopped mint and chilli to the peas. Add seasonings, lime juice then pulse quickly in blender, as the salsa should lumpy, then add crème fraîche.

#733. Mushy peas

Use dried peas and soak overnight. Wash and change the water then add an onion cut in two, thyme, celery stick and bay leaves. Simmer slowly till the peas are soft. Mash with a potato masher and add a knob of butter and seasoning. Serve with steak or fish.

#734. Crushed peas

Cook frozen peas in a small saucepan in butter and add lemon juice and finely sliced lemon zest. When cooked, lightly mash with a potato masher but keeping some of the texture of the pea shells. Add seasoning, olive oil and a little sour cream and mix in. Use as a base for fish or meat dishes on the serving plate.

#735. Crushed lemon peas

Boil the peas in salted water till cooked, strain then with a potato masher roughly mash the peas so that they still retain some texture. Drizzle in butter and lemon juice and add a few slices of finely sliced lemon zest.

#736. Green peas in cream

Boil the fresh peas in salted water to soft then drain well. Toss in a small knob of butter then pour in only a small amount of cream so that they are not drowning in liquid. A béchamel with cream could also be used as an alternative.

#737. Baked sweet potato batons

Wash the sweet potato then using a sharp knife, cut off both ends and cut the sweet potato into a large cube. Depending on the size of the sweet potato, it may be possible to cut the cube into batons approximately 10 x 10 x 60 mm. Place the batons in a roasting dish that has been buttered then pour in olive oil, orange juice, grated orange zest and a spoonful or two of demerara sugar. Roast the batons in the oven, turning them over while they are cooking and add a knob of butter as they near the end of the cooking cycle. Take care not to burn the sugar in the roasting pan.

#738. Baked sweet potatoes

Cut the sweet potato into discs and parboil till just soft. Bake in butter, cinnamon, brown sugar, honey and orange juice. The orange juice will evaporate and a butter syrup will form. Take care not to let the syrup burn because of too much heat.

#739. Ginger and maple sweet potato casserole

Peel and slice the sweet potatoes into 7 mm thick slices. Line a buttered casserole dish with the slices overlapping. Between each layer, place a layer of sliced onions and grated ginger and continue until three layers are completed. Pour melted butter over the sweet potatoes along with maple syrup. Bake in the oven at 180°C until the sweet potatoes are soft.

#740. Grilled sweet potatoes

Wash the sweet potatoes and parboil in cold salted water brought to the boil. Cook for 3–4 minutes, drain and allow to cool then cut lengthways in 5–7 mm wide strips. Grill the sweet potato pieces on a barbecue to get the grill marks on each side. Serve with a lime and coriander vinaigrette.

#741. Sweet potato with pecan nuts

Wash the sweet potatoes, cut a line around the circumference of the sweet potato to allow expansion and bake in the oven till the flesh is cooked. Remove from the oven and leave to cool slightly then cut in half and scoop out the flesh. Mix the flesh with butter and seasoning and add some fresh orange juice. Spoon the flesh back into the jacket and top with chopped pecan nuts.

#742. Sweet potato fries

Cut the sweet potatoes into batons 10 x 10 x 50 mm approximately. In a mixing bowl put oil, chopped rosemary, crushed garlic and seasoning. Dip the batons through the oil mix then bake on an oven tray till cooked, turning over during the baking period.

#743. Baked sweet potatoes

Wash the sweet potato, top and tail then slice the sweet potato lengthways into eight pieces. Place in a tray, add seasoning, oil and smoked paprika and mix thoroughly so that the oil and paprika are spread through all the pieces. Bake in the oven, turning them while they are cooking. When cooked, the sweet potatoes will be soft but hold their shape. Ideal as an accompaniment to grilled meat or fish dishes or with a dip.

#744. Sweet potato bake

Peel and wash the sweet potatoes then thinly slice. Using a meatloaf tin, butter the base and sides then put two layers of sweet potato on the base. Spread with previously made caramelised onions, then place another two layers and season. Continue layering until the tin is three quarter filled. Pour in vegetable stock, which will be absorbed by the sweet potato, top with knobs of butter and press down to compact the sweet potatoes. Oven bake till a paring knife can go through the potatoes without any resistance.

#745. Sweet potato fritters

Wash the sweet potatoes and cook in boiling salted water till just cooked, which will be indicated by a slight resistance to a knife into the centre of the vegetable. Allow to cool then slice across into 10 mm slices. Make a batter using eggs, flour, oil, seasoning then leave to rest for an hour. Dip the sliced sweet potato into flour then into the batter and deep fry till golden brown. Place on kitchen paper to drain.

#746. Caramelised sweet potato

Peel and cut the sweet potato into 20 mm thick rounds. In a roasting dish, pour a little vegetable oil. Smother the sweet potato in the oil, season and bake for 15 minutes at 190°C then turn the sweet potato over. At this point, the sweet potato should be caramelising. Add to the roasting pan chopped garlic and chicken stock and reduce the liquid, which will be absorbed by the sweet potato. Allow to caramelise again and keep turning over, adding more oil if required and brown sugar.

#747. Caramelised sweet potato with tomatoes and onions

Following dish #746: Peel and cut the sweet potato into 20 mm rounds. In a roasting dish pour a little vegetable oil. Smother the sweet potato in the oil, season then bake for 15 minutes at 190°C then turn the sweet potato over. At this point the sweet potato should be caramelising. Add to the roasting pan chopped garlic and chicken stock and reduce the liquid, which will be absorbed by the sweet potato. To the roasting pan, add sliced onions and whole cherry tomatoes. The onions will caramelise with the sweet potato but add a little more oil if required and brown sugar. Season well with ground black pepper and salt.

#748. Honey and cinnamon sweet potatoes

Peel the sweet potato and cut into 20 mm dice. Parboil in boiling salted water then drain well and spoon into a baking dish. Add a knob of butter, a little cinnamon over the top and bake in the oven till cooked. When the sweet potato is soft, drizzle with runny honey and turn the sweet potato through it ensuring that the honey doesn't burn under heat.

#749. Sweet potatoes and mushrooms

Peel and slice the sweet potatoes into 7 mm thick slices. Layer them in a buttered casserole dish overlapping then on the next layer use sliced onions, mushrooms and seasoning. Continue the layers till the top is reached. There are now three options:

1. Pour over milk and cream, some of which will be absorbed by the sweet potatoes.

2. Prepare an orange citrus sauce and pour it over the sweet potatoes.

3. Prepare a mushroom sauce by making a béchamel and adding cream and mushrooms.

With all options, bake in the oven till the sweet potatoes are soft.

#750. Sliced seasoned sweet potatoes

Wash the sweet potato and with a very sharp knife cut slices through the sweet potato crossways but only three quarters of the way through. Season the sweet potato and bake in the oven till cooked then use the following fillings to go in the sweet potato:

1. Place a piece of cheese in one slit then a slice of cooked bacon in the next, alternating each time. Put the sweet potato back in the oven to heat the bacon and melt the cheese.

2. In every slit place a slice of avocado then spoon over plain yoghurt with chilli and garlic. Don't reheat.

3. Place cooked bacon slices in every slit then pour maple syrup over the sweet potato and sprinkle with chopped pecan nuts.

4. In each slit place a piece of garlic butter then spoon over aioli sauce.

5. Mix maple syrup, chopped pecans, rosemary and a pinch of cinnamon and put some into each slit.

#751. Fried green tomatoes

Slice the green tomatoes into 15 mm thick slices. On a plate spread plain flour mixed with curry powder. Dip the tomato slices into the flour, egg wash then breadcrumb and fry in oil with crushed garlic. Fry both sides then place on kitchen paper to drain.

#752. Tomato bake

Slice the tomatoes in half and place in a buttered casserole dish. In a mixing bowl, combine half a cup of mayonnaise, garlic, half a cup of grated cheddar, seasoning, basil and mix well. Spread it over the tomatoes then top with a crushed sleeve of Ritz crackers and melted butter then bake. Use as a side or as a vegetarian dish on fettuccine.

#753. Tomato casserole

Tomatoes, garlic, mayonnaise, grated cheddar cheese, bacon, oregano and Snax biscuits. Remove top of tomato and scoop out the centre. Fill with a bread stuffing including bacon, onions, oregano, mayonnaise and grated cheese. Using a sleeve of Snax biscuits, smash with a rolling pin and sprinkle them over the top then bake in the oven.

#754. Breadcrumb and cheese stuffed tomatoes

Cut the top off the tomato and with a teaspoon remove the flesh and place in a bowl. To the bowl, add fresh breadcrumbs, fried diced onions, mixed herbs, grated cheese and chopped hazelnuts. Mix well and return the stuffing back into the tomato cavity. Bake in the oven then place the top back on the tomato and serve.

#755. Roast vegetable cakes

Peel and slice root vegetables into small chunky pieces then roast in the oven with garlic, rosemary and thyme. When cooked, remove from the oven. Meanwhile prepare mashed potatoes adding butter, cream and garlic. To the mashed potatoes add the roast vegetables and roughly mash keeping some chunkiness and colour. Mould the mixture into cakes, dip through panko breadcrumbs then fry in butter and oil till brown on both sides.

#756. Roast vegetables and quinoa

Select the choice of vegetables you require such as carrots, sweet potato, broccoli, capsicum, zucchini, eggplant, chunks of onion, and cut to even-size pieces where practicable. Roast in the oven, sprinkled with olive oil, garlic, sage and thyme. Prepare the quinoa as per instructions on the packet then set aside with a lid on to keep warm. When the vegetables are cooked, add to the quinoa and mix through. Add seasoning and drizzle over balsamic vinegar and olive oil mixed.

#757. Pickled vegetables

Slice red onions very thinly along with cucumber, carrots, capsicums and mangetout (snow peas). Put red wine vinegar, salt, sugar and fennel seeds in a bowl and stir well. Pour the liquid over the sliced vegetables ensuring they are all covered.

#758. Vegetable tagine

Make chermoula. Place chickpeas, aubergines, sweet potato, pumpkin, potatoes, tomato halves and any other vegetables in a pan. Pour over chermoula, add stock, cover and cook. Serve with plain yoghurt. **Chermoula**: Roast red capsicum, chopped coriander, oil, whole cloves, smoked paprika, cumin, lemon rind and juice, garlic.

19.

AVOCADOS

#	Dish	#	Dish
759	Guacamole	768	Avocado, Walnut And Feta Salad
760	Avocado Dressing	769	Avocado With Pomegranate Seeds
761	Avocado Chips	770	Avocado And Tuna Salad
762	Avocado, Marmite, On Toast Or Avocado And Tomato On Toast	771	Avocado And Grapefruit Salsa
763	Bacon, Avocado, Garlic Crouton	772	Avocado And Prawn Salad
764	Smoked Chicken And Avocado Sandwiches	773	Avocado Half
765	Avocado Pickles	774	Avocado Spread
766	Avocado Segments Wrapped In Bacon	775	Avocado Mashed With Sweet Chilli Sauce
767	Avocado Salsa	776	Avocado Enchiladas

#759. Guacamole

Mash the avocados and ensure no lumps. Add minced red onions, lemon juice, chilli flakes, chopped coriander, seasoning and mix in. Spoon into a serving dish.

#760. Avocado dressing

Mash the avocado flesh in a processor and add garlic, olive oil, lime juice and seasoning. Should it require thinning down, add a little water.

#761. Avocado chips

Remove the flesh from the avocado skin using a dessertspoon, keeping each half intact. Slice the flesh into segments then handling carefully, pass through flour, egg wash and breadcrumbs. Place on a baking tray lined with baking paper and bake in a hot oven till the breadcrumbs are browned. Serve with a dipping sauce.

#762. Avocado and Marmite on toast or avocado and tomato on toast

Generally viewed as a snack meal, avocado and Marmite on hot buttered wheat toast is something you love or hate. From the toaster, butter the toast then add a thin layer of Marmite. Add a layer of avocado which has been mashed with seasoning, balsamic vinegar and crushed garlic. That's it.

Avocado and tomato on hot buttered wheat toast is also a great snack item. Spread the hot toast with plenty of butter, then a layer of mashed avocado as above and then a layer of sliced fresh tomatoes. Add cheese by choice.

#763. Bacon, avocado, garlic crouton

Slice streaky bacon into small batons and fry till brown in oil and butter then allow to cool. Mash the avocado with crushed garlic, balsamic vinegar, lemon juice, seasoning then add the cold bacon pieces. Spread the avocado onto toasted grain bread brushed with garlic butter or onto ciabatta bread.

#764. Smoked chicken and avocado sandwiches

Slice smoked chicken into thin slices. Spread on toasted grain bread or buns the mashed avocado that has been mixed with mayonnaise and seasonings. Top with the smoked chicken, sliced brie and serve.

#765. Avocado pickles

Cut the avocado in half, remove the stone and remove the flesh with a dessertspoon and slice. In a saucepan, boil water, white vinegar, sugar and salt to make a brine then leave to cool. Add whole garlic bulbs and chilli flakes to the brine. When cold, add coriander leaf to the brine then neatly arrange the avocado slices in the jar and seal. Use on salad or with vegetables.

#766. Avocado segments wrapped in bacon

Remove half the avocado flesh from the skin and cut into segments. Wrap the individual segments in slices of streaky bacon, lay them on a baking tray covered in baking paper and bake in the oven until the bacon has cooked.

#767. Avocado salsa

Remove the flesh from the avocado and cut into dice. Dice fresh tomatoes and red onions the same way then drizzle the salsa with a balsamic vinegar, olive oil and lemon juice dressing.

#768. Avocado, walnut and feta salad

Lay a salad platter with lettuce leaves of choice such as iceberg, rocket, romaine. Cut the avocado in half and spoon over the flesh onto the lettuce. Cut feta cheese into 15 mm bite-size cubes and spread them over the bed of leaves. Top with precooked croutons then sprinkle with chopped walnuts. Drizzle with vinaigrette and serve. Sprinkle the avocado with lemon juice if the salad is not going to be consumed immediately.

#769. Avocado with pomegranate seeds

Cut the pomegranate in half and hold one half upside down over a mixing bowl then hit the skin with a spoon so the seeds fall into the bowl. Dress a plate with lettuce leaves of choice, top with diced avocado then sprinkle over chopped pecan nuts and pomegranate seeds and drizzle over a vinaigrette. The pomegranate seeds add a sharp tangy taste twist to the salad.

#770. Avocado and tuna salad

In a mixing bowl, place diced avocado, sliced cucumber, sliced red onions and sliced sun-dried tomatoes. With fresh tuna, fry quickly on a griddle plate browning on both sides and leaving griddle marks. When cold, cut the tuna steaks into 30 mm size pieces. Spread the salad over a plate that has a layer of lettuce on the base. Place the tuna on top along with precooked croutons. Drizzle with a balsamic vinaigrette and serve. Canned tuna can also be used in the salad.

#771. Avocado and grapefruit salsa

Remove the avocado flesh from the skin, keeping the flesh in the shape of the fruit. Slice the avocado flesh into segments then peel the grapefruit and segment the grapefruit. Place the avocado and grapefruit into a bowl and intertwine the different segments for presentation. In a frypan, caramelise bacon batons and leave to go cold. Sprinkle them over the avocado and grapefruit, drizzle with lemon juice and a dressing.

#772. Avocado and prawn salad

Place washed salad vegetables of choice such as iceberg lettuce, rocket, baby spinach on a small plate. Top with prawns that have been deveined, shell removed and fried, then diced avocado flesh. Prepare a vinaigrette of white wine vinegar, olive oil, chopped parsley, lemon juice and seasoning.

#773. Avocado half

To one half of an avocado add Worcestershire sauce, mayonnaise, Tabasco, lemon juice and seasoning. Mix into the avocado flesh and serve with crackers.

#774. Avocado spread

Remove the flesh from the avocado and place into a mixing bowl. Add chilli flakes, olive oil, lemon juice and seasoning, mix well then spread on toast or crackers.

#775. Avocado mashed with sweet chilli sauce

Split the avocado, scoop out the flesh and place in a mixing bowl. Add sweet chilli sauce, a touch of chilli flakes, lime juice and seasoning. Mix well and use as a spread on crackers, as a filling for potatoes/sweet potatoes or as a dip.

#776. Avocado enchiladas

Mashed avocados with chopped cashews, lemon juice and cooked chicken pieces. Mix together with an oil-based mayonnaise and spoon into the enchilada cups formed by sitting in muffin tray tins.

20.

SWEET POTATO AND POTATO SLICES

#	Dish	#	Dish
777	Pork And Peanut Butter	786	Preparation Of The Potato Slices
778	Bacon And Scrambled Eggs	787	Fried Pork And Peanut Butter
779	Baked Beans And Bacon	788	Maple Syrup, Bacon
780	Brie, Walnuts And Honey	789	Baked Beans, Bacon And Relish
781	Mayonnaise, Chicken	790	Brie, Honey And Walnuts
782	Avocado And Balsamic Vinegar	791	Mayonnaise, Chicken And Salad
783	Avocado And Bacon	792	Avocado And Balsamic Vinegar
784	Mozzarella And Tomato	793	Grated Cheese And Parmesan
785	Smoked Chicken And Blue Cheese		

Sweet potato slices

The sweet potato is peeled and sliced and then either fried in oil and butter or toasted in a toaster till cooked. Once cooked and while hot, spread with butter or the sauce that is going to be used. Sweet potato slices can be used as a side vegetable or as an accompaniment to drinks. Use sweet potatoes that have a good diameter and are around 12 cm long. This will then give a good serving. The slices can be treated like bruschetta and decorated accordingly.

#777. Sweet potato slices with pork and peanut butter

Spread with peanut butter then top with fried pork pieces that have been fried in oil, butter, grated root ginger, garlic, soy and hoisin sauce.

#778. Sweet potato slices with bacon and scrambled eggs

Spread the sweet potato slices with butter then spoon over ketchup. Lay crispy bacon on top then scrambled eggs.

#779. Sweet potato slices with bake beans and bacon

Spread the sweet potato with fruit chutney then hot baked beans that have been squashed with a potato masher, crispy bacon pieces and a fried egg.

#780. Sweet potato slices with brie, walnuts and honey

Spread the sweet potato with aioli, then slices of brie, chopped walnuts and drizzled with honey.

#781. Sweet potato slices with mayonnaise and chicken

Spread the sweet potato with mayonnaise then lay it on a made-up chicken salad, topped with cherry tomatoes and sliced spring onions.

#782. Sweet potato slices with avocado and balsamic vinegar

Spread the base with mashed avocado that has been mixed with balsamic vinegar then top with corn salsa.

#783. Sweet potato slices with avocado and bacon

Butter the base then add sliced tomato, mashed avocado and crispy bacon pieces.

#784. Sweet potato slices with mozzarella and tomato

Drizzle with dressing then top with mozzarella slices, tomato slices and basil.

#785. Sweet potato slices with smoked chicken and blue cheese

Spread with blue cheese then top with slices of smoked chicken, rocket, sliced tomato and crumbled blue cheese.

Potato Slices

786. Preparation of the potato slices

Cut the ends off the potato then slice into 8 mm thick slices lengthways being very careful while using the knife. Take two slices of the potato and fry until it is browned and cooked through. Then use the following toppings on the slices.

#787. Potato slices with fried pork and peanut butter

Spread with peanut butter and fried pork fingers. Add chopped coriander.

#788. Potato slices with maple syrup and bacon

Spread with maple syrup, top with crispy bacon then scrambled eggs.

#789. Potato slices with baked beans, bacon and relish

Heat then mash baked beans and spread on the potato. Top with crispy bacon, fruit relish and a fried egg.

#790. Potato slices with brie, honey and walnuts

Onto the hot potato slice, place a slice of brie, drizzle with honey and chopped walnuts.

#791. Potato slices with mayonnaise, chicken and salad

Spoon on a layer of mayonnaise then top with chopped chicken and salad.

#792. Potato slices with avocado and balsamic vinegar

Spread over a layer of mashed avocado that has been mixed with balsamic vinegar and top with a corn salsa.

#793. Potato slices with grated cheese and Parmesan

Sprinkle over grated cheese and Parmesan then grill.

21.

POTATOES

#	Dish	#	Dish
794	Scalloped Garlic Potatoes	811	Grilled Potatoes
795	Roasted Mashed Potato Cake	812	Sliced Potatoes, Courgettes And Capsicums
796	Hasselback Potato	813	Oven Baked Chips
797	Polenta And Parmesan Crumbed Potatoes	814	Roasted Potatoes In Duck Fat
798	Baked Potatoes Caprese	815	Potato With Lemon
799	Baked Potatoes With Sour Cream And Red Onions	816	Baked Garlic Potatoes
800	Baked Potatoes In Muffin Tins	817	Baked Jacket Potatoes
801	Mashed Potatoes With Wasabi	818	Hash Browns Baked
802	Mashed Potatoes And Chickpeas	819	Roast Potatoes With Sumac
803	Mashed Potato And Cauliflower	820	Roast Cubed Potatoes
804	Baked Potato Skins With Cheese And Bacon	821	Potatoes With Chimichurri Sauce
805	Grated Potatoes And Pinenuts	822	Parmesan Potato Wedges
806	Cajun Roasted Potatoes	823	Stuffed Potatoes With Garlic And Cheese
807	Smashed Roasted Potatoes	824	Blue Cheese Potato Gratin
808	Smashed Roasted Potatoes With Paprika And Lemon	825	Balsamic Roasted Potato Wedges
809	Potato Wedges Wrapped In Bacon	826	Battered Chips
810	Lemon And Garlic Roasted Potatoes		

#794. Scalloped garlic potatoes

Peel and slice the potatoes but as each potato is sliced, keep it together as in its whole shape by using toothpicks. Rub a casserole dish with butter then carefully place the potatoes in so that they maintain their original shape but are loosely held together. Chop garlic, rosemary and add mixed herbs then place in a saucepan of melted butter and heat on a low heat for 2 minutes. Spoon it over the potatoes and bake in the oven. When the potatoes are cooked, sprinkle over Parmesan and grated cheese and grill.

#795. Roasted mashed potato cake

Make a mashed potato keeping it quite dry but add butter, seasonings and a little cream. Spoon the mixture into an egg ring and pack tightly. Add cubes of cheese then remove the ring. Quickly fry streaky bacon, wrap it around the potato cake then bake.

#796. Hasselback potatoes

Using large potatoes, peel and cut in half lengthways. Place a wooden spoon on either side of the potato half which is cut side down, then slice every 5 mm down to the wooden spoons so that the potato is not cut through. Brush the potato with melted butter and roast in the oven in oil and butter until golden brown. The heat of the oven will cause the cuts to open out. Place whatever fillings are desired in the slits, for example cheese slices, cooked bacon pieces, sliced ham, sliced tomatoes or salami. Return to the oven, heat and serve.

#797. Polenta and Parmesan crumbed potatoes

Cut the potatoes into large chunky pieces approximately 25 mm in size then place in cold water, add salt, bring to the boil and cook till just soft. Mix together polenta and grated Parmesan cheese. Pour olive oil in with the potatoes, add polenta and Parmesan together and ensure all the potatoes are covered with the crumb mix. Pour oil into a frypan and fry the potatoes till brown all over. If there are a lot of potatoes to be cooked, do so in batches so the fat does not go cold and all the crumbs come off the potatoes.

#798. Baked potatoes Caprese

Bake large unpeeled potatoes in the oven till cooked through. Remove from the oven and slice down the centre with a knife 20 mm deep to create an opening in the cooked potato. Open out the potato then brush with garlic butter. Lay slices of mozzarella, cherry tomatoes halves and basil leaves in the opening. Wrap in tinfoil and bake for a further 10 minutes then serve.

#799. Baked potatoes with sour cream and red onions

Bake the potatoes as in #798. Make a slice through the middle then place in sliced red onions and top with sour cream. Wrap in foil, bake for 5 minutes then serve.

#800. Baked potatoes in muffin tins

Select the same-sized potatoes, wash, cut one end so that it stands upright and place in the muffin tins with the length being the high point. Bake in the oven till cooked. Cut off the top and with a teaspoon remove some of the cooked potato. In a bowl, mix the removed potato with cream, cream cheese, sliced ham, garlic and seasoning then spoon back into the potatoes. Return to the oven and bake for 10 minutes. Top with grated cheese and grill till the cheese is melted then serve. Any fillings can be devised to stuff the centre of the potato.

#801. Mashed potatoes with wasabi

Peel and cut the potatoes into rough equal sizes so that they all cook at the same time. When cooked, drain the potatoes well then place the saucepan back on the element to dry out the potatoes. Mash the potatoes with a masher or a ricer adding seasoning, butter and heated cream. While mixing in the butter and cream, add the wasabi in small measures to reach the desired taste.

#802. Mashed potatoes and chickpeas

As in dish #801, cook the potatoes and mash with butter and cream. The chickpeas can be added as hummus, simply as canned chickpeas that have been drained and washed, or as chickpeas roasted in the oven in oil, cumin, coriander and garlic. The latter presentation offers a brown chickpea against white mashed potatoes and a crunch and alternative textures.

#803. Mashed potato and cauliflower

Boil the peeled potatoes and cauliflower in the same saucepan till they are both cooked then drain well and mash together. Add fresh avocado, crushed garlic, chopped parsley, seasoning and olive oil. Mash well and serve.

#804. Baked potato skins with cheese and bacon

Wash the potatoes then cut the ends and sides of the potato off leaving around 10 mm of potato on each skin piece. Red-skinned potatoes are ideal for this. In a roasting tray, put diced bacon pieces and bake in the oven so that the fat renders off the bacon. Remove the bacon then place the potato skins flesh side down and bake so that they absorb the bacon flavour and fat. When cooked, turn the potatoes over, top with grated cheese and the cooked bacon then grill briefly in the oven. Top with cream cheese and sliced spring onions.

#805. Grated potatoes and pine nuts

Peel and grate the potatoes, put into a tea towel and squeeze out the liquid. Stir into the potato chopped dry-fried pine nuts, chopped coriander along with a pinch of chilli flakes. Mix in flour and stir then fry in oil and butter.

#806. Cajun roasted potatoes

Peel and cut the potatoes so they are of uniform size for roasting. Parboil the potatoes for 4 minutes in boiling salted water then drain through a colander. While draining in the colander, place a lid over the top and shake them well to rough up the sides. Place into a roasting pan with hot oil, crushed garlic and sprinkle over Cajun spice. Roast in the oven till the potatoes are crisp and brown then serve.

#807. Smashed roasted potatoes

Using potatoes of the same size, wash away any dirt and boil in salted water until cooked. Drain and place in a roasting tray then using your thumb, press down on the potato until it splits and flattens down slightly. Pour olive oil into the roasting dish and drizzle garlic butter and pesto over the top of the potato and bake. Remove from the oven and spoon sour cream and grated cheddar cheese over the top and grill till the cheese melts. Top with sliced spring onions and diced raw onions.

#808 Smashed roasted potatoes with paprika and lemon

Cook the potatoes as in dish #807. Smash the potato on a chopping board, sprinkle with butter, paprika and sliced lemon zest then bake for 10 minutes to crisp the potato.

#809. Potato wedges wrapped in bacon

Wash the potato then cut in half. Cut the half into four wedges and rub with oil then dip into a mix of pepper, salt and paprika. Wrap each wedge in a piece of streaky bacon then place on a baking tray. Bake slowly in the oven till cooked then serve immediately.

#810. Lemon and garlic roasted potatoes

Into a mixing bowl put olive oil, crushed garlic, lemon juice and finely sliced lemon zest. Mix well then add small potatoes that have been cut in half and leave for an hour. Heat a roasting pan on an element, add the potatoes with some of the oil and toss them around then bake in the oven at 200°C till cooked.

#811. Grilled potatoes

Into a mixing bowl put olive oil, lemon juice and grated lemon zest, chopped rosemary and crushed garlic. Slice the potatoes into 10 mm slices then place into the oil mixture. Using either a barbecue or a ribbed frypan, cook the potato slices, brushing with the oil as they cook. Place on a serving dish and top with cherry tomato halves, diced feta and black olives.

#812. Sliced potatoes, courgettes and capsicums

Peel and slice the potatoes, slice the courgettes and roughly chop the capsicums. Mix well in a bowl then add seasoning, oil and crushed garlic. Spoon half the mixture into a casserole dish, sprinkle with cheese then add the other half and more cheese. Add knobs of butter then pour in cream and bake in the oven till the potatoes are cooked.

#813. Oven-baked chips

Peel and slice the potatoes into the size of French fries. In a bowl, whisk olive oil, Italian seasoning, paprika and seasoning. Pour it over the chips, mix well then oven bake.

#814. Potatoes roasted in duck fat

Select potatoes of similar size and peel. Put into a saucepan with cold water and bring to the boil. When three quarters cooked, pour the potatoes into a colander and shake vigorously to roughen up the surfaces. On an element, place a roasting dish and spoon in duck fat to heat. Add the potatoes and shake the pan then oven bake, turning the potatoes while they are in the oven. Bake till golden brown and cooked through.

#815. Potato with lemon

Peel and dice potatoes into 20 mm cubes then cook in boiling salted water till just about cooked. Drain and pour into a buttered casserole dish. Top with diced onions, crushed garlic, lemon slices and bake in the oven till brown.

#816. Baked garlic potatoes

Wash the potatoes and cut each one into eight pieces. Dry them off on kitchen paper then place in a mixing bowl with oil and crushed garlic and spread out onto a roasting tray. Bake in the oven and turn over while they are cooking so they brown on all sides. While they are cooking, add to a mixing bowl panko breadcrumbs, grated Parmesan cheese, seasoning, melted butter and chopped parsley. When the potatoes are cooked, sprinkle with the crumb mix and leave in the oven for another 5 minutes then serve.

#817. Baked jacket potatoes

Cut an X in the top of the unpeeled, washed potatoes and bake in the oven till cooked through. Press the potato where the X has been cut and the potato flesh will open out. Drizzle into the flesh olive oil, seasoning and plain yoghurt.

#818. Hash browns baked

Hash browns can be either store-bought frozen or homemade. Lay the hash browns into a buttered casserole dish. In a frypan cook out diced bacon, garlic and sliced onions and spread over the top of the hash browns. Bake in the oven and when cooked, top with grated cheddar cheese and grill.

#819. Roast potatoes with sumac

Peel and cut the potatoes into similar-size pieces and place in a mixing bowl. Pour in olive oil, sumac and paprika. Mix the potatoes and ingredients well so that each potato is well covered. Place in a roasting pan with chopped garlic and cook at 190°C, turning during the roasting period.

#820. Roast cubed potatoes

Wash and peel the potatoes and cut into cubes 20 x 20 mm. Place in cold water and bring to the boil, drain then place in a baking tray and cook at 180°C in butter and oil, turning regularly so that all sides brown. Sprinkle over dried mixed herbs, thyme and cracked black pepper. When cooked, spoon onto a serving platter then drizzle over a dressing of capers, lemon juice and finely diced lemon zest, mustard, chopped black olives mixed in olive oil and red wine vinegar.

#821. Potatoes with yoghurt and chimichurri sauce

Using small potatoes of similar size, cook in boiling salted water. Drain well and press each one so that the skin breaks. Spoon over chimichurri sauce then natural yoghurt.

#822. Parmesan potato wedges

Slice unpeeled potatoes into wedges, fry in oil to give them a brown colouring then finish off cooking in a baking tray in the oven. On the baking tray, sprinkle Parmesan cheese and add raw onion rings. Once the potatoes are picking up a crust of the Parmesan on the pan base, add a tomato-based pasta sauce along with sour cream mixed in. Bake in the oven till the potatoes are cooked then serve.

#823. Stuffed potatoes with garlic and cheese

Wash large, unpeeled, equal-sized potatoes and with a sharp knife cut a thin line around the outside then bake in the oven till cooked. Allow to cool slightly then cut the potato in half through the expanded cut line you made previously. Scoop out the cooked potato but leaving a small amount still lining the potato shell. Place the potato flesh in a bowl, add crushed garlic, butter, grated cheese, seasoning and chopped parsley then mix well. Spoon back into the half potato shells, top with melted butter and grated cheese and bake in the oven for 10 minutes then grill to brown the cheese.

#824. Blue cheese potato gratin

Slice the peeled potatoes into 5–10 mm slices and place a layer on the base of a buttered casserole dish. Season and top with crushed garlic then add another layer of potatoes and garlic up to three layers. Pour over fresh cream till it just finishes under the top layer. Place in the oven with a tinfoil covering and cook until the potatoes are cooked through. Top the potatoes with crumbled blue cheese and a little grated cheddar. Return to the oven minus the tinfoil and grill for the last 5 minutes or until the top of the casserole is brown from the cheese being cooked. Grated cheese or crumbled blue cheese could be used between each layer for a stronger taste and béchamel could be used that has cream added as a way to reduce costs.

#825. Balsamic roasted potato wedges

Wash the potatoes but don't peel. Cut the potatoes in half then cut each half into four wedges. Place in a mixing bowl and pour over olive oil, balsamic vinegar, crushed garlic, dried mixed herbs and seasoning. Place the wedges in a roasting pan and cook at 200°C, turning every 15 minutes so the potatoes absorb the oil liquid and brown all over. Drizzle in more of the oil as it cooks.

#826. Battered chips

Peel the potatoes and slice into 10–15 mm sized chips. Precook the potatoes in boiling water for 4 minutes then drain and cool quickly. Prepare a batter from flour, eggs, milk, oil and baking powder. Rub the fries through seasoned flour then dip them into the batter and deep fry. Drain on kitchen paper then serve.

22.

VEGETABLE
AND POTATO
MISCELLANEOUS

#	Dish	#	Dish
827	Spinach And Garlic Potato Patties	849	Cauliflower Fritters With Bacon
828	Cauliflower Fritters	850	Potato Rosti
829	Cauliflower Fritters#2	851	Stuffed Portobello Mushrooms
830	Sweet Potato With Chorizo And Haloumi		**Potato Skin Fillings**
831	Polenta Chips	852	Cheeseburger Potato Skins
832	Cheese And Mashed Potato Pancakes	853	Bacon And Avocado Potato Skins
833	Potato And Lentil Patties	854	Avocado And Tomato Potato Skins
834	Roasted Capsicums With Feta And Black Olives	855	Bacon And Cheese Skins
835	Braised Capsicums With Garlic And Capers	856	Potato Skins With Prawns And Avocado
836	Sweetcorn And Ham Fritters	857	Potato Skins With Chorizo And Bacon
837	Potato Pancakes	858	Pancetta, Tomato And Feta
838	Avocado, Bacon And Egg	859	Broccoli And Cheese Sauce
839	Fried Potato Spice Mix	860	Meatballs In Potato Skins
840	Chicken Stuffed Capsicums	861	Cheese, Herb And Bacon Potato Skins
841	Vegetable Loaf	862	Potato Skin Sandwiches
842	Potato Crepes	863	Potato Skin Sandwich #2
843	Mashed Potatoes In Cabbage Leaves	864	Potato Skin Sandwich #3
844	Mashed Potato In Cabbage Leaves With Cheese Sauce	865	Potato, Sweetcorn And Zucchini Frittata

#827. Spinach and garlic potato patties

Prepare mashed potato keeping the mixture quite dry when adding butter and cream. In a frypan with 3 mm water, quickly wilt spinach adding a knob of butter and sliced garlic. Drain well and wring out in a dry tea towel. Put the spinach in with the mashed potato with a pinch of nutmeg and an egg. Mix well then shape into patties. Fry in butter and oil till brown on both sides then serve.

#828. Cauliflower fritters

Cauliflower cut into small florets, streaky bacon, Parmesan grated, self-raising flour, breadcrumbs, beaten eggs, garlic, chopped parsley, oil. Par-cook the cauliflower florets then drain. Fry bacon. Combine cauliflower, bacon, Parmesan, flour, breadcrumbs, eggs, garlic and parsley until a thick batter is reached. With a large metal spoon, place a spoonful at a time into a frypan with hot oil and butter. Turn over and brown the other side.

#829. Cauliflower fritters No. 2

Dry the cauliflower pieces after washing, place into a food processor and blitz till it looks like small rice granules. Add seasoning, garlic, onion, parsley, flour, grated Parmesan, a beaten egg then mix well. Spoon the fritter mix into a frypan and fry in an oil/ butter mix. Serve with yoghurt mixed with harissa and chopped coriander.

#830. Sweet potato with chorizo and haloumi

Peel and cut the sweet potato into cubes and cook in boiling salted water. Drain when nearly cooked and place on oven tray. Drizzle with oil, add garlic cloves, chilli and put in the oven. Slice chorizo into pieces and fry then add to sweet potato. In a frypan, fry mushrooms in butter, add chopped capsicums, smoked red capsicums and diced tomatoes. Add all to the sweet potato and season well. Fry sliced haloumi. Place all on a presentation tray, drizzle with olive oil and serve.

#831. Polenta chips

Milk, garlic, polenta, chopped sage leaves, Parmesan, seasoning. Heat milk and garlic then gradually whisk in polenta, reduce heat and keep stirring. Add Parmesan and press into a greased tray. Refrigerate then cut into chips and deep fry.

#832. Cheese and mashed potato pancakes

An ideal means of using any leftover mashed potato should there be any, however prepare mashed potatoes keeping the mixture on the dry side so that it can be moulded and holds its shape. Adding dry breadcrumbs or flour will assist. Into the mashed potato, add grated cheddar cheese, chopped parsley, sweated diced onions and seasoning. Mix the ingredients really well then mould the potato into 60 x 20 mm cakes, place on a baking sheet and put in the fridge to firm up. Dip through flour, egg wash and breadcrumbs then fry in oil till golden brown on both sides.

#833. Potato and lentil patties

Use leftover mashed potatoes or boil potatoes and prepare

mashed potatoes keeping the mix quite dry. Cook orange lentils till soft, drain well and add to the mashed potatoes. In a frypan, sweat off diced onions, garlic and add to the potato mash along with chopped parsley, seasoning and a beaten egg. Shape the patties and place on baking paper then leave in the fridge to firm up. Fry in oil and butter till brown on both sides.

#834. Roasted capsicums with feta and black olives

Cut the capsicums in half and remove the pith and seeds. Place a knob of butter inside then add a few canned chickpeas, black olives, fried onions and cherry tomato halves. Drizzle with olive oil, season then bake the capsicums until soft. Top with cubes of feta and basil leaves.

#835. Braised capsicums with garlic and capers

Cut the capsicums in half lengthways and remove pith and seeds. Place in a casserole dish and top with olive oil, chicken stock, anchovy fillets, capers and seasoning. Bake for 10 minutes at 180°C or till the capsicums are soft then remove from the oven. Drizzle with balsamic vinegar and serve.

#836. Sweetcorn and ham fritters

An ideal method of using up ham leftover from the Christmas celebrations. Pour a can of creamed sweetcorn into a mixing bowl and add to it chopped ham pieces around 10 x 10 mm cubes. In a mixing bowl, beat an egg with milk, oil then add flour, seasoning and crushed garlic. The batter should be quite thick. Then add the sweetcorn mixture to the batter. Heat oil and butter in a frypan then using a large spoon, place some of the corn mixture into the pan. Cook on both sides then place on kitchen paper to drain. Serve with crispy bacon slices.

#837. Potato pancakes

Prepare mashed potato adding salt, pepper, egg, flour, crushed garlic and mix well. Shape into small cakes approximately 60 mm in diameter then fry in butter with a little oil added. Fry on both sides, drain on kitchen paper and serve.

#838. Avocado, bacon and egg

Cover the inside of a small bowl with cling wrap then break an egg into it. Spin the egg around to make a seal then poach the egg in water for 4 minutes but keep it soft boiled. Cut the avocado in half and remove the stone and the flesh from the skin keeping the flesh whole. Place the freshly poached egg in the hole where the stone was. Put the other half of the flesh back to form a whole fruit again. Wrap in streaky bacon and fry in oil. Cut the avocado in half and serve.

#839. Fried potato spice mix

In a bowl, mix paprika, cayenne, thyme, garlic and onion powder along with salt and pepper. Using similar-size small potatoes, cook in boiling salted water till just cooked. Drain in a colander, dry and deep fry. Once the potatoes have been removed from the deep fryer, sprinkle over the mixture and toss the potatoes so to mix it through them all.

#840. Chicken stuffed capsicums

Slice the capsicums in half lengthways, then remove the pith and seeds. In a bowl, mix shredded cooked chicken, cream cheese, chopped chives, grated cheese, add seasoning and stir well. Spoon the mix into the half capsicum shells, bake and serve.

#841. Vegetable loaf

Grate courgettes and carrots. Sift flour, salt, cayenne, cumin, paprika and mustard then add grated cheese. Beat eggs with milk and melted butter then add to the flour and grated vegetables. Pour into a baking loaf tin and bake for 45 minutes at 180°C.

#842. Potato crepes

Grate the potatoes into a bowl then dry in a tea towel. Beat an egg and milk in a mixing bowl then add flour, baking powder and whisk to a smooth batter that holds well to the back of a spoon. Mix the batter into the grated potatoes, add seasoning, chopped parsley and ensure all is well mixed in. In a hot frypan, pour oil then batter to make small crepes 80 mm in diameter. Use the crepe to serve other vegetables on or serve with cream cheese on top.

#843. Mashed potatoes in cabbage leaves

Prepare a mashed potato mix adding butter, garlic, chopped parsley but keeping the mixture quite dry. Remove the outside leaves of a whole cabbage, cut away the white hard stalk area in the shape of a V then par-cook the leaves in boiling salted water till softened. Plunge into iced water to stop the cooking of the leaves then dry and place on a chopping board. Into the cold mashed potato add a beaten egg, mix well then shape some of the potato into a cylinder. Brush the cabbage leaf with melted butter then place the potato on top and fold the leaf into a package. Place into a buttered casserole seam side down. Brush them with butter and bake quickly in the oven then under a grill. Cooked bacon or tomatoes could also be added to the potatoes.

#844. Mashed potatoes in cabbage leaves with cheese sauce

Prepare the potato filling and the cabbage leaves as in dish #843.

Add any different ingredients to the potato or inside the cabbage leaf as required then fold. Prepare a cheese sauce and spoon it over the top of each cabbage leaf but don't fill the casserole with the sauce as it could cause the cabbage rolls to break apart. Top with grated cheese, bake then grill in the oven before serving.

#845. Cannellini beans and bacon

In a frypan, cook diced onions and garlic in oil then add bacon pieces and rosemary. Once brown, add diced tomatoes and chicken stock. Reduce then add the cannellini beans, season and stir.

#846. Crumbed ham and cheese potato balls

Using cold mashed potato, place into a mixing bowl and add grated cheese and sliced ham. Mix into the potato along with seasoning and chopped parsley. Mould the mixture into round balls. Put through flour, egg wash and panko breadcrumbs and deep fry.

#847. Corn and bacon fritters

Prepare a batter of eggs, flour, milk, seasoning and beat well. Fry chopped onion and bacon pieces and leave to cool then add to the batter along with chopped coriander, corn kernels, grated cheese and miso paste. Fry the fritters in oil, cooking both sides, then drain on kitchen paper.

#848. Crostini with meatballs

Cut a baguette into slices and toast. Rub with garlic butter. Place a small cooked meatball on top, add tomato sauce, grated cheese and grill briefly.

#849. Cauliflower fritters with bacon

Cut the cauliflower into florets and cook in boiling salted water until soft. Place quickly under cold water then chop the cauliflower into smaller pieces. Place the cauliflower in a bowl along with chopped capsicum, chopped parsley, crushed garlic, a pinch of chilli flakes and self-raising flour, mix in then add eggs and beat to a thick mix. Slowly pour in milk and stir until the batter thickens and holds on the back of a spoon. Put oil into a frypan, spoon in the batter and brown on both sides. Once cooked through, place on kitchen paper to drain. Serve with plain yoghurt and chopped coriander.

#850. Potato rosti

Peel and grate the potato and remove all the moisture in a tea towel. Add fried onion and seasoning to the mix. Spoon onto an oiled baking sheet and press down so that they spread out or fry in oil and butter in a frypan. Serve under meat or fish.

#851. Stuffed portobello mushrooms

Remove the stalks from the mushrooms, brush with butter and grill in the oven. Dice onions, fresh tomatoes, garlic and fry in a frypan in oil and butter till lightly brown. Cut sirloin or fillet steak into goujons or little finger-sized pieces then fry in hot oil but keep them rare. Spoon the onion mixture into the mushroom then top with the steak, a cherry tomato and a slice of bocconcini. Bake briefly in the oven then serve.

Potato skin fillings and toppings

With a sharp knife cut a slit around the circumference of the unpeeled potatoes lengthways then place in a baking dish. Bake the potatoes in their skins and when cooked, cut in half, scoop out the potato flesh and hold in another bowl. Leave the potato skin with 4–5 mm of potato inside the shell so that it holds its shape and doesn't collapse. Brush with melted butter then add fillings.

#852. Cheeseburger potato skins

Bake the potatoes in their skins, cut in half and scoop out the potato flesh. Prepare a Bolognese sauce with beef mince, garlic, Italian herbs, tomato paste and tomatoes. When cooked, line the base of the potatoes with the sauce, top with sliced fresh tomatoes, grated mozzarella cheese and bake.

#853. Bacon and avocado potato skins

As in dish #852, bake the potatoes, cut in half lengthwise and remove most of the potato flesh. Fry the bacon in a frypan till it is crisp then set aside. Remove the flesh from the avocado, mash with balsamic vinegar and seasoning then fill the potato skins. Top with bacon pieces and serve.

#854. Avocado and tomato potato skins

Deep fry the potato skins (see 'Potato skin fillings and toppings' above) and place on kitchen paper to absorb the excess oil, then place in a roasting pan. Chop fresh tomatoes, place on the cooked potato skins and bake in the oven. Once reheated, spoon onto serving platters and top with sliced avocado segments.

#855. Bacon and cheese skins

Using some of the potato flesh that has been removed from the baked potatoes, mix with butter, pepper and salt then spoon back into the shells. Top with cooked bacon pieces and grated cheese then oven bake.

#856. Prawns and avocado

Mash the avocado with some of the potato flesh, butter and seasoning then spoon back into the potato shells. Fry the prawns in butter quickly and place on top of the avocado. Top with mayonnaise and chopped spring onions.

#857. Potato skins with chorizo and bacon

Deep fry the potato skins (see 'Potato skin fillings and toppings' above) and place on kitchen paper to drain. Slice chorizo into 15 mm pieces and fry in oil, garlic and smoked paprika. Chop the bacon into small pieces and fry with the chorizo. Once the chorizo and bacon are cooked, spoon onto the deep-fried potato skins and drizzle over the oil from the chorizo. Place in the oven for 10 minutes to reheat all the ingredients then serve.

#858. Pancetta, tomato and feta

Bake the potatoes in their skin till they are cooked through. Cut in half lengthways and spoon out the cooked potato flesh leaving a thin lining of potato around the walls of the skins. In a bowl, mix some of the potato flesh with diced tomato and feta cubes and spoon back into the potato shells. Roll the pancetta and arrange on top then bake in the oven.

#859. Broccoli and cheese sauce

Prepare the potatoes as in #858. Make a cheese sauce using a selection of cheeses desired. Cut the florets from the broccoli and cook in boiling salted water until just cooked then drain and plunge into cold water to stop the cooking. Mix the broccoli with the cheese sauce and spoon into the potato shells, cover with grated cheese, crumbled feta, bake then serve.

#860. Meatballs in potato skins

Prepare and cook beef meatballs. Using potatoes or sweet potatoes, wash without peeling then bake in the oven till the flesh is cooked. Allow to cool then cut in half lengthways and scoop out the flesh. Make mashed potato patties out of the scooped-out flesh. Leave approximately 8 mm of flesh on the inside of the skins, brush with melted butter and grill to harden the skins. Place the potato skins on the serving plate then spoon the meatballs and sauce into the skins and serve with the potato patties.

#861. Cheese, herb and bacon potato skins

Deep fry the potato skins till golden brown (see 'Potato skin fillings and toppings' above), place on kitchen paper to drain then place in a roasting pan. Cut streaky bacon into batons and fry in oil till caramelised. Spoon them over the potato skins and then sprinkle over grated cheese and bake in the oven till the cheese has melted. Season then add chopped parsley and a touch of cayenne if desired.

#862. Potato skin sandwich

Bake a potato in its skin and when soft allow to cool then cut in half lengthways. Scoop out the flesh into a bowl but leave about 8 mm of potato still on the skin. Trim the bottom off one half so the potato lies flat on a chopping board. Spread with mayonnaise, cheese, fried bacon, sliced tomato and avocado. Place the other half of the potato back on top and serve with a salad.

#863. Potato skin sandwich No. 2

Prepare the potato skin as in #862 then spread with sun-dried tomato pesto, mayonnaise, ham, rocket and drizzle with balsamic vinegar. Top with the other half.

#864. Potato skin sandwich No. 3

Prepare the potato skin as in #862 then on one half add a fried hamburger, mayonnaise and mustard, rocket, sliced beetroot and sliced tomato. Top with the other half and drizzle with a dressing.

#865. Potato, sweetcorn and zucchini frittata

Grate peeled potatoes, place in a clean tea towel and wring out excess liquid. Add to the bowl a can of whole kernel sweetcorn and sliced zucchini. Break eggs into another bowl, beat lightly and pour into the vegetables. Add grated tasty cheese, broken feta and seasoning. Pour all into a casserole dish that has been buttered then bake in the oven (180°C) till just cooked. Top with deep fried potato skins around the edge of the frittata.

#866. Stuffed pumpkin with mince and potatoes

Slice around the top of the pumpkin stem and remove. Ensure that the pumpkin is stable while cutting through the top and take great care not to injure yourself while using the knife cutting through the top of the pumpkin. With a dessertspoon clean out the seeds and pith from the inside of the pumpkin then add pepper, salt and olive oil. In a frypan, cook diced onions, mixed herbs, pork and beef mince, canned tomatoes so that it becomes a thick sauce by reducing. In another saucepan, cook and prepare mashed potatoes. Mix both the mince and the mashed potatoes together and spoon into the pumpkin then place the top back on the pumpkin. Place on a baking tray and bake in the oven till a sharp knife pierces the skin of the pumpkin easily. Serve with a brown onion sauce and deep-fried potato skins to give the dish texture.

#867. Smashed potatoes

Select small new potatoes and cook in boiling salted water till soft. Gently smash the potatoes with a thumb so that the skins break and place in a serving bowl. To the potatoes add chopped parsley, sliced gherkins, diced onions, capers and mayonnaise. Season well and combine all the ingredients. Serve hot or cold.

#868. Potato balls with cheese topping

Using leftover mashed potatoes, place in a mixing bowl and add chopped parsley, grated cheese and a beaten egg. Mix well then roll the potato mix into balls 40 mm in diameter. Put through flour, egg wash and breadcrumbs and fry the balls. Cover well as the hot oil could leak into the potato and blow it apart. When golden brown, place on a baking tray, top with grated cheese and grill to melt the cheese on top. Place each ball on a deep fried potato skin large enough to hold the potato ball.

23.

VEGETARIAN

#	Dish	#	Dish
869	Vegetarian Meatballs	884	Tofu And Chickpea Curry
870	Stir Fried Tofu And Rice	885	Aubergine Stack
871	Tofu Custard	886	Eggplant Pizza
872	Fried Tofu	887	Aubergine And Tomato Bake
873	Chickpea And Pumpkin Curry	888	Babaganoush
874	Roasted Chickpeas	889	Sweet Potato Curry With Chickpeas
875	Chickpea, Chilli And Sweet Potato In Pomodoro Sauce	890	Carrot And Sweet Potato Fritters
876	Lentils	891	Vegetarian Cottage Pie
877	Roasted Chickpeas #2	892	Coconut Curried Lentils
878	Chickpeas With Satay Sauce	893	Falafel
879	Chickpea And Zucchini Tagine	894	Vegetarian Patties
880	Chickpea And Vegetable Tagine	895	Vegetarian Lentil Crepes
881	Vegetable Fritter Burger	896	Roast Vegetable Couscous
882	Mushroom Burger	897	Pearl Barley With Toasted Hazelnut
883	Black Bean And Sweet Potato Burger	898	Grilled Polenta With Roasted Tomatoes And Bocconcini

#869. Vegetarian meatballs

Cauliflower, quinoa, brown rice, garlic, spices, egg, oats, garlic and seasonings. Cook and cool the quinoa and brown rice then in a food processor process all together. Put the mix into the fridge and allow to cool then mould into balls. Fry in vegetable oil and drain on kitchen paper.

#870. Stir-fried tofu and rice

Cook the rice and allow to cool. Prepare sliced onions, carrots, celery, green beans and capsicum along with grated root ginger and crushed garlic. Fry the vegetables in vegetable oil then add in the tofu which has been cut into cubes. Pour in soy, hoisin and fish sauces and toss the pan to mix it through the vegetables. Season and serve with rice.

#871. Tofu custard

Dice the tofu into cubes then fry quickly in oil and garlic. The tofu should be firm. Fry sliced shiitake mushrooms and garlic together then add sliced capsicums, spring onions and chopped coriander. In a glass jug, mix miso paste, which has been mixed with hot water and cooled, with beaten eggs, which will form the custard. In a ramekin put the tofu and vegetables then pour in the warm miso and egg mix. Season and bake in the oven in a water bath till set.

#872. Fried tofu

Remove the tofu from the packet and place in a dish with a flat base. Spoon over teriyaki sauce and add sliced garlic and ginger. Keep in the fridge and turn the tofu to allow all sides to absorb the sauce. Heat oil in a frypan and place the block of tofu in the pan. Turn over and brown the other side then remove from the pan. Cut into blocks then place on a salad. Spoon over the teriyaki sauce, season and serve.

#873. Chickpea and pumpkin curry

Peel and cut the pumpkin into 15 mm cubes and set aside. In a saucepan, put oil and sweat off diced onion, diced root ginger, crushed garlic, then add grated turmeric, cardamom seeds, curry powder, cumin and allow to heat gently. Add the pumpkin and allow to brown then pour in a can of chopped tomatoes and coconut milk or stock, whichever is the choice. Bring to a gentle simmer and as the pumpkin starts to soften, add a drained, washed can of chickpeas. Check the seasoning and taste then serve over rice with naan bread and chutney.

#874. Roasted chickpeas

Drain and wash a can of chickpeas and dry on kitchen paper. In a mixing bowl, add cumin, oregano, sweet paprika, sumac, turmeric, cayenne, sesame seed and mix well. Place the chickpeas in the bowl and mix well then roast in the oven in olive oil.

#875. Chickpea, chilli and sweet potato in pomodoro sauce

Peel and cut the sweet potato into cubes around 15 mm. Place in a saucepan with cold salted water, bring to the boil and simmer till just soft then drain. Spoon into an oven casserole then add a can of drained, washed chickpeas with chopped fresh tomatoes. Spoon over chilli flakes then pour over pomodoro sauce. Bake in the oven for 20 minutes then check for taste and seasoning.

#876. Lentils

Place the lentils in a saucepan with cold water but no salt then simmer gently until cooked. In a frypan, sauté diced onions, chopped celery, chopped capsicum and sweat through. Add chopped garlic and diced ginger if desired. Pour in vegetable stock to just cover the lentils and simmer for ten minutes, season and serve.

Note: Fresh or tinned tomatoes can be used in place of or in conjunction with the stock to give a different taste. Potatoes cut into 15 mm cubes can also be added to the lentils along with any other vegetable.

#877. Roasted chickpeas No. 2

Using canned chickpeas, drain well, wash and dry on kitchen paper then pour into a bowl. Put in oil, crushed garlic and buffalo sauce then spoon into a roasting pan. Cook in the oven for 45 minutes or till the chickpeas have dried off with only a small amount of sauce still in the dish. **Buffalo sauce:** Requires a store-bought hot sauce like a pomodoro with chillies. Place in a processor with apple cider vinegar, Worcestershire sauce, garlic, paprika and seasoning. Whisk in melted butter until it has emulsified. It is a very hot spicy sauce.

#878. Chickpeas with satay sauce

Peel and cook small cocktail-size onions from cold salted water and simmer slowly. When nearly cooked, drain and place in a roasting dish with vegetable oil and crushed garlic and roast at 190°C until brown. While the onions are roasting, add canned chickpeas which have been drained and washed. Allow to cook and mix with a wooden spoon while roasting. Other vegetables could also be roasted with the onions at the same time.

Roast peanut sauce: In a roasting dish, dry roast the peanuts and leave to cool. Place in a food processor and blitz to a rough paste. Add garlic, soy sauce, sesame oil, brown sugar, fish sauce, chilli flakes and lime juice. Blitz again to mix all together then season. Add water to thin the sauce down to a pouring liquid. Use with vegetables or barbecue dishes.

#879. Chickpea and zucchini tagine

In a frypan, slowly cook diced onions with the spices cardamom, turmeric, ginger and nutmeg, batch fry a choice of root vegetables such as sweet potato, pumpkin, parsnip and butternut then place into the tagine. When all the ingredients have been browned, deglaze the pan with the stock and the pomodoro sauce and add to the tagine. Cook on an element for 30 minutes then add chickpeas, dried apricots and dates. Continue to cook for another 30 minutes then check to see if the sweet potatoes are cooked, check seasoning and serve with couscous. A tagine is a North African/Middle Eastern cooking vessel (as well as the name of the dish cooked in one). As an alternative, use a large saucepan with lid.

#880. Chickpea and vegetable tagine

Peel the vegetables selected for the tagine then cut into similar sizes. For root vegetables, start them first by placing into a tagine if there is one available or into a saucepan with a lid. With vegetables like potatoes, carrots, pumpkin, sweet potato, pour over stock so that it comes up to three quarters of the vegetables. A tagine is tall and conical so that the steam goes up the chimney, can't escape and trickles down back into the food at the bottom thus creating a stronger flavour. Along with the stock add root ginger, garlic, turmeric, cardamom, cinnamon and Moroccan seasoning. As the root vegetables start to get soft, add vegetables such as courgettes, Brussels sprouts, green beans and chickpeas. When all the vegetables are cooked, remove with a slotted spoon, drizzle over some of the sauce and top with sliced almonds.

#881. Vegetable fritter burger

Grate suitable vegetables to form the fritters, for example carrots, onions, pumpkin, parsnip, celery, garlic, ginger and beetroot. Add flour to the grated vegetables and mix in then add an egg keeping the mixture like whipped cream. Add in grated cheese, chopped cashew nuts and chopped parsley. Mould the mixture into patties and fry in oil and butter till brown on both sides. Cut a burger bun in half and toast. Spread the top and bottom with mashed avocado and balsamic vinegar. To the bottom add rocket, sliced beetroot, tomatoes, the fritter and minted yoghurt then put the top on and serve.

#882. Mushroom burger

Depending on choice of availability of mushrooms and what each individual choice is, select enough to fit on a burger bun. Using portobellos, remove the stalk and fry in butter and garlic in a frypan on both sides then leave to cool. Lay stalk side up and add some grated mozzarella, sliced tomato and grilled haloumi. Drizzle with olive oil and season then bake in the oven. Slice the burger bun in half and toast till brown then spread with butter. Put rocket, beetroot slices and the portobellos on the burger base, top with aioli and add the bun top and serve.

#883. Black bean and sweet potato burgers

Boil the peeled and cut sweet potato then mash, adding butter and seasoning but keeping the mix quite dry. To the sweet potato mash add canned black beans, crushed garlic, diced onion, chopped spring onion, breadcrumbs, sweet chilli sauce, a beaten egg and seasonings. Mould into burger patties and fry in oil. Other additives could be turmeric, cumin, coriander. Cooked lentils and couscous could also be added as additional ingredients.

#884. Tofu and chickpea curry

Cut firm tofu into cubes approximately 20–30 mm in size. Fry the tofu in oil to brown then set aside. In the same pan, fry diced onion, sliced pumpkin, grated ginger, crushed garlic, a can of drained chickpeas, baby spinach then pour in a store-bought korma curry paste. Allow to heat through then pour in coconut milk, stir and season. Return the tofu to the pan, heat and serve on rice. Serve with chutney and naan bread.

#885. Aubergine stack

Cut two slices off the aubergine so that there are two circles then cut a large tomato into two slices. Fry them all in hot oil till they are brown on both sides then set aside. Once cool, place the aubergine on a plate. With a cheese slicer, slice Parmesan cheese and lay the aubergine on it. On top, place the tomato and to that add a slice of mozzarella. Repeat the layering then dress the stack with an oil, basil and balsamic dressing.

#886. Eggplant pizza

Slice the eggplant into 15–20 mm slices and fry in oil and garlic in a frypan on both sides till the eggplant is cooked. Place the slices on a baking tray and spread with pizza sauce. Top with fresh tomato slices and any selected vegetables such as mushrooms, zucchini or caramelised onions. Top with grated mozzarella and bake in the oven for 10 minutes or until the top is cooked.

#887. Aubergine and tomato bake

Cut the aubergine into 20 mm size dice then rub through flour, egg wash and breadcrumbs, fry to brown the pieces then bake in the oven to complete the cooking. Sauté off diced onion, sliced capsicum, zucchini and place to one side. Lay half the aubergine in a buttered casserole then add half the onion mixture, top with sliced tomato, torn basil leaves and grated cheese. Repeat the layers a second time then bake in the oven for 30 minutes.

#888. Baba ghanoush

Char grill the aubergine over a barbecue or naked flame to burn off the skin. Leave to cool then remove most of the skin and chop the aubergine into pieces. Roast the aubergine in the oven with tomatoes, capsicums, onions and garlic. When cooked, put in a food processor then mix in tahini, lemon juice and seasoning. Process till a smooth paste is achieved.

#889. Sweet potato curry with chickpeas

Dice an onion and sweat off in a saucepan in coconut oil then add cumin, ground coriander, cinnamon, mustard seeds, fenugreek, turmeric, grated root ginger and garlic. Keep on a low heat as the spices release their oils then add in diced sweet potatoes, diced capsicum and continue cooking. Add in a store-bought curry paste, coconut milk and simmer. Using a can of chickpeas, drain and roast in the oven in oil and garlic. Allow to brown but not burn then pour into the sweet potato curry and stir in. Check seasoning, taste then serve on rice. Depending on how hot you desire the curry to be, you can use a hot curry paste or add chillies to the strength of heat desired.

#890. Carrot and sweet potato fritters

Grate a carrot and sweet potato into a bowl. Add in grated root ginger, crushed garlic and finely diced shallots. Prepare a batter of self-raising flour, eggs, olive oil, seasoning and pour onto the grated vegetables. If you like hot spicy fritters, chopped chillies can also be added. Allow the mixture to sit in the fridge for an hour then fry in an oil/butter mixture and brown on both sides. Grated cheese or Parmesan can also be added.

#891. Vegetarian cottage pie

Soak lentils for two to three hours, wash then cook in simmering non-salted water until soft. They can also be cooked without soaking. In a saucepan, fry diced onions, diced carrots, celery and peas. Add tomato paste then a can of chopped tomatoes. Bring to a simmer then add in the cooked lentils and stir well. Check seasoning, taste then pour into a casserole dish and leave to cool. Prepare mashed potato adding cream, butter and seasoning. Spread it over the lentil mix and bake in the oven till cooked through.

#892. Coconut curried lentils

Diced onion, garlic, root ginger, chilli, curry powder, capsicum, pumpkin cubes, cooked lentils, cumin, coriander, turmeric, stock, canned tomatoes, half can coconut milk. In a saucepan in coconut oil, fry the onion, ginger, garlic, capsicum, curry powder, cumin, chilli, turmeric and coriander on a low heat then add the lentils and a can of chopped tomatoes, pumpkin and bring to a simmer. Add coconut milk and top up with stock if required. Simmer gently until the pumpkin is soft. Check seasoning and taste. Serve on rice with naan bread.

#893. Falafels

Canned chickpeas, tahini, egg, lemon juice, cumin, garlic, lemon zest, ground coriander, chilli flakes. Blitz the ingredients in a food processor then fold in flour, baking powder, chopped parsley and leaf coriander. Shape into small balls then flatten to make patties and fry in butter and oil. **Yoghurt sauce**: Plain yoghurt, chopped coriander, grated lemon zest and juice, cumin.

#894. Vegetarian patties

In a mixing bowl, place chopped tofu, canned cooked lentils drained, hummus, chopped onion, beaten egg, sliced garlic, chopped parsley, almond meal, seasoning and chopped cashews. Mix well, and to roll the mix into patties it needs to be quite dry. Use more almond meal or rice flour to dry the mixture. Roll the mix into small balls about the size of golf balls then press down on a clean chopping board. Fry in oil and brown on both sides.

#895. Vegetarian lentil crepes

Prepare the lentils as in dish #891 and leave to go cold. Prepare a crepe mix, make the crepes and place on top of each other on a tray. Roll the lentil mix into cylinder shapes, place in the middle of the crepe and roll it up. Place in a buttered casserole, pour over pomodoro sauce and bake in the oven till cooked.

#896. Roast vegetable couscous

Roast zucchini, sliced aubergine and carrots, chopped capsicums, sliced pumpkin and sweet potato in the oven in oil and crushed garlic. In a saucepan, boil vegetable stock or water then add couscous, place a lid on the saucepan and set aside. When the liquid has been absorbed, fluff up the couscous with a fork, adding a knob of butter and seasoning, then spoon onto a serving plate. Top with the roast vegetables and spoon some of the couscous over the top. Fry strips of haloumi cheese in oil then add to the top of the vegetables, drizzle with olive oil and serve.

#897. Pearl barley with toasted hazelnut

Prepare the pearl barley as you would a rice risotto. In a large saucepan sweat off diced onions, carrots, celery in oil then add the barley and mix well so that the barley gets well coated in oil. Slowly add vegetable stock stirring continuously while the barley thickens to the point that it is nearly cooked. Keep on a low element and stir to prevent from drying and burning. At the end, add a large knob of butter and Parmesan cheese then check seasoning. In a dry frypan place sliced hazelnuts and allow to just brown. Serve the barley with the hazelnuts sprinkled over the top.

#898. Grilled polenta with roasted tomatoes and bocconcini

Prepare the instant polenta as per packet instructions keeping it thick. Pour onto a baking dish lined with buttered baking paper, keeping it 20 mm thick, then cool. Bake vine tomatoes in the oven leaving the vine connected, drizzling with balsamic vinegar and olive oil. Slice the cold polenta into 60 mm squares and fry on a grill plate to leave grill lines. Top with the hot tomatoes and sliced bocconcini.

24.

SALADS

#	Dish	#	Dish
899	Asparagus And Cherry Tomato Salad	914	Grape Salsa
900	Asparagus And Egg Caesar Salad	915	Nicoise Salad
901	Warm Avocado Salad	916	Seafood Salad With Mango
902	Avocado, Sour Cream And Olive Oil	917	Hawaiian Prawn Salad
903	Bacon And Avocado Salsa	918	Couscous Salad
904	Broccoli Salad	919	Roast Vegetable Salad On Spinach With Avocado Dressing
905	Roasted Butternut Squash	920	Chicken Panzanella
906	Chicken Caesar Salad	921	Potato And Tuna Salad
907	Chickpea Salad With Dates	922	Roast Vegetable Salad
908	Roast Cauliflower And Chickpea Salad	923	Grilled Potato Salad
909	Warm Salmon Salad	924	Warm Potato Salad
910	Waldorf Salad	925	Grated Beetroot And Carrot With Ginger Dressing
911	Tabbouleh	926	Salmon Salad
912	Sliced Aubergine Salad	927	Roasted Tomato, Garlic And Lentil Salad
913	Pickled Salad	928	Prawn, Smoked Mussel, And Avocado Salad
		929	Butternut, Cranberry And Quinoa Salad

#899. Asparagus and cherry tomato salad

Trim the root ends of the asparagus, slice the spears in half, barbecue then place in a flat-bottomed bowl. Cut the cherry tomatoes in half and add to the bowl then add a good serving of chopped parsley. Mix well together then dress with an oil, balsamic and lemon dressing.

#900. Asparagus and egg Caesar salad

Poach, grill or barbecue the asparagus then cool. Lay cos lettuce on a salad platter, and add soft-boiled eggs cut in half, croutons, anchovies and Parmesan cheese. Drizzle with Caesar salad dressing and serve.

#901. Warm avocado salad

In a frypan, fry garlic and sesame seeds in oil on a medium heat. Add deseeded cucumber which has been diced into 20 mm dice. Remove the stone from the avocado then chop the dice the same size as the cucumber. To the cucumber add a few chilli leaves then the diced avocado and pour in a little apple cider vinegar. Spoon out onto a serving plate before the avocado gets hot.

#902. Avocado, sour cream and olive oil

Place the avocado in a food processor then add sour cream along with a small pinch of chilli flakes if desired. Blitz the mix then add oil slowly till it emulsifies. Season and pour into a small jug to serve.

#903. Bacon and avocado salsa

Chop the bacon into batons and fry in butter till crisp. Dice avocado and slice red onions and mix into a bowl with the bacon. Add in chopped chilli and dressing.

#904. Broccoli salad

Cut the broccoli into florets then slice in half. Season then add apple cider vinegar, diced onions, roasted peanuts, cranberries, balsamic and natural yoghurt. Mix well together and serve cold.

#905. Roasted butternut squash

Peel and slice the butternut into uniform pieces 20 x 20 mm, parboil for 2 minutes then drain and roast in the oven with oil, fresh thyme, crushed garlic and diced bacon pieces. When the butternut is nearly cooked, add a few slices of sun-dried tomatoes. Drain off the oil and spoon the butternut into a salad bowl. Add a dressing and serve the dish warm or cold.

#906. Chicken Caesar salad

Cos lettuce, pan-fried chicken breasts, crispy bacon pieces, anchovy fillets, garlic croutons, poached egg, Caesar dressing and shaved Parmesan. Placed the cos lettuce onto the serving plate, top with sliced chicken, bacon, anchovies and croutons. Top with a very soft poached egg, drizzle with Caesar dressing, grate Parmesan cheese over the top and serve.

#907. Chickpea salad with dates

In a mixing bowl put olive oil, cumin, cinnamon and crushed garlic. Using canned chickpeas, drain, wash and add to the bowl. Top with fresh grated carrots, chopped dates, chopped coriander, sliced chilli and whole shelled pistachios. Mix well, season and serve on a salad platter.

#908. Roast cauliflower and chickpea salad

The cauliflower can be roasted whole or cut into florets and roasted to brown and 80 per cent cooked through but still retaining a little crunch. While the cauliflower is roasting in the oven, also pour in the drained canned chickpeas, sliced capsicum and parboiled onions. Add crushed garlic and chopped thyme while the vegetables are roasting. When cooked, leave to cool. Set up the serving plate with lettuce leaves and place the roasted vegetables on top of the lettuce. Drizzle with a dressing and serve.

#909. Warm salmon salad

Wash and cut potatoes into roughly 35 mm pieces. Parboil for 5 minutes in boiling water then roast in the oven in oil, butter and garlic. When the potatoes are soft, add skinned and boned salmon to the pan in the oven and cook through. Remove the pan from the oven and leave to cool. Meanwhile slice red onions and cook stalks of fresh asparagus. Place the warm potatoes into a mixing bowl then add the sliced red onion and chopped parsley. Spoon the mix onto a serving platter which is covered in lettuce leaves, tear the cooked salmon apart and dot it over the potatoes. Add the warm cooked asparagus and pour over an oil-based mayonnaise. Slices of smoked salmon could also be added or used instead of fresh salmon.

#910. Waldorf salad

A fruit and nut salad that came into being in the late 1800s and served at the Waldorf Hotel. Core the apples and dice along with celery. Place into a mixing bowl along with seedless grapes and mix in an egg mayonnaise, lemon juice and seasoning. Serve the salad on a layer of lettuce, or individual lettuce leaves can be used as cups for individual serves.

#911. Tabbouleh

Cook the bulgur wheat and leave to go cold. Place in a mixing bowl and add a lot of chopped mint, parsley and cucumber that has been deseeded and skinned. Drizzle with olive oil then add garlic, chopped tomato, finely sliced lemon zest and lemon juice. Mix well then season and serve.

#912. Sliced aubergine salad

Slice the aubergine and fry in a frypan with crushed garlic, thyme and sage along with thinly sliced butternut and thickly sliced tomatoes. Brown the vegetables on both sides then place on kitchen paper to drain. With lettuce underneath, lay two slices of aubergine on the plate and top with the butternut and tomatoes. Drizzle with an oil dressing then spoon on a harissa yoghurt mix. Garnish with spring onions.

#913. Pickled salad

Slice red onions and cucumber. Into a small mixing bowl put apple cider vinegar with a teaspoon of sugar and a drop of water. Stir and mix well then pour it over the red onions and cucumber. Season and top with chopped coriander.

#914. Grape salsa

Red grapes mixed with sliced red onions, sliced smoked red capsicum and chopped spring onions. Drizzle with olive oil and red wine vinegar.

#915. Niçoise salad

Lettuce, tuna, red onions, sliced capsicums, green beans, diced tomatoes, cucumber sliced, croutons, anchovies, capers, boiled potatoes, olives and hard-boiled egg segments. Place the lettuce into a bowl then top with diced cooked potatoes, cooked cold whole green beans, cooked egg segments and so on before adding the smaller items such as olives, capers, croutons and drizzle with a dressing.

#916. Seafood salad with mango

Seafood salad can be as expensive as you wish to make it using lobster, crab, oysters, fresh tuna, prawns, mussels or whatever you might like to use as ingredients. With at least three or four types of seafood, prepare and cook then leave to cool in the fridge. Trim the seafood down to a size that will match most of the ingredients being used, for example cut the lobster into pieces the size of a half-cooked mussel. Gently mix the seafood together on a tray and add in diced fresh mango that has been mixed with sliced lemongrass. Drizzle with a dressing and spoon onto a serving platter. Serve with lemon wedges and mayonnaise.

#917. Hawaiian prawn salad

In a bowl, add fresh sliced apples and pineapple cut into small pieces and also add sliced red onions, spring onions, capsicums, chillies and spoon onto a layer of lettuce leaves. Top with cooked prawns and drizzle with vinaigrette.

#918. Couscous salad

Cook the couscous as per packet instructions and leave to cool. Prepare the salad vegetables — diced capsicum, diced tomato flesh, deseeded cucumber, torn leaves of basil and celery — and add to the couscous. Drizzle in lemon juice, olive oil, seasoning and top with chopped coriander.

#919. Roast vegetable and spinach salad with avocado dressing

Select vegetables desired such as carrots, sweet potatoes, pumpkin, parsnip, capsicums, courgettes and prepare for roasting. The root vegetables will start the roasting process in garlic, rosemary and thyme, then the softer vegetables will follow for the last 20 minutes. Turn during cooking so that they all brown. Leave to cool then place on a salad platter. Spread baby spinach through the vegetables and drizzle over avocado dressing.

#920. Chicken panzanella

Breadcrumb slices of chicken breast and fry in oil. Cut sourdough bread into 30 mm cubes, sprinkle with oil and crushed garlic and bake in the oven. In a bowl, whisk balsamic vinegar and oil then add sliced red onion, anchovy fillets and their oil, black and green olives, halved cherry tomatoes, baked sourdough cubes and mix well. Spoon this over rocket on a serving plate, place the cooked chicken around the sides and serve.

#921. Potato and tuna salad

Cook new baby potatoes in boiling salted water till just cooked then drain well and cool. Cut in half and place in a serving dish. Arrange over the top of the potatoes a drained can of tuna, rocket, black olives, cooked fresh whole beans and cherry tomatoes. Drizzle with balsamic vinegar then with mayonnaise that has had lemon juice added. Arrange anchovy fillets over the top and serve.

#922. Roast vegetable salad

Use a variety of root vegetables such as carrots, sweet potato, pumpkin, courgettes and capsicums cut into 10 x 50 mm batons and oven roast in oil and garlic then leave to cool. Set the roasted vegetables on rocket and tomatoes. Spoon over dressing and serve.

#923. Grilled potato salad

In a mixing bowl, put olive oil, crushed garlic, chopped rosemary, lemon juice/ grated lemon zest and mix well. Slice raw potatoes, place in the mixing bowl and leave for an hour. Cook the potatoes on a barbecue or on a ribbed frypan to give the grill marks. When they are cooked, leave to cool. In a salad bowl, place rocket then the cooked potatoes and top with a blue cheese dressing. Add cubed pieces of feta and black olives and serve.

#924. Warm potato salad

Prepare boiled potatoes and leave to cool. Slice spring onions, celery and garlic and mix with mayonnaise. Dice the potatoes and place in a bowl. Pour over the mayonnaise, mix well. As an option, you could poach two eggs keeping them very soft and puncturing while sitting on top of the salad so that the yolks dribble through the salad.

#925. Grated beetroot and carrot with ginger dressing

Grate the cooked beetroot and carrot and place into a mixing bowl. To the bowl add grated root ginger and apple. Prepare an oil and malt vinegar dressing with grated root ginger, chopped coriander and seasoning. Drizzle and serve.

#926. Salmon salad

Dice the fresh salmon fillet into 25 mm cubes and place in a mixing bowl. In another bowl put sesame oil, soy sauce, grated ginger and garlic, fish sauce and mix well then pour it over the salmon. Leave for 3 hours then fry in oil and leave to cool. Sprinkle with sesame seeds. Prepare a salad of lettuce, avocado, tomatoes, blue cheese then top with the salmon. Spoon over a little of the marinade and serve.

#927. Roasted tomato, garlic and lentil salad

Place the cherry tomatoes in a roasting tin with olive oil, seasoning, dried mixed herbs and two whole cloves of garlic that have their tops cut off. Slow roast at 160°C till the tomatoes start to dry out. Remove and leave to cool. Into a bowl, spoon the tomatoes and garlic minus their paper shells then add a can of drained lentils. Season, pour on dressing and serve.

#928. Prawn, smoked mussel and avocado salad

Using prawns already cooked and smoked mussels, place in a bowl and mix together with sliced red onions, baby spinach and diced avocado flesh. Season, drizzle with vinaigrette and serve in lettuce cups.

#929. Butternut, cranberry and quinoa salad

Slice the butternut into 10 mm cubes and cook in boiling salted water until soft and cooked through then drain in iced water and dry on kitchen paper. Mix in a bowl with dried cranberries, roasted pine nuts and cooked quinoa. Drizzle with a ginger vinaigrette and spoon onto a serving platter.

25.

SAUCES/
DRESSINGS/
MARINADES

951	Lemon Ginger Marinade	984	Roast Tomato Sauce
952	Ginger And Sesame Seed	985	Ranch Dressing #2
953	Lasagne/Bolognese Style Sauce		**Sweet Sauces**
954	Peach And Apricot Glaze	986	Caramel Sauce
955	Pork Gravy	987	Rum Caramel Sauce
956	Port And Prune Sauce	988	Rum Butter And Pistachio Sauce
957	Roast Garlic Gravy	989	Coffee And Rum Sauce
958	Sesame Soy Vinaigrette	990	Caramel Whisky Sauce
959	Teriyaki Sauce	991	Hot Fudge Sauce
960	Teriyaki Marinade	992	Iranian Custard
961	Ranch Dressing	993	Cream And Almond Milk
962	Dry Ranch Dressing	994	Star Anise Syrup

#930. Alfredo sauce

Warm together butter and cream then add in sour cream, crushed garlic, seasonings and dried oregano. Whisk well then add in the Parmesan cheese till the sauce is smooth then serve.

#931. Quick Alfredo sauce

Add cream cheese and butter to a saucepan and then garlic and milk. Put in grated Parmesan and seasoning then place on a medium heat whisking continually. Cook for 6 minutes and allow to reduce slightly. When cool it becomes thicker than while in the saucepan so it is not necessary to reduce too far. Pour in cream to thin the sauce where necessary.

#932. Anchovy rosemary mayonnaise

To an egg-based mayonnaise, stir in anchovy fillets, chopped rosemary and parsley. Stir well and season, remembering that anchovy fillets in cans/jars already have a high salt content.

#933. Avocado pesto

Avocado flesh, basil, cashews, lemon juice, garlic, olive oil, freshly grated Parmesan cheese and seasoning. Place all ingredients in a food processor and pulse so that it does not become a totally smooth paste. Drizzle in olive oil to get consistency.

#934. Quick cheese sauce

Grate the cheese into a mixing bowl, add seasoning and spoon in cornflour and mix well. In a saucepan, heat the milk until just beginning to simmer then pour in the cheese mix and stir with a whisk while it thickens. Allow the cornflour to cook out, check the seasoning and use as required.

#935. Fried ginger, coriander and basil pesto

Chop the ginger and lightly fry in oil with chopped garlic then leave to cool. In a food processor, process coriander, roasted pine nuts, basil, drizzle in olive oil and add Parmesan. Check for taste and seasoning.

#936. Walnut pesto

Into a food processor, put walnuts, garlic, basil, Parmesan then drizzle in virgin olive oil and pulse. Season and serve.

#937. Brazil nut sauce

In a saucepan, mix white torn crustless bread, milk powder, a small amount of water, garlic and gently heat to a smooth paste. Add cream and stir in. In a processor, blitz Brazil nuts to a rough grind then add to the saucepan with milk and cream then season.

If the sauce is too creamy, add a little white vinegar. Serve with meat, poultry.

#938. Maple balsamic vinaigrette

In a mixing bowl, put balsamic vinegar, Dijon mustard, maple syrup and stir well. Into this drizzle olive oil then add salt. Check taste then it's ready to use.

#939. Cashew nut dressing

In a processor mix dry-fried cashews, soy, garlic and oil along with a little hot water. Blitz to a smooth liquid, season and serve. Can also be served as a sauce for chicken.

#940. Carrot and ginger dressing

Into a food processor put olive oil, white vinegar, chopped carrots, spring onion, minced ginger, soy sauce, honey and seasoning. Blitz the mix then pour into a sauce jug.

#941. Cauliflower sauce

Cut the cauliflower into florets and cook in boiling salted water. Drain well and add butter then put into a food processor and process till the resultant sauce still has some lumps in it. Season then add sour cream and serve with roast or grilled meat.

#942. Cherry vinaigrette

Pitted cherries, balsamic vinegar, olive oil, crushed garlic, red wine vinegar and seasoning. Place in a food processor and pulse. Serve with pork.

#943. Chimichurri sauce

Fresh mint, basil, chives and chillies chopped and placed in a bowl. Add capers, seasoning, lime juice and zest then olive oil to make it thick but wet. Use on grilled steak. Let the steak rest then slice across the grain. Spoon the sauce onto a serving plate and place the sliced steak on top then spoon a little more sauce on top.

#944. Coriander, lime and mustard dressing

Mix the mustard and chopped coriander in a bowl then add lime juice, oil and runny honey.

#945. Roast garlic and aioli sauce

Prepare or use store-bought aioli. In the oven, roast five garlic cloves that have had their heads cut off. When cooked, squeeze the cloves into the sauce and mix in. Check for seasoning and use over meat, poultry, fish.

#946. Tomato dressing

Slow bake tomatoes with garlic then add olive oil and balsamic vinegar and blitz in a blender.

#947. Roast garlic vinaigrette

Roast garlic cloves in the oven till brown. Mash in a mortar and pestle then mix in olive oil and vinegar 2:1.

#948. Blue cheese and aioli sauce

Prepare or use store-bought aioli as in #945 including the garlic and also add crumbled blue cheese to the sauce.

#949. Mascarpone cream sauce

Mascarpone, grated Parmesan, butter, nutmeg, seasoning, cream. Melt butter, add mascarpone and stir. Add nutmeg then Parmesan and lower the heat. Add seasoning and thin with cream.

#950. Mint and pistachio pesto

Pistachio nuts, Parmesan cheese, garlic, mint and olive oil. Place the nuts, garlic and mint in a food processor and blitz. Drizzle in olive oil then add the Parmesan. Check for seasoning.

#951. Lemon ginger marinade

Red pepper flakes, lemon juice and zest, honey, soy, finely diced root ginger and oil. Whisk all the ingredients together.

#952. Ginger and sesame sauce

Sesame oil, toasted sesame seeds, garlic, grated root ginger, soy and honey. Combine all ingredients in a jar, shake well then use as a dressing for chicken or vegetables.

#953. Lasagne/Bolognese style sauce

In a roasting pan, cook the mince until dried out and brown as though it is dehydrated then remove and set aside. In another roasting pan, grill tomato halves till very brown but not black. Into a heavy-based saucepan put sliced onions in oil and cook slowly till they begin to turn brown. Add brown sugar, butter and continue cooking. In another saucepan, sweat off diced carrots, celery and onions then add red wine and chopped garlic. Add beef stock and reduce then add the dried mince and tomatoes and continue cooking. Once it reaches a sauce thickness, remove from the element, season and use in dish required.

#954. Peach and apricot glaze

Put equal quantities of peach and apricot jam in a saucepan, pour over rum and heat slowly, stirring continuously. Add in a cinnamon stick, honey and brown sugar. Reduce slowly without burning. When the glaze becomes thick, remove from the heat and leave to cool. Use over pork dishes and desserts.

#955. Pork gravy

When the pork has finished roasting in the oven, remove to another tray and keep warm. Into the roasting pan, put peeled sliced apple segments and cider. If cider is not available then use chicken stock, beer or Guinness. Allow to reduce and lift the pan drippings for flavour then thicken with cornflour and water and check seasoning.

#956. Port and prune sauce

Cut the prunes in half and place into a small saucepan. Add port, orange juice/zest, stock, brown sugar and grated ginger. Bring to a simmer, add butter and allow to reduce. Check for seasoning and thicken with cornflour mixed with water if necessary.

#957. Roast garlic gravy

Head of garlic, chopped onions, dried mixed herbs, soy sauce, oil, vegetable stock and a roux of butter and flour. Roast a whole head of garlic till the cloves are brown. Fry the onion and herbs in a frypan till brown, then add the garlic along with the butter. Stir the pan well to pick up the pan bits then stir in an equal quantity of flour. Allow the roux to brown slowly without burning then add vegetable stock — whisk while adding the stock and don't allow to create lumps. Simmer very gently adding soy sauce and seasoning. Allow to reduce then check for seasoning. Any stock can be used but this sauce is suitable for vegetarian dishes.

#958. Sesame soy vinaigrette

Into a bowl put soy sauce, a few drops of sesame oil, dry-fried sesame seeds, honey then mix well and add olive oil slowly. Add seasoning.

#959. Teriyaki sauce

Put water, soy, honey into a small saucepan, heat gently and whisk. Add white vinegar, crushed pineapple, garlic, ginger and whisk. Thicken with cornflour mixed with water then add sesame seeds.

#960. Teriyaki marinade

Apple juice, white vinegar, crushed garlic, soy sauce and diced root ginger. Mix all ingredients in a food processor adding honey or brown sugar to sweeten the liquid.

#961. Ranch dressing

Buttermilk, garlic, onion, chives, parsley, dill, pepper, paprika and mustard seed mixed into mayonnaise.

#962. Dry ranch dressing

Dried parsley, ground pepper, salt, garlic powder, milk powder, onion powder and thyme. Mix well together. For use in slow-cooker dishes.

#963. Redcurrant jelly gravy

Red wine, beef stock, redcurrant jelly and sheet gelatine. Place the gelatine in cold water to soak then remove from the bowl. Heat the other ingredients in a saucepan and stir well. Check taste and seasoning and let cool. Then add the sheet gelatine and pour into ice cube trays to set. Serve with roast beef or lamb.

964. Tomato and garlic sauce

Fresh tomato flesh, clump of garlic cloves roasted, oregano, diced onions, tomato paste, basil, brown sugar and seasoning. Roast the tomato, onion, garlic briefly in oil and butter along with oregano. Put into a mixing bowl, removing the garlic from its paper covering. Add in tomato paste, basil, sugar and stir well, drizzling in a little oil. Pour into a saucepan, gently simmer and reduce. Put through a food processor or a sieve, or leave chunky if that is what you prefer. Check seasoning and serve.

#965. Ginger and miso dressing

Finely dice root ginger and heat gently in a few drops of sesame oil and vegetable oil. Mix a tablespoon or two of miso paste with water and add to the saucepan with the ginger and allow to emulsify. Season and serve.

#966. Lamb dressing

Into a mixing bowl, add minced garlic and anchovy fillets along with some of the anchovy oil. Slowly add cubes of butter, mix with a balloon whisk and emulsify the ingredients. Season well and use over roast lamb or cooked vegetables.

#967. Lime juice, fish sauce, garlic, chilli

Mix all the ingredients together then mix in soft avocado flesh to thicken the sauce. Season and serve.

#968. Walnut and sherry dressing

Mix 10 ml walnut oil with 2 ml sherry and 2 ml pomegranate syrup. For use over salads or fish dishes.

#969. Yoghurt and curry marinade

Using plain Greek yoghurt and a store-bought curry sauce, add lime juice and brown sugar. Use for chicken, lamb, fish.

#970. Tzatziki

Cup of yoghurt, crushed garlic, half cup cucumber flesh seedless and skinless, and a tablespoon of chopped mint.

#971. Red onion jam

Red onions sliced, butter, brown sugar and balsamic vinegar. Toss the onions in butter and keep on a low heat till soft and beginning to colour. Add sugar and balsamic vinegar and continue cooking. The mixture will reduce and become a little thicker in texture. Be careful not to allow it to burn.

#972. Chermoula sauce

Chopped parsley, coriander leaves, mint leaves, crushed garlic, cumin, chilli, lemon juice, paprika, turmeric, olive oil. Blend all ingredients in a food processor till smooth.

#973. Wasabi mayonnaise

To egg mayonnaise, add wasabi and lime juice to taste.

#974. Yoghurt, avocado, oil and wasabi dressing

Place the yoghurt and avocado into a food processor and blitz.

Add oil and wasabi and stir in along with seasoning. Use with salmon dishes.

#975. Roast peanut sauce

In a roasting dish, dry roast the peanuts and leave to cool. Place in a food processor and blitz to a rough paste. Add garlic, soy, sesame oil, brown sugar, fish sauce, chilli flakes and lime juice. Blitz again to mix all together, season. Add water to thin the sauce down to a pouring liquid. Use with pork, vegetables or barbecue dishes.

#976. Peanut sauce

Roasted salted peanuts, tamarind pulp, chilli, crushed garlic cloves, root ginger, chopped shallots, sticks of lemongrass, coriander, peanut oil, brown sugar, kecap manis, sweet chilli sauce. Place in a food processor and blitz.

#977. Sriracha mayonnaise

Stir together 250 ml homemade mayonnaise, 80 ml sriracha, 50 ml lime juice and seasonings.

#978. Crack sauce

Barbecue sauce, brown sugar, lime juice and crushed garlic. Use to cook pork chops or chicken.

#979. Vodka sauce

Sauté onion in butter and brown. Add vodka, reduce, add crushed tomatoes, season then at the end add cream and simmer very gently. Serve with pasta, salmon or prawns.

#980. Jack Daniel's sauce

For serving with fried or grilled steak. Collect any pan drippings from the cooking of the steak and add a knob of butter, Worcestershire sauce, Dijon mustard, crushed garlic and 150 ml Jack Daniel's. Pour into a small saucepan and reduce then thicken with cornflour mixed with water.

#981. Coriander and lime marinade

Chop coriander and place into a bowl. Drizzle in olive oil, lime juice and grated zest, grated root ginger, garlic and chilli flakes. Stir well, add seasoning then use for chicken, fish, beef, pork.

#982. Barbecue sauce/marinade

Grate apples into a mixing bowl then add soy sauce, maple syrup, cinnamon, nutmeg, ketchup and star anise. Mix well and brush over the meat being cooked.

#983. Spring onion and miso butter

To soft butter, mix in miso paste and sliced spring onions. Put it in cling wrap, form into a tube 25 mm in diameter and place in the fridge. When required, cut a slice off the roll and place on the hot food items. Great served on fried fish.

#984. Roast tomato sauce

Roast tomatoes attached to the vine along with diced tomatoes, chopped garlic, oregano, thyme, torn bread pieces and olive oil then pass through a sieve to remove the skins. Add tomato paste to the purée then place in a food processor and blitz. Check seasoning and add a spoonful or two of brown sugar should the tomato taste be too acidic. Finish with oil and red wine vinegar.

#985. Ranch dressing No. 2

Mix powdered garlic and onion, chopped dill and parsley. Into another bowl mix mayonnaise, buttermilk, sour cream and lemon juice. Mix both bowls together to complete the ranch dressing.

Sweet sauces

#986. Caramel sauce

Sugar, cream, butter and vanilla essence. Pour the sugar into a heavy-based pan and heat slowly so that it begins turning brown — do not stir but swirl the pan if necessary. Reduce heat, add butter and mix in. Stir over low heat and pour in cream and vanilla essence.

#987. Rum caramel sauce

Follow as in #986 and when adding the butter, pour in the dark rum and mix with a whisk. Then add the cream and vanilla.

#988. Rum butter and pistachio sauce

In a saucepan, melt the butter then add brown sugar and stir together. Remove from heat and pour in cream then return to a reduced heat and stir till it begins to thicken. Pour in rum and chopped pistachios.

#989. Coffee and rum sauce

Prepare a short black coffee and place in a saucepan. Heat and add 200 g brown sugar, 150 ml rum, vanilla paste, pinches of cinnamon, cloves and nutmeg. Bring to the boil to reduce, thicken with arrowroot mixed with water then add a knob of butter and mix well.

#990. Caramel whisky sauce

Butter, brown sugar, cream, whisky. Warm butter and sugar, mix well and heat till it turns colour. Reduce heat, add cream and bring to a boil then simmer for 5 minutes stirring. Remove from the heat and slowly pour in the whisky.

#991. Hot fudge sauce

Mix together butter, cream, honey, brown sugar, cocoa and salt in a saucepan and heat. Remove from heat and stir in broken chocolate pieces and vanilla paste.

#992. Iranian custard

In a mixing bowl, pour almond milk, add cornflour mixed with milk, rose water and cardamom seed. Heat to bring out the flavour of the spice, and the sauce will also thicken due to the cornflour. Separate three eggs and stir the three egg yolks into the sauce, stirring well. As the custard thickens, remove from the heat and sprinkle with chopped pistachios and almonds.

#993. Cream and almond milk

Heat almond milk with maple syrup in a saucepan and bring to a simmer. Reduce heat and pour in cream then thicken the sauce with arrowroot mixed with water. Sweeten the sauce with sugar, vanilla essence and dry-fried chopped almonds.

#994. Star anise syrup

Bring water, sugar, star anise, cinnamon stick and orange zest to the boil in a small saucepan and reduce the boiling liquid.

Remove from the element once the syrup starts to thicken and holds to a wooden spoon.

26.
DESSERTS

#	Dish	#	Dish
995	Almond Crumble	1015	Caramel Ice Cream
996	Banana, Orange And Chocolate Crepes	1016	Chocolate Slice
997	Baklava	1017	Chocolate Truffles
998	Bread And Butter Pudding	1018	White Chocolate Coconut Cream Sauce
999	Tarte Tartin	1019	White Chocolate Cake Black Doris Plums
1000	Brandy Snaps	1020	Strawberry Mille Feuille
1001	Brandy Cups	1021	Caramelised Bananas And Strawberries In Filo
1002	Banana Fritters	1022	Mock Ice Cream
1003	Apple Roll	1023	Layered Ice Cream
1004	Homemade Ice Cream	1024	Pineapple Bowl
1005	Caramelised Figs	1025	Tiramisu
1006	Feijoa And Apple Crumble	1026	Stuffed Pears
1007	Maple Dumplings	1027	Baked Chocolate Bar
1008	Marshmallow Crumble	1028	Peach Souffle Omelette
1009	Ice Cream (Quick Home Method)	1029	Strawberries, Tortillas And Ice Cream
1010	Hot Fudge Sauce	1030	Chocolate Bar Lasagne
1011	Crepes	1031	Baked Pears
1012	Caramel Gel	1032	Poached Rum And Raisin Pears
1013	Baked Figs In Maple Syrup		
1014	Hazelnut And Coconut Macaroons For Ice Cream Sandwiches		

#995. Almond crumble

Mix together flaked almonds and crushed almonds in a mixing bowl. Add vanilla extract, maple syrup, melted butter, breadcrumbs and salt and stir well. Spoon it over the ingredient that requires the topping then bake and grill to brown the top. Use this crumble on fruit dessert dishes, but it can also be used on meat, poultry and vegetables.

#996. Banana, orange and chocolate crepes

Prepare a crepe batter, leave to rest in the fridge for an hour then make large crepes. Make an orange sauce with caramel, orange juice, zest and Grand Marnier, cut the bananas in half and cook briefly in the orange sauce then leave to cool. Wrap the banana in the crepe and spoon over chocolate fudge sauce.

#997. Baklava

Into a mixing bowl, place chopped dates, sliced almonds, chopped pistachios and hazelnuts, chopped walnuts, lime juice and zest. Mix well then add liquid honey mixed with rose water. Line a baking tin with six sheets of filo pastry and spread over the nut mix. Top with four sheets of filo pastry, brush with butter and complete another two layers of filo pastry and nuts, pour over the honey mixture then bake in the oven. Drizzle over more honey mixed with rose water and leave to cool.

#998. Bread and butter pudding in ramekins

Butter the ramekins, dust with sugar and set aside. In a mixing bowl, mix chocolate drops, assorted nuts and dried fruit mix. In another bowl mix eggs, milk and cream with sugar. With a pastry cutter, cut a ring of bread to fit into the ramekin, brush with butter, spoon over some nuts and dried fruit then pour in some egg mix. Continue layering until the ramekin is full then bake in the oven in a roasting dish containing water three quarters of the way up the ramekin.

#999. Tarte Tatin

Prepare a caramel using sugar and water then when it has turned amber, pour it into an oven-friendly frypan. Line the pie dish with fruit such as pears, apples, bananas, forming a pattern with them and keeping the fruit close together. Cover with a sheet of puff pastry, pushing the edges of the puff pastry down the inside of the frypan, then bake. When the pastry is cooked, turn over so the fruit and caramel are on top in presentation form and the pastry forms the base.

#1000. Brandy snaps

Sugar, golden syrup, butter. Melt all together and add ginger and baking soda. Mix in enough flour to make it fairly stiff. Put one dessertspoon for each snap onto an oiled baking sheet. Keep them apart as they will spread out as they bake. Remove from tray and roll around an oiled wooden spoon handle.

#1001. Brandy cups

Flour, golden syrup, butter, ginger, sugar, baking powder. Cream butter and sugar then add warmed syrup, mix well and add ginger and flour and lastly baking powder. Rub muffin cups with oil. Place a dessertspoon of the mixture onto a baking sheet and bake. The dough will spread as it bakes. When cooked, carefully lift it off the baking tray with a spatula, place it over the muffin tin and shape in situ. Fill with fruit or ice cream and drizzle over a sauce.

#1002. Banana fritters

Prepare a batter with self-raising flour, baking powder, milk, eggs. Keep the batter thick then add a chopped chilli and some roasted desiccated coconut. Roll the banana on a bench to soften, cover with flour then add to the batter and mix in. Cook the fritters in a deep fryer or in a saucepan on the stove. When cooking on the stove, don't leave the saucepan unattended in case the oil overflows. Serve with a rum sauce.

#1003. Apple roll

Slice the apples into thin slices. Roll out puff pastry and cut into 50 mm strips. Using a store-bought almond paste, spread it over the puff pastry then line it with the apple slices. Sprinkle on muscovado sugar and roll up the pastry then place on a baking try and bake.

#1004. Homemade ice cream

Heat evaporated milk and bring to the boil. Add condensed milk, fresh cream and cardamom then cornflour and stir for a minute. Remove from heat and cool. Blend with a mixer to remove any lumps then deep freeze. Melts very quickly. Could add chopped pistachio nuts.

#1005. Caramelised figs

Prepare a caramel from sugar and water. Add the fig halves and make sure they are all coated. Sprinkle on balsamic vinegar and coat with the pan sauce.

#1006. Feijoa and apple crumble

Peel and cut tart-tasting apples into small cubes, peel and cut feijoas and place them all in a bowl. Mix cinnamon, nutmeg, caster sugar, orange juice and zest. Mix all the ingredients together then pour into a buttered casserole dish leaving enough room for the crumble mix to be placed on top. Prepare the crumble from flour, butter, cinnamon, nutmeg, brown sugar and wholemeal oats. Spread it over the top of the fruit and bake until the crumble is cooked and the fruit is soft.

#1007. Maple dumplings

Make the dumplings by rubbing butter into flour to which baking powder is added. Mix to a dough by adding in milk and vanilla but handling the dough lightly. Make a sugar syrup by mixing sugar and water and reducing then pour in Maple syrup. Roll patties out of the dough then oven bake. When all the dough is cooked through, dip them into the syrup so they absorb some of it. Orange juice or rum can be added to the syrup depending on choice.

#1008. Marshmallow crumble

Copy the same procedure as in #1006. Peel and cut tart-tasting apples into small cubes and place in a bowl with chopped pecans and desiccated coconut. Mix in cinnamon, nutmeg, caster sugar, orange juice and zest. Mix all the ingredients together then pour into a buttered casserole dish leaving enough room for the crumble mix to be placed on top. Prepare the crumble from baby marshmallows, flour, butter, cinnamon, nutmeg, brown sugar and wholemeal oats. Spread it over the top of the fruit and bake until the crumble is cooked and the fruit is soft.

#1009. Ice cream (quick home method)

Squeeze two each of oranges and lemons then slice and cook the zest in a water and sugar mix then cool. Put the zest into a bowl, adding 250 g icing sugar and stir. The juices will dissolve the icing sugar. Add 500 ml pouring cream and whisk with a stick beater till just creating peaks. Pour into an ice cream mould and put into the deep freeze for at least 12 hours. Serve with a chocolate sauce — try a Snickers or Mars bar melted then cream added for extra decadence.

#1010. Hot fudge sauce

Caster sugar, brown sugar, cocoa, flour, evaporated milk, water, butter, vanilla essence, cream, butter, vanilla essence. Put sugars, cocoa, evaporated milk and flour mixed with water into a small saucepan and heat stirring all the time. When thickened, turn down the heat and add butter and vanilla essence. Finally add cream to taste.

#1011. Crepes

Cold milk, flour, eggs, sugar, melted butter and oil. Into a mixing bowl break the eggs, add milk, sugar then sifted flour and mix with a whisk. Finally pour in melted butter and oil. Leave the batter to rest in the refrigerator for an hour then make the crepes.

#1012. Caramel gel

Melt butter and salt in a heavy-based saucepan then add water, sugar and corn syrup. Don't stir. Keep the sides of the pot clean using cold water and a pastry brush. When it starts to colour and is a light amber, remove from the heat and with a wooden spoon beat in butter and vanilla. Add lemon juice for acidity, which should keep the caramel runny.

#1013. Baked figs in maple syrup

Cut the figs in half and place in a casserole then brush with butter and sprinkle with brown sugar. Bake slowly in the oven then drizzle with maple syrup and Grand Marnier. Allow to bake further, taking care not to burn the sugar on the base of the casserole. Serve with the sauce in the casserole and with cream.

#1014. Hazelnut and coconut macaroons for ice cream sandwiches

Add flour, caster sugar, chopped hazelnuts, coconut and salt to a food processor and mix. In a separate bowl beat egg whites with salt until stiff then add food colouring and vanilla extract. Slowly add the flour to the beaten egg whites, taking care not to beat the air out of the mix. Place in a piping bag and pipe onto baking paper on a baking tray. Bake in the oven till cooked then place on a wire rack to cool. Layer ice cream between each one and serve.

#1015. Quick ice cream

Pour 600 ml cream into a bowl and beat till thick and just forming peaks then add to a can of condensed milk. Fold in a pot of caramel (store-bought) and do so gently. Pour the mixture into a mould lined with cling wrap and freeze.

#1016. Chocolate slice

Prepare a chocolate ganache and when completed keep warm. In a flan tin, blind bake a sugar pastry base. When cooked, cool then spoon in the ganache and allow to cool. Decorate with sliced fresh fruit.

#1017. Chocolate truffles

Prepare a chocolate ganache and leave to go cold. With a dessertspoon, slide through the ganache and roll into balls then place on greaseproof paper. Sprinkle over cocoa powder and roll the truffles around in it then refrigerate.

#1018. White chocolate coconut cream sauce

In a saucepan, pour fresh cream with coconut cream. To this add desiccated coconut and sugar. Thicken with cornflour then add white chocolate buttons. Use over baked desserts or ice cream.

#1019. White chocolate cake with Black Doris plums

Make a Genoese sponge and leave to cool. Cut in half and spoon over plum jam and cream then return the top half. Make a white chocolate ganache using white chocolate, cream, a knob of butter and vanilla extract. Melt the ganache in a bowl over a saucepan containing hot water but don't let the base of the bowl touch the water. Stir with a wooden spoon. Once it is melted into a warm sauce, set aside to cool slightly then with a palette knife coat the top and sides of the cake with the ganache. Poach halved Black Doris plums in a sugar and rum syrup. Cool and serve with the white chocolate cake.

#1020. Strawberry mille-feuille

Using store-bought puff pastry, cut three oblong layers 120 x 80 mm. Line all sides and ends with strips of pastry 20 mm wide and placed on the pastry with egg wash used between the strips. Brush each layer with egg wash and bake at 200°C till the puff pastry has risen and cooked. Leave the pastry to go cold on a wire rack. Prepare a strawberry bavarois/custard and leave to go cold. Spoon the bavarois onto the base layer, top with sliced strawberries then add a second layer of the cooked pastry. Complete that layer then the same on the top layer. Decorate the top with strawberries and cream and serve.

#1021. Caramelised bananas and strawberries in filo

Prepare a caramel by melting sugar in a heavy-based frypan and as it turns colour to caramel ensure that it does not burn. Add knobs of butter and swirl while the pan is off the heat and finish with cream. Add the bananas and strawberries to cook and then remove. Once the fruit is cold place some of the fruit onto a square of four filo pastry sheets that have been brushed with melted butter. Fold the pastry over the fruit, brush with butter and bake.

#1022. Mock ice cream

Using a frozen packet of fruit such as blackberries, mix in a food processor. Add half a tub of yoghurt, a little lime juice and runny honey to sweeten. Once mixed, place in deep freeze till required.

#1023. Layered ice cream

The ice cream is sandwiched between layers of puff pastry or filo pastry. Bake the discs or store buy them if practicable. If baking in-house, sprinkle the pastry with crushed pistachio nuts before baking. The diameter of the rings should be around 7 cm and use at least three layers per serve. Put one layer of pastry on the plate then a roll of ice cream. Drizzle with a flavoured sauce such as chocolate or strawberry then lay another disc on top. Finish off with a disc on top then piped cream, nuts and sauce.

#1024. Pineapple bowl

Cut a pineapple in half lengthways. With a sharp knife cut through the flesh in a criss-cross direction to free up the flesh then remove with a spoon into a bowl without putting a hole in the skin. Prepare a sugar syrup adding a cinnamon quill. To the syrup add rum, Cocoriba and mint leaves and pour it over the pineapple to marinate. Return the cubed pineapple back to the pineapple skin and dress with mint leaves.

#1025. Tiramisu

Dip sponge fingers in sweetened black coffee and crème de cacao then line the base of the mould. Melt chocolate in a double boiler ensuring the bottom of the bowl with the chocolate in it does not touch the water. Add salt and sherry to the chocolate. Whisk egg yolks and stir into mascarpone. Whisk the egg whites and fold into the mascarpone mixture. Layer the chocolate and custard with sponge fingers in between then refrigerate.

#1026. Stuffed pears

Remove the core with an apple corer then stuff the centre with a mixture of raisins, sultanas, pine nuts, butter, brown sugar and rum. Bake the pears in the oven and serve with a butterscotch sauce.

#1027. Baked chocolate bar

Lay a sheet of store-bought puff pastry on the bench then on top lay a block of Whittaker's or Cadbury chocolate. Check that both sides of the puff pastry overlap over the top of the chocolate bar then lay the puff pastry sides back out on the bench. Slice both sides of the pastry into strips 15 mm wide but still attached to the puff pastry base. Additions of jam or crushed nuts can be added to the top of the chocolate then fold the strips back over the pastry so that the chocolate bar is fully enclosed. Brush with egg wash and bake at 220°C till the pastry is brown. Cut and serve immediately.

#1028. Peach soufflé omelette

Separate egg yolks from whites and place the whites into a clean mixing bowl that does not have any fat on the sides. Pour cream and caster sugar onto the egg yolks and stir well. Whip the egg whites to a stiff foam then stir into the egg yolk mix. Before starting the omelette preparation, peel the peach and poach in a sugar syrup or use canned peaches. Heat the peach segments in butter and muscovado sugar and keep warm. Fold the egg white into the egg yolks mixture and pour carefully into a hot omelette pan with butter melted in it. Top with the peaches then place straight into a hot oven and do not open the oven until the omelette has risen and set. The omelette should slide out of the pan onto a serving plate. Serve with ice cream and cream.

#1029. Strawberries, tortillas and ice cream

On a standard dinner plate scoop out four or five balls of ice cream. Top with strawberries and into the ice cream balls push the corners of tortilla chips so that they sit sticking out and also form a platform over the top of the ice cream. Drizzle over strawberry sauce then complete a second layer as the first. For the top layer place one or two ice cream balls then drizzle hot chocolate sauce over the whole dish and serve quickly with pouring cream. This dish can't be made ahead so have all the ingredients ready to assemble when required.

#1030. Chocolate bar lasagne

Line a dessert dish with chocolate biscuits completely covering the base. Oreos could be used as an option. Top with whipped cream which has been sweetened with icing sugar and vanilla essence. Slice your favourite chocolate bar and spoon it over the top and drizzle with chocolate or caramel sauce. Complete two layers then place briefly in the deep freeze to harden up before serving.

#1031. Baked pears

Remove the skin off the pears, remove some of the core from underneath and cut a thin slice off the base so that the pear sits evenly in the saucepan. Then prepare a cooking liquid of water, red wine, brown sugar, cinnamon stick and honey and poach the pears gently till just cooked then remove from the liquid and cool. When cold, using store-bought puff pastry, slice off strips 20 mm wide and wrap around the pear starting at the base and working up. Cover the whole pear, brush with egg wash and bake at 200°C till golden brown. Make a sauce from the cooking liquor by checking on sweetness, add crème de cassis and thicken with cornflour and water. Serve with ice cream and cream.

#1032. Poached rum and raisin pears

Make a syrup of sugar, water, cloves and cinnamon. Simmer to reduce the sauce then add raisins, lemon juice, grated lemon zest and dark rum. Peel the pears, cut in half and deseed. Poach the pears in the liquor till soft then remove with a slotted spoon and place on a wire rack to drain. Thicken the sauce with arrowroot mixed with water, check the taste and spoon it over the pears.

27.

PIZZA TOPPINGS

#	Dish	#	Dish
1033	Avocado And Chilli	1053	King Prawn
1034	Salami And Pickle	1054	Margherita
1035	Roasted Chicken And Mayonnaise	1055	Chicken And Caramelised Onion
1036	Chicken And Peanut Butter	1056	Tasman
1037	Salami, Avocado And Chilli	1057	Florentina
1038	Fillet Steak	1058	Peking Duck
1039	Fresh Salmon	1059	Neopolitana
1040	Hamburger	1060	La Reine
1041	Fillet Steak #2	1061	Capricioza
1042	Hawaiian	1062	Gardinera
1043	Chicken Tikka	1063	Siciliana
1044	Aubergine And Feta	1064	Bombay
1045	Bocconcini And Tomato	1065	Mediterranean
1046	Smoked Chicken	1066	Quattro Stagioni
1047	Feta And Chicken	1067	Brie
1048	Roma	1068	Smoked Chicken
1049	Spicy Mexican	1069	The Mexican
1050	Chorizo	1070	Smoked Salmon
1051	Chermoula Chicken Pizza		
1052	Prosciutto		

Basic ingredients to prepare a home-made pizza

Toppings

Many toppings come by direct association with restaurants or fast food outlets, and so rages the argument whether pineapple should be served on a pizza. You can stick to those toppings that are standard or create your own or add accompaniments to the standard description. Fried mushrooms sliced or whole, sun-dried tomatoes, sliced capsicums, artichokes are items that can be used in addition to other ingredients. You are making the pizza, so you give it soul the best way you know how.

Pizza dough

Flour, yeast, warm water, salt, brown sugar, olive oil. Combine the warm water, yeast, sugar and olive oil. Stir and leave for the yeast to prove. Sift the flour and salt together into a bowl, make a well in the centre and pour in the yeast liquid. Sprinkle a little flour over the yeast mixture and leave covered for a few minutes. Using hands, slowly mix the liquid and incorporate the flour to form the dough. Remove the dough from the bowl, place on a floured board and knead gently. Cover and leave to prove in a warm place then knead again. Knead again then roll into a ball that will fit the pizza pan once it has been rolled.

Pizza sauce

Fresh tomato flesh, roasted garlic cloves, oregano, diced onions, tomato paste, dried basil, brown sugar, olive oil and seasoning. Roast the tomatoes, onions and the garlic briefly in oil and butter along with oregano. Pour it into a large saucepan, add in tomato paste and muscovado sugar and stir well, drizzling in oil. Gently simmer and reduce the sauce. Either put through a food processor and sieve or leave chunky if that is what you prefer. Check seasoning and serve.

Method

With a rolling pin roll out proved pizza dough and line the round pizza tin. Brush the inside edge of the pizza tin with oil to hold in place and prevent the dough from shrinking. Spoon the pizza sauce over the dough, keeping it away from the edges of the dough. If the sauce spills over the dough it will cause the crust to stick to the pan. Place the appropriate ingredients on the pizza sauce, top with grated mozzarella, drizzle with a garlic-flavoured olive oil, season then bake in the oven.

Fast pizza dough

Two cups of self-raising flour to one cup of Greek yoghurt.

Pizza recipes

#1033. Avocado and chilli pizza

Top the pizza sauce with sliced avocado and fresh tomatoes and sprinkle gently with chilli flakes.

#1034. Salami and pickle pizza

Place sliced salami and sliced pickle on the pizza.

#1035. Roasted chicken and mayonnaise pizza

Tear apart a roast chicken that has been cooked specifically for pizzas. Spread the torn cooked chicken meat over the pizza then drizzle with mayonnaise.

#1036. Chicken and peanut butter pizza

Fry chicken pieces in oil and butter till cooked through. At the same time prepare a peanut/satay-style sauce to go with it. When the chicken is cooked, cut into suitable-sized pieces and leave to cool. In a small saucepan, heat chopped peanuts slowly in a dry pan (that is, with no oil). When heated, add coconut milk, chilli flakes, peanut butter, soy sauce and fish sauce. Simmer gently till the sauce begins to thicken. Season and set aside. Place the chicken on the pizza, drizzle with the satay sauce, add any other toppings and bake.

#1037. Salami, avocado and chilli pizza

Top the pizza sauce with sliced salami and avocado and sprinkle gently with chilli flakes.

#1038. Fillet steak

Thinly sliced fillet steak (10 mm) cooked in a frypan with garlic very quickly. Place on pizza pastry that has tomato sauce on. Add caramelised onions, sliced cooked mushrooms and béarnaise sauce.

#1039. Fresh salmon

Bake salmon fillet and flake. Place on top of the pizza. Top with sun-dried tomatoes, sliced red onions, mozzarella and grated cheese. Top with hollandaise sauce and crème fraîche before serving.

#1040. Hamburger

Make small flat burger patties and fry first to brown on each side in oil and garlic. When cold, place on pizza base which has pizza sauce on it, top with caramelised onions and sliced tomatoes.

#1041. Fillet steak

Thinly slice fillet steak and quickly fry in oil and garlic to brown on both sides then leave to cool. Dress the pizza with capsicum, sliced red onions, sliced tomatoes and caramelised onions. Top with the fillet steak then complete the preparation and serve.

#1042. Hawaiian

Ham and pineapple pieces topped with grated cheese.

#1043. Chicken tikka

Cook diced chicken in tikka sauce. Spoon chicken over tomato pizza sauce, spoon over chutney, plain yoghurt and grated cheese.

#1044. Aubergine and feta

Cut an aubergine into slices and fry in oil and garlic. When brown, place on kitchen paper to drain off any excess oil. When cold, lay the aubergine onto the pizza, top with slices of fresh tomato and crumbled feta.

#1045. Bocconcini and tomato

Top with sliced bocconcini then fresh sliced tomato over the top.

#1046. Smoked chicken pizza

Cut the smoked chicken into slices and lay it on the pizza. Top the chicken with sun-dried tomatoes, sun-dried tomato pesto with sliced green capsicums.

#1047. Feta and chicken pizza

Use chicken of choice whether that be roasted or fried. Top with caramelised red onion and then with cubed feta.

#1048. Roma pizza

Slices of buffalo mozzarella and fresh basil leaves.

#1049. Spicy Mexicana

Slices of pepperoni, char-grilled capsicum, sliced red onions, chilli sauce and jalapeños.

#1050. Chorizo pizza

Sliced chorizo fried in oil then left to cool, sliced portobello mushrooms, baby spinach, paprika and chilli flakes.

#1051. Chermoula chicken pizza

Pan-fried chicken brushed with chermoula sauce, sliced red onions and cashew nuts. **Chermoula sauce**: Chopped parsley, coriander leaves, mint leaves, crushed garlic, cumin, chilli, lemon juice, turmeric, olive oil. Blend all ingredients in a food processor till smooth.

#1052. Prosciutto pizza

Sliced prosciutto, sliced artichokes, sun-dried tomatoes and shaved Parmesan.

#1053. King prawn pizza

Whole king prawns pan fried in oil, sliced chorizo pan fried, wilted spinach, sliced mushrooms and smoked paprika.

#1054. Margherita pizza

Fresh diced tomato flesh, fresh torn basil leaves, bocconcini slices and grated mozzarella.

#1055. Chicken and caramelised onions

Cover the pizza base with shredded chicken, caramelised onions, oven-baked capsicums and grated mozzarella.

#1056. Tasman pizza

Baked salmon fillet diced, steamed mussels, prawns, oysters, cooked calamari with mozzarella cheese. Topped with aioli sauce once cooked.

#1057. Fiorentina pizza

Spinach, eggs, olives, diced tomatoes, garlic oil and mozzarella grated.

#1058. Peking duck pizza

Sliced Peking duck, hoi sin sauce, bok choy, sliced red onions, cucumber.

#1059. Neopolitana pizza

Sliced buffalo mozzarella, whole black olives, basil leaves, sliced tomatoes, cracked black pepper and oregano.

#1060. La Reine pizza

Sliced ham, sliced salami, sliced tomatoes, whole fried mushroom and black olives.

#1061. Capricciosa pizza

Sliced ham, buttered leeks, black olives, capers, capsicum, egg and anchovies.

#1062. Giardiniera pizza

Fresh roasted vegetables of the day marinated in oil and garlic with rosemary.

#1063. Siciliana pizza

Sliced ham, fresh basil leaves, olives and anchovies.

#1064. Bombay pizza

Chicken diced in a pineapple and coconut curry and topped with mango chutney.

#1065. Mediterranean pizza

Feta, sun-dried tomato, capers, red onions, artichokes, basil, olives and capsicum.

#1066. Quattro stagioni

Sliced salami, olives, shrimps, anchovies, capers, sliced peppers, sun-dried tomatoes, sliced ham, basil and garlic.

#1067. Brie pizza

Sliced brie, sun-dried tomatoes, sliced ham and wilted spinach.

#1068. Smoked chicken

Sliced smoked chicken, caramelised onions, sliced tomatoes and grated mozzarella cheese.

#1069. The Mexican

Sliced peppered salami, jalapenos, sliced onion, sliced fresh chilli, chutney, smoked sliced bell peppers, mozzarella.

#1070. Smoked salmon

Top the base with sliced fried courgette, capers, smoked salmon and sliced capsicum, and when cooked top with lemon cream cheese.

28.

MISCELLANEOUS

#	Dish	#	Dish
1071	Bacon And Cheese Butter	1087	Salsa Cheesecake
1072	Chilli And Lime Butter	1088	Griddle Cakes
1073	Upmarket Toasted Sandwich	1089	Stuffing For Poultry
1074	Smokey Tomato Dahl	1090	Hot Dog Onion Rings
1075	Tempura Batter	1091	Cheese And Bacon Sticks
1076	Bread Crumbed Haloumi	1092	Lebanese Fattah
1077	Miso Glaze/Dressing	1093	Sesame Seed Sticks
1078	BBQ Sauce/Spaghetti	1094	Camembert Fries
1079	Caramelised Onions And Anchovy Tarts With Black Olives	1095	Chicken And Broccoli Fritters
1080	Fried Ravioli	1096	Crepes Cordon Bleu
1081	Naan Bread	1097	Fried Ham With An Orange And Honey Glaze
1082	Naan Bread Topping	1098	Sausages In A Bread Wrapper
1083	Double Cooked Cheese Souffle	1099	Breakfast Bread Rolls
1084	Sun-Dried Tomato Pesto	1100	Blue Cheese And Walnut Butter
1085	Avocado Hummus	1101	Chorizo And Bean Casserole
1086	Seafood Pastry Snacks		

#1071. Bacon and cheese butter

Soft butter, streaky bacon fried till it's crispy then crumbled, grated cheese, chopped parsley. Mix the ingredients together and place on a sheet of cling wrap. Roll the butter into a 30 mm diameter roll within the cling wrap and tie both ends. Hold in the fridge to harden then cut off slices as required to use on meat, fish, vegetables.

#1072. Chilli and lime butter

Soft butter, chilli flakes, grated lime zest and juice, chopped cilantro. Prepare and roll as in #1071.

#1073. Upmarket toasted sandwich

Cut a 40–50 mm slice off a piece of whole white loaf. Using a very sharp knife, cut a slice in the bread 20 mm in from the edge all the way round and remove most of the centre and grill in the oven. There should still be a complete base on the bottom. Soften a segment of blue cheese and mix in some Worcestershire sauce. Form a 10 mm ridge around the hole in the bread with the blue cheese and put some in the centre. Again, quickly grill then remove from the oven. In the hole, place two egg yolks and bake quickly so that the whole sandwich is hot.

#1074. Smoky tomato dhal

Cooked dhal, tomato halves, onion, garlic, root ginger, smoked paprika, cumin, cardamom seeds, fresh coriander. Fry the onions, garlic, root ginger, paprika, cumin and cardamom seeds in oil in a frypan. When transparent, add in the cooked dhal and heat. When hot, spoon the dhal into the tomato halves and serve.

#1075. Tempura batter

Self-raising flour mixed with soda water. Mix well. The batter is quite thin but roll the ingredient in flour first before placing in the batter.

#1076. Breadcrumbed haloumi

Slice the cheese into thick slices then put through flour, egg wash and breadcrumbs. Fry in oil and butter. Serve as a canapé, a side dish or on a savoury meat dish as a topping.

#1077. Miso glaze/dressing

White miso, sake or sherry, soy, sugar and rice vinegar. Mix well together. Lamb can be marinated in this dressing before cooking; roast aubergine slices can be brushed while roasting.

#1078. Barbecue sauce

Brown sugar, soy sauce, grated ginger, crushed garlic, honey, oil and ketchup. Mix in a bowl then brush it over the items to be barbecued. Continue brushing while the barbecue is in progress.

#1079. Caramelised onion and anchovy tarts with black olives

With a sheet of puff pastry, cut out circles to fit a muffin tin. Butter the moulds, place the puff pastry into them, poke with a table fork on the base then bake in the oven at 200°C. Remove from the oven and cool. Spoon in caramelised onions, top with anchovies and black olives.

#1080. Fried ravioli

Cook the ravioli in boiling salted water but undercook. Drain then fry in sage butter and oil till golden brown and serve with tomato salsa and Parmesan. (This is not an Italian-friendly recipe!)

#1081. Naan bread

Plain flour, salt, yeast, water, yoghurt, oil. Sift flour and salt.

Make a well add a little warm water, yeast, oil then leave to sit with a pinch of flour sprinkled over the yeast. Leave in a warm place for 15 minutes. Once bubbles appear in the yeast, add the yoghurt and more warm water and start making the dough. Once a smooth dough is reached, place back in the bowl, cover with a clean tea towel and sit till it doubles in size. Knock it back, divide equally and roll out with a rolling pin then fry in oil on both sides.

#1082. Naan bread topping

Spoon over the top with a pizza-style tomato sauce then top with cooked prawns, squid, mussels. Spoon over some cheese sauce, top with grated cheese and crumbled feta then grill in the oven.

#1083. Double-cooked cheese soufflé

Make a roux, add milk, egg yolks, cream and grated cheese. Fold in egg whites and cook in a buttered ramekin. Turn out onto coupe dish or dessert plate, pour over double cream, kirsch and sprinkle with grated cheese.

#1084. Sun-dried tomato pesto

Tomato paste, chopped basil, olive oil, garlic, sun-dried tomatoes, diced onion, brown sugar, oregano and pine nuts. Pour a little of the sun-dried tomato oil into a saucepan and add onions, garlic, brown sugar, oregano. Reduce heat and add tomato paste and pine nuts. Pour the mix into a food processor, add basil and pulse. Check seasoning then add the sun-dried tomatoes and mix by hand.

#1085. Avocado hummus

In a food processor, add drained can of chickpeas, tahini,

avocado flesh and garlic bulbs. Pulse until a paste is reached. Add olive oil and seasoning to achieve a spreadable paste.

#1086. Seafood pastry sticks

With a sheet of store-bought puff pastry, place on a bench and cut into four equal squares. For the filling use whatever selection of seafood is desired, however it needs to be dry. Roughly chop prawns and mussels into small-size pieces and wrap in a dry tea towel or cloth. Spoon onto the four squares across the width. Brush the edges of the pastry then roll the pastry squares and seal. Brush the whole tube with egg wash and bake in the oven at 200°C till brown.

#1087. Salsa cheesecake

In a food processor, process Snax biscuits or similar till a crumb mix is achieved. Pour in melted butter, mix well and lay it in the base of a spring-form tin to a depth of 7 mm and bake in the oven. Again in the food processor, beat cream cheese, sour cream and grated cheese then slowly add eggs. Fold in store-bought salsa and chilli flakes and pour on top of the crust. Bake in the oven at 160°C for 40 minutes. Top with a coating of sour cream and sliced fresh tomatoes.

#1088. Griddle cakes

Prepare a batter using flour, eggs, milk and seasoning. Add whole kernel corn, chopped parsley and grated cheese. In a frypan, sweat off diced bacon, onions, chopped capsicums and garlic then stir into the batter when cold. Fry the cakes in vegetable oil and garlic until brown on both sides.

#1089. Stuffing for poultry

Roughly chop prunes, apricots, walnuts and pistachios then fry in butter. Add diced root ginger, garlic, cardamom, coriander, cherries and chopped dates. Leave to cool then spoon into the poultry and bake.

#1090. Hot dog onion rings

Peel and slice large white onions into 15 mm wide slices and separate then place on baking paper which is on a baking tray. Fry and slice the hot dogs into approximately 15 mm sized pieces. Prepare a béchamel sauce and cook out but keep the sauce thick so that it pours with the assistance of a spoon. Place the cold sausage pieces into a mixing bowl, add some of the cold béchamel sauce and mix. Spoon the mixture into the onion rings then place in the freezer to freeze the onion ring mixture. The next day, flour, egg wash and breadcrumb the onion rings then fry and serve.

#1091. Cheese and bacon sticks

Slice 20 x 20 mm sticks off a block of cheese. Fry streaky bacon in a frypan till well-cooked but not crispy then leave to cool. When cold, wrap a piece of the streaky bacon around the cheese stick then place on a piece of puff pastry. Fold the pastry over to enclose the cheese and bacon and seal the edges with egg wash. Brush the whole stick with egg wash and bake at 200°C till golden brown.

#1092. Lebanese fatteh

Cut flat breads into small crouton-size pieces, fry in oil and place in the bottom of a casserole dish then top with chickpeas. In a saucepan, sauté diced onions, garlic, cinnamon and pepper then add lamb and beef mince and cook. In a blender mix yoghurt, garlic, mint, pepper then pour it over the chickpeas. When the mince meat is cooked, ladle it over the yoghurt and top with roasted pine nuts and chopped parsley.

#1093. Sesame seed sticks

Toast and butter both sides of white sliced bread then remove the crusts. In a mixing bowl put the chicken mince, Thai curry paste, sliced spring onions, crushed root ginger, garlic, egg white and breadcrumbs. Mix well and add seasoning, flour if necessary to dry out the mix, which should be spreadable with a knife. Spread the paste thickly (6 mm) over one side of the toast then cut into three fingers. Dip the chicken paste side into the sesame seeds then fry seed side down in oil and butter. Turn over and briefly fry the base side then serve hot with **dipping sauce**: rice wine vinegar, caster sugar, fish sauce, soy sauce, chopped coriander and sliced chilli.

#1094. Camembert fries

Cut a round of camembert in half widthways then cut into strips at least 10 mm. Put the slices through flour, egg wash and breadcrumbs then fry. Serve with mayonnaise and salad.

#1095. Chicken and broccoli fritters

Chicken mince (or pork), crushed garlic, egg, panko crumbs, cooked broccoli florets, diced onions and grated cheese. Mix well together in a bowl, mould the paste into fritters and place on an oiled baking tray then bake in the oven. Turn over and continue cooking till cooked through.

#1096. Crepes cordon bleu

Prepare crepes approximately 20 cm in diameter and leave to cool. Brush with butter and wholegrain mustard then overlay with thin slices of ham and sliced Swiss cheese. Roll the crepes to form a cigar shape, place in a buttered casserole dish and heat in the oven. Top with grated cheese and grill to brown the cheese. Serve with hollandaise sauce.

#1097. Fried ham steak with an orange and honey glaze

In a frypan, fry the ham steak in oil and butter and brown on both sides. In a mixing bowl add orange juice, whole cloves, finely sliced orange zest, honey, orange marmalade, grated ginger, mustard and mix well. To the ham, add another large knob of butter then pour in the orange mix and bring to the boil then allow to simmer gently to finish cooking the ham. Check for seasoning and serve. Sliced chilli could also be added if desired.

#1098. Sausages in bread wrapper

Fry the sausages in oil and crushed garlic till brown then cool. With a piece of white sliced bread, remove the crusts and roll with a rolling pin to flatten the bread out. Roll the cold, cooked sausage in the slice of bread then dip into beaten eggs and cream mixed together. Fry the roll in oil, turning on all sides till nicely brown all over.

#1099. Breakfast bread rolls

Buy bread buns large enough for a single serve. With a sharp knife remove the top then remove the bread from centre of the bun. Line the base of the bun with cooked sliced bacon then top with a spoonful of baked beans, a few pieces of cooked and broken potato rosti. Spoon over melted butter and bake the bun in the oven. After 5 minutes, break an egg into the cavity, top with grated cheese and bake until the egg is just cooked then serve.

#1100. Blue cheese and walnut butter

In a food processor place blue cheese and soft butter and allow to mix. Drizzle in Worcestershire sauce, olive oil and chopped walnuts. Spoon the cheese mixture onto a sheet of cling wrap, shape into a cylinder 25 mm in diameter and place in the deep freeze for 30 minutes to set.

#1101. Chorizo and bean casserole

Slice the chorizo into thin slices and brown in oil in a frypan. While the chorizo is frying, add sliced onions, garlic and sliced capsicum. Turn down the heat and add drained red beans, a can of chopped tomatoes and small cherry tomatoes that have been oven roasted.

29.

TAKE-OUT/ LUNCHES

#	Dish	#	Dish
1102	Corned Beef And Cabbage Turnover	1107	Chicken Baguette Carprese
1103	Chicken And Sesame Noodle Pot	1108	Pork And Peanut Butter Wrap
1104	Jar Salad	1109	Waffle Sandwiches
1105	French Bread Stuffed With Bolognese Sauce	1110	Steak And Roast Vegetable Wrap
1106	Chicken Baguette	1111	Tortillas

#1102. Corned beef and cabbage turnovers

Place a store-bought sheet of puff pastry on a chopping board and cut a circle 16 cm in diameter. Using cooked corned beef, cut or pull into smaller pieces and place in the centre of the pastry. Top with cooked cold cabbage and a half teaspoon of wholegrain mustard over the mix. Fold the pastry over and seal the join with egg wash. Brush the top with egg wash and bake in the oven at 200°C until golden brown. Two tablespoons of mustard sauce or cheese sauce could also be used over the cabbage.

#1103. Chicken and sesame noodle pot

In the base of the jar, put sesame oil, crushed garlic, diced root ginger and chilli. Add leftover cooked chicken, baby spinach, coriander leaves, cooked cold noodles. Top with a spoonful of coconut oil. Add more filling to pack the jar. At work, top the jar with boiling water for a few minutes then eat with chopsticks.

#1104. Jar salad

Into the base of an Agee jar, pour a generous layer of pesto. Next is diced tomatoes, roast diced beetroot, carrots then top with quinoa. Add baby spinach, cubed feta, olive oil and seasoning.

Leftover meat or canned tuna could also be added, as could other vegetables of choice.

#1105. Baguette stuffed with Bolognese sauce

Prepare a Bolognese sauce as for spaghetti Bolognese then leave to cool. Cut a baguette into four sections then take one of the sections and remove the inner centre bread with a long bread knife. Drizzle in some melted garlic butter then slide in sliced cheese. Spoon in the sauce so that the roll is full. Spoon over the top some melted garlic butter then bake. Eat like a sausage roll.

#1106. Chicken baguette

Cut the baguette into 12 cm lengths and using a sharp knife, remove the bread centre. Slice a chicken breast into thin slices and flour, egg wash and breadcrumb then fry in oil and butter and leave to cool. Wrap the chicken in slices of smoked cheese and before pushing it down the centre of the bread loaf, spoon in some garlic butter. Heat in the microwave if desired.

#1107. Chicken baguette Caprese

Cut the baguette into a 12 cm lengths then cut in half lengthways. Spread the inner roll with garlic butter and toast till melted. Leave to cool then top with slices of mozzarella, then cooked chicken pieces. Add cherry tomatoes cut in half and chopped basil. Drizzle with olive oil then wrap in cling wrap.

#1108. Pork and peanut butter wrap

Leftover roast pork, pulled pork or pork chops can be used. Chop the pork into finger-length pieces and mix with sliced raw onions and chopped spring onions along with a small amount of sweet chilli sauce. Lay the wrap on a chopping board. Spoon peanut butter into a small bowl then add chilli flakes, butter, curry, coconut cream and seasoning. Mix well then spread it over the wrap. Top with the pork mixture then roll up the wrap and place in cling film.

#1109. Waffle sandwiches

Prepare the waffle batter as per the waffle iron maker's instructions and make the waffles. Ideal as sandwiches to be taken to work or the beach. Fill with beef or chicken fillings or bacon and eggs.

#1110. Steak and roast vegetable wrap

Use the cut of steak that you prefer. Sirloin or rump would be perfect. Marinate if required or leave plain. Prepare some small diced roast vegetables and roast in oil, butter, rosemary and garlic. Cook the steak to required degree of cooking then leave to go cold. When the vegetables are cold, spread aioli onto the wrap and top with the cold roast vegetables. Slice the steak into thin slices and lay them over the top of the roast vegetables. Add mustard of choice if required, roll up the wrap and cling wrap.

#1111. Tortillas

Having two tortillas to make a sandwich for a take-out lunch, many fillings can be used so make whatever fillings you like. Here's one to start. With a sharp knife cut slices from the block of cheese. Place a dry frypan on the element and place a tortilla in it. While it is heating, lay the cheese on top keeping a 20 mm clear edge all the way round. Top the cheese with slices of pepperoni then place a second tortilla on top. Turn the sandwich over and cook the other side then place onto the chopping board. Allow to cool then cut and wrap for lunch.

30.

DRINKS

#	Dish	#	Dish
1112	Turmeric Health Drink	1132	Watermelon Cooler
1113	Fruit Infused Vodka	1133	Coffee Float
1114	Margarita Sangria	1134	Coconut Coffee
1115	Blackcurrant Tea Sangria	1135	Coffee Mocha
1116	Berry Or Strawberry Vodka	1136	Feijoa, Vodka And Apple Juice
1117	Hunters Rum	1137	Limoncello
1118	Chocolate Mudslide	1138	Café Tonic
1119	Whisky Cream	1139	Iced Coffee
1120	Oreo Baileys Shake	1140	Irish Coffee
1121	Irish Coffee Cream	1141	Affogato
1122	Pineapple Margarita	1142	Whisky And Peach Cooler
1123	Pino Colada Pineapple	1143	Lemonade With Basil And Fresh Lemon Juice
1124	Ginger And Lemon Rum	1144	Coffee With Brandy And Orange Zest
1125	White Wine Slushies	1145	Mulled Wine
1126	Bourbon Milkshakes	1146	Moscow Mule
1127	Ginger Tea	1147	Strawberry Daquiri
1128	Jack And Coke Slushie	1148	Bourbon On Smoked Ice
1129	Vodka, Honey And Lemonade Slushie	1149	Whisky Sangria
1130	Cherry Sangria	1150	White Wine Ice Cubes
1131	Vodka Fruit Punch		

#1112. Turmeric health drink

Coconut milk, turmeric powder, piece grated root ginger, honey and pepper. Grate the root ginger and mix all ingredients together and pour it over ice.

#1113. Fruit-infused vodka

2 cups fruit to 2–3 cups vodka. Strawberries are ideal for this. Leave for at least 3–5 days or longer. Strain into a clean bottle. The same process could be used for white wine. Peaches and mango are also ideal for this drink.

#1114. Margarita sangria

To 1 bottle wine add 1½ cups tequila, 1 cup triple sec, 1 cup orange juice, ½ cup lemon juice, sliced orange and lemon slices.

#1115. Blackcurrant tea sangria

4 cups water, 2 blackcurrant tea bags, sugar, fresh blackcurrants, lemon slices, white wine. Infuse all ingredients into boiling water.

#1116. Berry or strawberry vodka

2 punnets fresh strawberries cut in half, add them to a bottle of vodka and mint leaves then pour into a preserving jar with a lid. Boil 2 cups sugar to 1 cup water and simmer to a syrup. When cool, add to the strawberries and leave for 4–5 days. Serve with lemonade if necessary. Other fruits can be used.

#1117. Hunter's rum

6 shots rum, 12 whole cloves, sliced lemon, 55 g caster sugar, 6 cups water, 90 g butter, 6 cinnamon sticks. Place all ingredients into a small saucepan, simmer then serve warm.

#1118. Chocolate mudslide

120 mls vodka, 120 mls Kahlua, 120 mls Baileys Irish Cream, 4 cups vanilla ice cream, chocolate syrup. Mix the vodka, Kahlua

and Baileys in a jug then pour it over the ice cream along with chocolate syrup.

#1119. Whisky cream

250 ml fresh cream, 1 can condensed milk, 350 ml whisky, 1 tsp instant coffee, 2 Tbsp chocolate syrup, 1 tsp vanilla. Mix all ingredients in a jug and pour it over ice.

#1120. Oreo Baileys shake

Put ice cream into a blender with ice and crush then add 8 Oreo cookies. Add fresh cream, 4 shots vodka and 4 shots Baileys Irish Cream. Pour into glasses and top with whipped cream.

#1121. Irish coffee cream

200 ml Baileys Irish Cream, 80 ml vodka, 80 ml black coffee, 50 ml cream and ice. Mix all ingredients together and pour.

#1122. Pineapple margarita

Into a mixing jug pour 1 litre pineapple juice, 500 ml orange juice, 100 ml lime juice, 250 ml tequila and 250 ml triple sec. Stir well and pour into a small cocktail glass with a lime slice on the glass.

#1123. Piña colada pineapple

Cut the top off a pineapple and remove the centre flesh. Place in a food processor and blitz adding coconut cream, piña colada and spicy rum. Pour it back into the pineapple shell and serve with straws.

#1124. Ginger and lemon rum

Mix ginger beer and sliced lemon zest with dark rum, pour over ice and serve.

#1125. White wine slushies

In a blender, put in white wine (approximately 500 ml) and add the equivalent of 2 peaches which have been frozen. Canned peaches could also be used but drain and freeze first. Top up with soda water and fresh mint and blitz. Pour into wine glasses.

#1126. Bourbon milkshakes

Vanilla ice cream, honey, bourbon, pinch of cinnamon, vanilla, cream. Blitz in a blender and pour into cold glasses.

#1127. Ginger tea

4 cups water, 2 Tbsp grated root ginger or 1 heaped tsp ground caraway seeds. Heat in a saucepan for 5 minutes on a gentle heat then cool. Add lemon slices and honey to sweeten.

#1128. Jack and Coke slushie

Pour Jack Daniel's into ice cube trays and place in the freezer. When making the drink, place the soft JD ice cubes in a blender with ice cubes. Blitz quickly and pour into a glass. Add Coke and top with a slice of lemon and mint leaf.

#1129. Vodka, honey and lemonade slushie

Pour the vodka into ice cube trays and place in the freezer. They won't set like ice cubes but will ice up. Turn out the vodka ice and place in a food processor with ice cubes. Pour in honey and blitz quickly. Pour the mix into glasses that contain ice cubes and top up with lemonade.

#1130. Cherry sangria

Fresh cherries, white wine and amaretto. Remove the stones from the cherries and place the cherries in a bowl, pour in the white wine and leave overnight. Add amaretto to sweeten the drink then serve.

#1131. Vodka fruit punch

Oranges, lemons, grapefruit, apple juice, ginger ale and fresh mint. Top up with vodka or any other suitable liquor as desired.

#1132. Watermelon cooler

Cut the watermelon and remove the rind. Put into a food processor along with a little sugar and lime juice and pulse. Add a small amount of water if necessary, or use vodka instead.

#1133. Coffee float

1 cup coffee, 1 Tbsp cocoa, scoop ice cream, 50 ml Kahlua. Mix coffee and cocoa then pour in Kahlua and finally add the ice cream.

#1134. Coconut coffee

1 cup coffee, 3 tsp coconut oil, 2 tsp desiccated coconut, 2 Tbsp butter, 80 ml vodka. Place all ingredients into a blender and blitz.

#1135. Coffee mocha

Pour coffee into ice cube trays and freeze. Place the frozen cubes in a tall glass, squeeze over chocolate syrup, Kahlua and top with milk.

#1136. Feijoa, vodka and apple juice

Peel feijoas and chop into dice. Add to pouring jug then pour in vodka and apple juice over ice. Add a few drops of Angostura bitters and stir well.

#1137. Limoncello

12 smooth-skinned lemons, 1 litre vodka, 750 g caster sugar. Peel the lemons but ensure no pith is on the zest, as it creates a bitter taste. Pack into a sterilised jar until it is packed full. Pour over the vodka and cover the lemon peel. Seal the jar and store away from light for a minimum of 2 days. When ready to bottle, make a syrup from the sugar and simmer till the syrup thickens. Cool the syrup and remove the lemon strips away from the vodka. Add the syrup to the vodka, stir well and bottle. Store a bottle in the deep freeze.

#1138. Café tonic

A glass of crushed ice, 60 ml cold espresso. Top up with a can of tonic water.

#1139. Iced coffee

A glass of ice, chilled coffee, condensed milk.

#1140. Irish coffee

2 Tbsp Irish cream, 1 Tbsp cream, cocoa, caster sugar, vanilla essence, 1 shot espresso, 1 tot Irish whiskey. Top with chocolate/ vanilla ice cream and chocolate shavings.

#1141. Affogato

2 scoops vanilla ice cream in a coffee cup, top with double-shot hot espresso or strong filtered coffee. Top with shaved chocolate and chopped nuts.

#1142. Whisky and peach cooler

In a saucepan boil 8 cups water. In a frypan add 2 skinned, sliced fresh peaches, 1 cup sugar and 1 cup water then boil allowing the peach to break up. Strain the peach juice through a sieve into the saucepan of water, adding lemon juice and 2 cups whisky and allow to go cold and hold in the fridge. Serve in a long glass with mint and lemon segment.

#1143. Lemonade with basil and fresh lemon juice

Tear basil leaves and place in a jug. Cut and squeeze fresh lemons and pour the juice into the jug. Slice a lemon into 8 lemon wedges and add to the jug then top with lemonade.

#1144. Coffee with brandy and orange zest

Carefully remove the zest off an orange and lemon and leave off the white pith, which will taste bitter. Into the peel, place 3 whole cloves in each piece of the orange and lemon. Pour the long black coffee into a saucepan adding brandy and the orange and lemon peel. Heat gently and add sugar. Stir with a cinnamon stick, add Drambuie to accentuate the flavour and enjoy.

#1145. Mulled wine

1 litre red wine, 6 strips each of lemon zest and orange zest using a potato peeler for ease of removing the zest. Place the wine in a saucepan with the zest along with 6 whole cloves without the bulbs on the end of the clove, 200 ml kirsch liqueur, 250 g sugar,

a split vanilla bean, a cinnamon stick and 400 ml water. Bring to the boil and simmer. Add slices of orange and lemon and cool and leave in the fridge.

#1146. Moscow mule

In a glass over ice, pour vodka, lime juice, ginger beer and top off with mint leaves.

#1147. Strawberry daiquiri

Fresh and frozen strawberries, rum, lime juice. Place all in a blender and mix well. Keep a few fresh strawberries back for garnishing the glass.

#1148. Bourbon and smoked ice

In a large glass Pyrex dish, fill with clean water then place in a covered barbecue and smoke the water for approximately 60 minutes. Strain the water through a filter and taste the strength of the smoke. More water can be added if required to dilute slightly. Use whatever moulds you have available to be able to freeze and produce large ice blocks. In a glass, pour bourbon, add the smoked ice block then a little water or mix as required but not diluting the smoked ice block too much.

#1149. Whisky sangria

Into a glass jug pour red wine 5:1 of whisky then put a cinnamon quill into the jug along with sliced apples. Stir and serve.

#1150. White wine ice cubes

Buy a bunch of white grapes, wipe down and place in a Ziploc bag and deep freeze. Two or three grapes will cool down a nice white wine without diluting the drink.

GLOSSARY AND CULINARY TERMS

Arborio rice — A short-grain rice generally used for risottos.

Arrabbiata — An Italian sauce of tomatoes, onions, garlic and chilli used over pasta.

Bain-marie — A hot-water bath to keep food warm or to cook food without burning. For example when melting cooking chocolate, the chocolate is placed in a smaller pot or bowl which sits in a larger pot of hot water; or when cooking a terrine in the oven, the terrine is placed in a baking dish which has hot water in it.

Baklava — A Greek dessert using filo pastry, honey and nuts.

Béchamel — A sauce made with equal quantities of flour and butter then slowly adding warm milk to make a rich smooth sauce to which other things such as chopped parsley and grated cheddar can be added. Ensure that once the milk has been added, it simmers very gently to cook the flour out. If the sauce is going to be held aside, brush the top with melted butter to stop a skin forming.

Beignets — Fritters or deep-fried items such as battered anchovy fillets.

Beurre manié — Equal quantities of flour and soft butter mixed together. Pieces of the dough are dropped into a casserole or sauce to thicken it while stirring.

Beurre noisette — Nut brown butter which is used for pan frying fish or vegetables items. Take care the butter does not burn, which in turn will alter the taste of the finished product.

Blanch — To precook in boiling water then dropping in ice water to stop the cooking and retain the colour, especially in vegetables.

Blind bake — A term meaning to precook the pastry base. In making a savoury or dessert pie and using a short pastry on the base, it needs to be cooked first otherwise it will go soft due to the liquid from the pie. Line the pie dish then cover with baking paper and use rice or baking beads on top of the paper and allow to cook. Leave to cool and brush with melted butter to seal the pastry before adding the filling.

Breadcrumbs

a. For crumbing meat and vegetable products:

Made from stale bread and put through a food processor. If using fresh bread, then leave in a baking dish in the oven on a very low heat for an hour to dry out. The food item needs to be put through flour, egg wash and breadcrumbs before frying or deep frying. Panko breadcrumbs are a well-known type found in supermarkets.

b. Breadcrumb stuffing:

Keep the breadcrumbs wet if using for a stuffing of meat, poultry or fish. Use white crustless bread and moisten with orange juice, milk or water as required. For stuffing, the bread could also be torn into small pieces.

Canapé — A cushion of bread or pastry on which are served various foods both hot and cold. Depending on function and the requirements of a customer, canapés, crostini, bruschetta should be small enough to eat in one mouthful. As the canapés are passed around, plates are not generally used while guests are standing. So, while holding a glass in one hand, the other hand is selecting.

Caramelisation — Relates to the browning of items being cooked in a frypan or pot. For chicken or beef, it will be the browning of the items to seal in the flavour. For vegetables, it will be onions that brown because their natural sugars will colour.

Carbonara — A sauce for pasta which includes bacon, Parmesan, egg and cream.

Cartouche — A lid made out of greaseproof paper to use over a saucepan to keep moisture in while the product is cooking. Take a piece of greaseproof paper and fold in half, then in half again. Fold in half again then place the pointed end at approximately the centre of the pot or pan. Tear off any paper hanging over the edge of the saucepan and unfold. This circle of paper should fit the pot perfectly.

Casserole/Dutch oven — An earthenware or metal fireproof dish with a lid for oven use. The casserole dish could also be Pyrex. A casserole is also the name of the stew that is cooked in the dish, and casseroling is cooking (meat and poultry) in a casserole dish.

Ceviche — A raw fish dish marinated in lemon juice and olive oil.

Chateaubriand — Head of a fillet of beef.

Chicken breast pocket — Lay the chicken breast on a chopping board skin side down. Provided the breast is whole, the chicken fillet should still be intact on the top side of the breast. Open this out but leave attached. On the opposite side, using a very sharp knife, cut a pocket without breaking the skin. This area can now be used for stuffing. Fold the fillet back into its position and tie the breast with string or cotton or wrap streaky bacon around it and secure with toothpicks.

A pocket can also be made by inserting a very sharp knife into the chicken breast from where the bone is attached. A filling can be inserted such as soft garlic butter or herbed cream cheese then closed up with a toothpick.

An alternative pocket can be created by placing the chicken breast skin side down and using a very sharp knife cut the chicken breast two thirds of the way through and open it out so it takes the shape of a butterfly. Lay the filling on one side of the chicken, fold the second side back and hold in place with butcher's twine or wrap with streaky bacon.

Chilli rating — Scoville Heat Units (SHU)

2,480,000 — Dragon's Breath (Wales, UK)

2,200,000 — Carolina Reaper

1,400,000 — Black Mama

1,041,427 — Bhut Jolokia

500,000–1,000,000 — Scotch Bonnet, Red Savina Habanero

250,000–500,000 — Long Slim Cayenne

100,000–250,000 — Tabasco

50,000–100,000 — Thai Hot

5000–25,000 — Jalapeño, Serrano

Chorizo — A Spanish pork sausage containing garlic, paprika and chilli.

Concasse — Coarsely or roughly chopped for example onions and tomatoes.

Cottage pie or shepherd's pie — Shepherd's pie uses leftover lamb or mutton and refers to the shepherds that herded the sheep. Cottage pie was also known as a means of using up leftover roast meat.

Coulis — A thick sauce made of puréed fruit.

Crepe — A very thin pancake which is usually folded or rolled with a filling or a sauce. A pancake is thicker like a pikelet and smaller in diameter. Crepes are served as a breakfast stack with maple syrup but can also be used as a snack.

Croquettes — Usually cooked foods which you mould into a cylindrical shape, flour, egg wash and crumb then deep fry, for example turkey croquettes or potato croquettes.

Croutons — Either baked pastries to be served with grilled or casserole dishes, or fried cubes or slices of bread to be served with soup or meat dishes.

Deglaze — A term meaning to dissolve the residue in the base of a frypan or pot that has been used to fry something and which has excellent flavour. Water, stock, wine or spirits can be used to deglaze.

Dhal — Cooked curried lentils with spices and served with meat, poultry, vegetables or rice.

Dukkah — A dry spice and nut mixture from the Middle East and eaten in conjunction with bread and olive oil. Also used as a spice with vegetables.

Egg wash — A beaten egg which can include milk or water and used in pastry work to brush over pastry before baking or using to seal pastry seams in pies.

Escalope — A thin slice of boneless meat, for example an escalope of veal for schnitzel.

Falafel — Ground chickpeas and spice made into a paste, moulded into balls or patties and fried.

Fricassee — A white casserole in which the meat, fish or poultry is cooked in stock, then the sauce is made from the cooking liquid using a velouté.

Frittata — A European-style egg omelette with the mixture added in and cooked on the element and in the oven. The omelette is not folded.

Frying medium — When frying food products in salted butter, it is a good choice to add a little vegetable oil as it increases the frying temperature without the butter burning. Salted butter will tend to burn with heat and become beurre noisette. Too much heat with butter alone will create beurre noir or black butter. If butter alone is the required medium to cook with then melt a packet of butter over a gentle heat in a thick-based saucepan and allow to simmer. The salt and whey will separate and when left to go cold the natural butter can be removed leaving the remains in the saucepan.

Frypan/skillet — For the purposes of this book, they are the same cooking implement but just different terminology for different countries. The frypan/skillet should be able to be used on the elements and in the oven, so the handles need to be made of appropriate metal material.

Ghee — Clarified butter used in Indian and Middle Eastern cookery.

Halloumi — Goat's/sheep's milk cheese. Of a hard texture which is good for frying and holding its shape.

Harissa paste — A North African hot, saucy, spicy paste which is orange in colour. Used in collaboration with other ingredients, stir into natural yoghurt so that it leaves a marbled pattern and use as a dip.

Hoisin sauce — A Chinese sauce used in stir-fried foods.

Hummus — A chickpea paste used as a spread or dip or as a coating for roast vegetables.

Jamaican jerk — In general it consists of allspice, chilli and pepper but other similar spices can also be added.

Julienne vegetables — The slicing of vegetables to the size of matchsticks.

Jus/gravy — A French term for unthickened gravy, jus is as thin as any other liquid and usually made when adding alcohol or stock to a roasting pan or frypan to take up the flavours left behind when the meat was cooked. Jus lie is the term for a gravy that is thickened by a roux or cornflour.

Kirsch — A cherry liqueur.

Korma — A curry sauce based on cardamom and yoghurt.

Lamb

- **Lamb** is a sheep that has reached six months and because of age is very tender.
- **Hogget** is a sheep that is two years old and tends to have a stronger flavour.
- **Mutton** is a sheep that is four years old plus, has a stronger flavour than the other two but tends to be a little fatty and requires a lot slower cooking.

Language terminology — English and US

English	US
Beef mince	Ground beef
Beetroot	Beets
Butter — a knob of butter is 30 g	Butter — a stick of butter is 4 oz (113 g)
Capsicum	Bell pepper
Coriander	Cilantro
Cornflour	Corn starch
Frypan	Skillet
Grill	Broil
Icing sugar	Powdered sugar
Spring onions	Green onions/scallions
Stock	Broth

Lardons — Batons of bacon.

Leaf gelatine — Has the appearance of bubble wrap plastic sheeting. Soak first in water before adding to mousse or terrines.

Mascarpone — An Italian cream cheese made from cow's milk.

Mirepoix — A mirepoix of vegetables is a base of root vegetables used in the bottom of a roasting dish in which roast meat is placed. This prevents the roast from frying on the bottom of the pan and the vegetables can be used in the gravy at the end of the cooking. The term is also applied to a mixture of diced vegetables which are served on a plate as a side.

Miso — Fermented soy bean paste that can be used as a soup or stock.

Panzanella — Italian bread salad from large cubes of bread with tomatoes, olives, basil and dressing.

Pasta — Pasta comes in various types and shapes to suit their purpose. It is cooked in boiling salted water till al dente or 'to the tooth'. Here is a guide to the uses of some of the pasta available in the supermarkets.

- **Ravioli** — Stuffed pasta parcels which are meat or vegetable filled. They are poached in boiling salted water then tossed in garlic oil or butter and served with a sauce which could be béchamel, pesto, tomato or a butter sauce.
- **Penne** — A small hollow pasta tube which is used to absorb meat and sauce into the tube and cling to the outside. It is also used in some baked pasta dishes.
- **Spiral/fusilli** — The corkscrew-style pasta is ideal for lifting pieces of chunky meat or sauce being caught in the pasta, e.g. Bolognese.
- **Cannelloni** — Hollow tubes to be filled with a mixture of choice, e.g. raw beef mince, tuna, prawns or vegetarian. Cooked in a béchamel sauce, a pasta tomato sauce or a combination of both.
- **Spaghetti** — One of the most well-known pastas. Long, thin and cooked in boiling salted water till al dente or 'to the tooth'. Can be served with most sauces or just tossed in oil and garlic and served with Parmesan cheese.
- **Black pasta** — Also known as 'squid ink' pasta. Great when served with seafood in a cream or tomato-based sauce.
- **Lasagne pasta** — Used in dry or fresh form for lasagne but also can be used to roll and envelop food then cooked in béchamel or tomato sauces.

Pot roasting — A term given to cooking a good-quality piece of meat in a casserole in liquid either in the oven or on top of the stove. The meat is usually of excellent quality but with the inclusion of slow cookers, almost any cut of meat can be used.

Potatoes — types and uses

- **Jersey Benne** — High water content, low starch.
- **King Edward** — Good for roasting. Fluffy texture.
- Smooth inside.
- Boiling, braising and casseroles.
- **Desiree Red Skin** — Ideal for mash or creamed potatoes.
- **Rua** — Like Desiree not too waxy and not too starchy.
- Between smooth and fluffy.
- For most cooking methods.
- **Desiree** — The everything potato.
- **Agria** — Fluffy inside and will absorb a lot of liquid.
- **Piper** — Good all-round potato like King Edward. Fries well.
- Fluffy inside.
- For chips, baking, roasting, mashing, wedges.

Preserved lemons — Whole lemons that have been preserved in a salt brine. Used in Middle Eastern dishes.

Ragout — A casserole which has been slow cooked using a slow cooker, in the oven or on the stove. Generally utilising the poorer cuts of meat, e.g. ragoût de boeuf.

Sauces — Most of the classic sauces are derived from a main sauce. Listed below are the main basic sauces and their derivatives, i.e. béchamel, velouté, Espagnole, tomato and hollandaise.

Basic sauce

Béchamel =	Cream	Cheddar	Mornay	Nantua	Soubise
Milk	Cream	Cheese	Gruyere	Cream	Diced onion
roux	Lemon	Worcestershire	Cream	Butter	Simmered in béchamel
		Mustard	Butter	Paprika	
				Diced shellfish	

Velouté =	Bercy	Allemande	Supreme	Auroa	Cardinal
Stock	Fish stock	Veal stock	Chicken stock	Allemande sauce	Fish stock
roux	Shallots	Egg yolk	Mushrooms	Tomato paste	Cream
	White wine	Cream	Cream	Butter	Cayenne
	Butter	Lemon			lobster

Espagnole =	Chasseur	Chateaubriand	Bordelaise	Robert	Duxelle
Brown stock	Mushrooms	White wine	Red wine	Onion	Onion
Brown roux	Shallots	Shallots	Shallots	Mustard	Mushrooms
	White wine	Lemon	Bay leaf	Sugar	White wine
	Tomatoes	Tarragon	Thyme	Butter	Tomatoes

Tomato =	Creole	Spanish	Milanaise	Neapolitan	Bolognese
Tomato	Onion	Creole	Mushrooms	Garlic	Mirepoix
Vegetable purée	Celery	Mushrooms	Butter	Olives	Ground meat
	Garlic	Olives	Ham	Anchovy	Red wine
	Pepper			Capers	Oregano
	Thyme				
	Cayenne				

Hollandaise =	Béarnaise	Mousseline	Maltaise	Grimrod	Choron
Butter	Shallot	Whipped cream	Orange juice	Saffron	Béarnaise
Egg yolk	Tarragon		Orange zest		Tomato paste
	vinegar/				Cream
	reduction				

Sauté — To toss food in a frypan to keep it on the move using a little oil or butter so that it colours all over, e.g. sauté potatoes or mushrooms. Can also relate to some meat products which are sautéed and would usually be meat of high quality.

Sweat — To cook in butter or oil without adding any colour to the ingredient, e.g. diced onions being cooked.

Tagine — A North African method of cooking. The name relates to the container used to cook this dish, as well as the dish itself. The lid is tall and conical, which allows the steam to go up, collect at the top of the cone and then fall back into the food without evaporating and creating a stronger flavour. An oven-friendly saucepan with a lid can create the same method of cooking on an element or in the oven. It needs to be slow cooking.

Thickening agents — There are various methods available which are suitable for thickening sauces, casseroles, gravies or dessert sauces.

a. Roux — A mixture of flour and butter used to make sauces. The ratio of flour to butter can change depending on the type of sauce being made. A béchamel has equal quantities of flour and butter whereas a brown sauce will have a higher ratio of flour to butter and cooked longer to slowly brown the flour without burning.

b. Cornflour — Cornflour diluted with a little water added to form a slurry can be used to thicken small liquid quantity sauces like lemon juice being used to serve with a fish dish. It is important to add the cornflour slurry very slowly and stirring at all times so that it doesn't congeal in one spot and cause the sauce to become lumpy.

c. Arrowroot — Very much the same as above in cornflour. Use only for small quantity liquids to be thickened and allow to gently simmer to allow the arrowroot to cook out.

d. Egg yolk — Egg yolks can be used to thicken hot and cold sauces. A cold sauce using egg yolks is mayonnaise made from oil. Hollandaise sauce is made using warm egg yolks and an egg custard is also made using egg yolks to thicken the sauce. Sauces thickened with egg yolks can also split easily so take care when making.

e. Potatoes — Raw potatoes can be added to thicken casserole dishes, e.g. curry where no other thickening agent is used. Mashed potatoes can also be used to thicken some casserole dishes as can dried potato flakes.

f. Rice and lentils — Adding uncooked rice or lentils to a casserole or soup will absorb some of the liquid and assist it to thicken.

g. Butter — Knobs of butter into a hot sauce which is still on an element can thicken a sauce by emulsifying, but constant stirring is required.

h. Beurre manié — Beurre manié is a measure of equal quantities of flour and butter. The butter is softened and the flour mixed into it. It is added to a casserole that requires thickening by peeling off pieces of the beurre manié and putting into the liquid. The heat of the casserole will melt the butter and the flour will thicken. Keep stirring while the butter is being added, otherwise lumps will form.

Vegetables — The rule of thumb for cooking vegetables are:

1. All vegetables grown in the ground are cooked in cold salted water and brought to the boil, e.g. sweet potato, parsnip, swede. The exception is new potatoes, which are cooked in boiling salted water.

2. All vegetables above the ground that are to be cooked are placed into boiling salted water.

Velouté — A sauce made from a roux and similar to a béchamel, however this roux is cooked a little longer on the element than the béchamel roux. The cooking liquid from the simmering meat is used to thicken this sauce.

Temperature, weight and liquid conversions

Temperature			Liquid			Weight	
°C	°F		Ml	Fl. oz		Metric	Imperial
0	32		60	2		20 g	¾ oz
100	212		80	2 ½		60 g	2 oz
120	250		125	4		125 g	4 oz
130	270		160	5		180 g	6 oz
140	280		180	6		250 g	8 oz
150	300		250	8		500 g	1 lb
160	320		500	16		1 kg	2 lb
180	360		625	20			
200	390		1000	32			
250	480						

METHODS OF COOKING

Roasting

Roast cooking times

- Beef, 35 min per kg
- Lamb, 45 min per kg
- Mutton, 45 min per kg
- Veal, 55 min per kg
- Pork, 55 min per kg
- Chicken, 90 min per bird

The above times are approximate for planning purposes.

Roasting is used for the best cuts of meat, game, poultry and vegetables. Use a roasting pan with deep sides. Line the bottom of the roasting dish with root vegetables or onion halves so that the meat is kept off the bottom of the pan and the bottom of the meat doesn't fry. Crushed bulbs of garlic, rosemary and thyme can be added to the vegetable base to give flavour to the meat. The meat should be browned and sealed first either on the stove in a frypan or starting off in a very hot oven around 200°C for 15 minutes then turned down to around 160°C for the rest of the cooking period. At regular intervals during cooking take the oven tray out and with a large spoon pour the pan liquid back over the meat. This is known as basting. Once the meat is cooked and removed from the oven it needs to be covered with baking paper or tinfoil and left to rest for at least 15 minutes. Use the vegetables in the bottom of the pan as the basis for a gravy by adding flour and allowing to brown slowly then adding stock. Once the sauce is made either strain it or put it all through a blender/food processor then check for viscosity and taste.

Grilling

There are three ways of grilling:

- Over heat — as in barbecue or grill/hotplate on the kitchen stove.
- Under heat — under the oven grill or using a salamander.
- Between heat — between electric grill bars.

Grilling meat, poultry or fish requires first-class cuts to be used. The food to be grilled may be marinated first which will add extra flavour. The food items should be rubbed with oil so that they do not stick to the grill bars. Timing of grilling the food depends very much on the thickness of the meat/poultry being used so continual practice and experience will help to make that decision. Grilled steak, chops, fillets, chicken breasts should be cooked on one side first then turned only once during its cooking time. There are some who believe that the meat should be turned constantly during its cooking period, so believe and do whatever you think is best. Because grilling uses a direct hot heat, it is easy to overcook the meat, poultry or fish and dry it out. During cooking, once the meat is nicely browned, move it to the cooler part away from the heat source so that it continues to cook slowly. Also make use of the grill mark patterns to add a good presentation of the dish. Like roasting, allow the meat to rest for 15 minutes before cutting or serving.

If you have a meat thermometer, the following are guides to achieve degree of cooking:

- Steak rare, 140°C
- Steak medium rare, 148°C
- Steak medium, 150°C
- Steak medium well done, 155°C
- Steak well done, 160°C

To achieve the above temperatures, the steaks need to be approximately 20 mm plus in thickness and kept out of refrigeration for at least 45 minutes before grilling.

Frying

There are three ways of frying:

- Shallow frying — using a frypan for shallow fat mediums.
- Sauté — very similar to shallow but using only first-class meat/vegetables.
- Deep frying — using a deep-frying vat and temperature controlled.

All frying is using first-class cuts of meat or products from meat, poultry, fish, vegetables and some pastry products. Shallow frying can use olive or vegetable oil alone or a mix of oil and butter. The butter gives a nutty flavour while the oil gives the frypan a higher cooking heat point without burning. Chops, chicken breasts, fish fillets, fish cakes, corn fritters and vegetables are items that shallow frying is suitable for. Allow the items to rest after cooking.

Sautéing is completed in a frypan and it is very similar to number one but in this instance, once the item is cooked, the pan is deglazed with stock or wine and sauce made and served with the sautéed item. The food mentioned is completely cooked in this pan and the sauce made so the meat has to be A grade. Casseroles and stews also have their ingredients browned in a frypan but because they need long, slow cooking, this is not termed sautéing.

Deep frying is usually completed in a specifically designed deep fat fryer that is thermostatically controlled. Deep frying food in a pot on the stove in a household environment is done but it can be dangerous, especially when attention is drawn away and the fat is uncontrolled. Items to be deep fried usually are coated in some form with either a batter or a crumbing mix. The items do need to be well coated otherwise the hot fat will get through into the food item and possibly damage it. Ice cream and chocolate bars can be deep fried but they do need a proper coating to encase them.

When frying any of the above in large quantities it is best to batch fry so that the pan and the frying medium doesn't get too cool. But keep a bottle of oil next to a deep fryer in case the oil needs to be cooled to prevent overflow.

Poaching

This is cooking in a liquid which is just on boiling point where the top of the liquid is just moving. Water, stock or milk is used for poaching. It is used for cooking fish, seafood, chicken, fruit or vegetables and the most well-known one of poached eggs.

Steaming

This term is used for cooking by moist heat, but the item is not immersed. Steam pots are usually two-layered with the liquid on the bottom and the perforated pot on top. It is known to be one of the best ways to cook vegetables which helps retain their vitamins. Chinese food also uses the same principle with the bamboo baskets.

Stewing

Cooking food in a liquid which will be a stock or a sauce. The main ingredient in stewing is usually a tougher, coarser or cheaper cut of the joint, and the stewing which, like poaching, is keeping the cooking liquor just turning over for a longer time period to make the meat tender.

Sous vide

Sous vide is a method of cooking used in the catering industry and now the equipment is available for the domestic kitchen. Sous vide is cooking in a resealable plastic bag in a controlled-temperature water bath. The temperatures are usually a lot less than boiling or simmering therefore don't cause meat muscle to toughen. Steak can be cooked sous vide with cracked pepper and a sprig of rosemary added. Once cooked, the steak can be briefly grilled or barbecued to add colour.

Braising

This method of cooking is a combination of roasting and stewing in the oven in a pan that might have a tight-fitting lid or tinfoil is used to seal the ingredient in the baking dish. Braising keeps the cooking liquid and the ingredients together and can be used for all types of meat, poultry, fish and vegetables.

Pot roasting

Pot roasting is cooking good-quality cuts of meat or poultry in a casserole with a tight-fitting lid. This method retains all the juices and flavours of the joint and its sauce. Tagine cooking from North Africa uses the same principle and is now a popular method of cooking.

Baking

This is a method of cooking using mainly a dry heat for the cooking of bread, buns, cakes and pastries. Some ovens dispense water as in steam during their baking process but that is to keep the oven temperature moist.

Paper bag

A similar method of cooking to casseroling in that the ingredients are sealed inside a brown paper bag or tinfoil. This method of cooking applies to quality cuts of meat, poultry, fish and vegetables. The main food ingredients could be laid on a bed of vegetables with a little stock, lemon/orange juice or cut tomatoes added. The paper bag is sealed or in case of using foil, lay the ingredients in baking paper then in foil and seal the joints of the foil by entwining together to form the seal. Place in a pan then in the oven. Take care on opening because the steam coming out of the bag can burn.

ABOUT THE
AUTHOR

Food, hospitality, kitchen design, airline catering and travel have all been part of the author's life. Juttee Armiss is a pen name. She first appeared in a four-book autobiographical novel series.

Follow Juttee: https://www.facebook.com/jutteearmissauthor/